TWILIGHT IN ITALY AND OTHER ESSAYS

David Herbert Lawrence was born into a miner's family in Eastwood, Nottinghamshire, in 1885, the fourth of five children. He attended Beauvale Board School and Nottingham High School, and trained as an elementary schoolteacher at Nottingham University College. He taught in Croydon from 1908. His first novel, *The White Peacock*, was published in 1911, just a few weeks after the death of his mother to whom he had been extraordinarily close. His career as a schoolteacher was ended by serious illness at the end of 1911.

In 1912 Lawrence went to Germany with Frieda Weekley, the German wife of the Professor of Modern Languages at the University College of Nottingham. They were married on their return to England in 1914. Lawrence had published *Sons and Lovers* in 1913; but *The Rainbow*, completed in 1915, was suppressed, and for three years he could not find a publisher for *Women in Love*, completed in 1917.

After the war, Lawrence lived abroad and sought a more fulfilling mode of life than he had so far experienced. With Frieda, he lived in Italy, Sicily, Sri Lanka, Australia, New Mexico and Mexico. They returned to Europe in 1925. His last novel, *Lady Chatterley's Lover*, was published in 1928 but was banned in England and America. In 1930 he died in Vence, in the south of France, at the age of forty-four.

Lawrence's life may have been short, but he lived it intensely. He also produced an amazing body of work: novels, stories, poems, plays, essays, travel books, translations, paintings and letters (over five thousand of which survive). After his death Frieda wrote that, 'What he had seen and felt and known he gave in his writing to his fellow men, the splendour of living, the hope of more and more life . . . a heroic and immeasurable gift.'

Stefania Michelucci was born in Vinci, near Florence, and graduated from Pisa University with a doctoral dissertation on Thom Gunn's poetry. She taught for a period at Arizona State University, specializing in Contemporary American Poetry. Her research has been carried out at the universities of Genoa and Milan, including a project on *The Functional Aspects of Places and Space in D. H. Lawrence's Narrative*. In addition, she has published various critical articles on the shorter fiction and travel writing of D. H. Lawrence.

John Worthen is advisory editor for the works of D. H. Lawrence in Penguin Twentieth-Century Classics. Currently Professor of D. H. Lawrence Studies at the University of Nottingham, he has published widely on Lawrence; his acclaimed biography, *D. H. Lawrence: The Early Years 1885–1912*, was published in 1991. He has also edited a number of volumes in the authoritative Cambridge Lawrence Edition, whose texts Penguin Twentieth-Century Classics are reproducing.

D. H. LAWRENCE

TWILIGHT IN ITALY AND OTHER ESSAYS

EDITED BY PAUL EGGERT
WITH AN INTRODUCTION AND NOTES
BY STEFANIA MICHELUCCI

PENGUIN BOOKS

PENGUIN BOOKS

Published by the Penguin Group

Penguin Books Ltd, 27 Wrights Lane, London w8 5TZ, England
Penguin Books USA Inc., 375 Hudson Street, New York, New York 10014, USA
Penguin Books Australia Ltd, Ringwood, Victoria, Australia
Penguin Books Canada Ltd, 10 Alcorn Avenue, Toronto, Ontario, Canada M4V 3B2
Penguin Books (NZ) Ltd, 182–190 Wairau Road, Auckland 10, New Zealand

Penguin Books Ltd, Registered Offices: Harmondsworth, Middlesex, England

This edition first published by Cambridge University Press 1994
Published with new editorial matter in Penguin Books 1997
1 3 5 7 9 10 8 6 4 2

Printed in England by
Clays Ltd, St Ives plc

Contents

Note on the Penguin Lawrence Edition

D. H. Lawrence stands in the very front rank of English writers this century; unlike some other famous writers, however, he has always appealed to a large popular audience as well as to students of literature, and his work still arouses passionate loyalties and fervent disagreements. The available texts of his books have, nevertheless, been notoriously inaccurate. The Penguin Lawrence Edition uses the authoritative texts of Lawrence's work established by an international team of scholars engaged on the *Cambridge Edition of the Works of D. H. Lawrence* under its General Editors, Professor James T. Boulton and Professor Warren Roberts. Through rigorous study of surviving manuscripts, typescripts, proofs and early printings the Cambridge editors have provided texts as close as possible to those which Lawrence himself would have expected to see printed. Deletions deliberately made by printers, publishers or their editors, accidentally by typists and printers – at times removing whole pages of text – have been restored, while house-styling introduced by printers is removed as far as possible. The Penguin Lawrence Edition thus offers both general readers and students the only texts of Lawrence which have any claim to be the authentic productions of his genius.

Acknowledgements

I am deeply indebted to Dr Paul Eggert for his pioneering scholarship in the original Cambridge University Press edition of *Twilight in Italy and Other Essays* (1994). Special thanks to Professor John Worthen for the professionalism, intelligence, patience and the extraordinary sense of humour with which he guides those working with him. I would like to thank Professor Giovanni Cianci and Professor Giuseppe Sertoli for their invaluable suggestions, Professor Massimo Bacigalupo for his scholarly encouragement and Dr Ronald Packham for his most useful advice. I would finally like to acknowledge the great debt which I owe to all the people in Gargnano who put up with my presence in the summer of 1995 while I was working on this edition.

Chronology

1885   David Herbert Richards Lawrence (hereafter DHL) born in Eastwood, Nottinghamshire, the fourth child of Arthur John Lawrence, collier, and Lydia, née Beardsall, daughter of a pensioned-off engine fitter.

1891–8   Attends Beauvale Board School.

1898–1901   Becomes first boy from Eastwood to win a County Council scholarship to Nottingham High School, which he attends until July 1901.

1901   Works three months as a clerk at Haywood's surgical appliances factory in Nottingham; severe attack of pneumonia.

1902   Begins frequent visits to the Chambers family at Haggs Farm, Underwood, and starts his friendship with Jessie Chambers.

1902–5   Pupil-teacher at the British School, Eastwood; sits the King's Scholarship exam in December 1904 and is placed in the first division of the first class.

1905–6   Works as an uncertificated teacher at the British School; writes his first poems and starts his first novel 'Laetitia' (later *The White Peacock*, 1911).

1906–8   Student at Nottingham University College following the normal course leading to a teacher's certificate; qualifies in July 1908. Wins *Nottinghamshire Guardian* Christmas 1907 short-story competition with 'A Prelude' (submitted under name of Jessie Chambers); writes second version of 'Laetitia'.

1908–11   Elementary teacher at Davidson Road School, Croydon.

1909   Meets Ford Madox Hueffer (later Ford), who begins to publish his poems and stories in the *English Review* and recommends a rewritten version of *The White Peacock* (1911) to William Heinemann; DHL writes *A Collier's Friday Night* (1934) and first version of 'Odour of Chrysanthemums' (1911); friendship with Agnes Holt.

1910   Writes 'The Saga of Siegmund' (first version of *The Trespasser*, 1912), based on the experiences of his friend, the Croydon teacher Helen Corke; starts affair with Jessie

Chambers; writes first version of *The Widowing of Mrs. Holroyd* (1914); ends affair with Jessie Chambers but continues friendship; starts to write 'Paul Morel' (later *Sons and Lovers*, 1913); death of Lydia Lawrence in December; gets engaged to his old friend Louie Burrows.

1911 Fails to finish 'Paul Morel', strongly attracted to Helen Corke; starts affair with Alice Dax, wife of an Eastwood chemist; meets Edward Garnett, publisher's reader for Duckworth, who advises him on writing and publication. In November falls seriously ill with pneumonia and has to give up school-teaching; 'The Saga' accepted by Duckworth; DHL commences its revision as *The Trespasser*.

1912 Convalesces in Bournemouth. Breaks off engagement to Louie; returns to Eastwood; works on 'Paul Morel'; in March meets Frieda Weekley, wife of Ernest, Professor at the University College of Nottingham; ends affair with Alice Dax; goes to Germany on a visit to his relations on 3 May; travels, however, with Frieda to Metz. After many vicissitudes, some memorialized in *Look! We Have Come Through!* (1917), Frieda gives up her marriage and her children for DHL; in August they journey over the Alps to Italy and settle at Gargnano, where DHL writes the final version of *Sons and Lovers*.

1913 *Love Poems* published; writes *The Daughter-in-Law* (1965) and 200 pp. of 'The Insurrection of Miss Houghton' (abandoned); begins 'The Sisters', eventually to be split into *The Rainbow* (1915) and *Women in Love* (1920). DHL and Frieda spend some days at San Gaudenzio, then stay at Irschenhausen in Bavaria; DHL writes first versions of 'The Prussian Officer' and 'The Thorn in the Flesh' (1914); *Sons and Lovers* published in May. DHL and Frieda return to England in June, meet John Middleton Murry and Katherine Mansfield. They return to Italy (Fiascherino, near La Spezia) in September; DHL revises *The Widowing of Mrs Holroyd*; resumes work on 'The Sisters'.

1914 Rewrites 'The Sisters' (now called 'The Wedding Ring') yet again; agrees for Methuen to publish it; takes J. B. Pinker as agent. DHL and Frieda return to England in June, marry on 13 July. DHL meets Catherine Carswell and S. S. Koteliansky; compiles short-story collection *The Prussian Officer* (1914). Outbreak of war prevents DHL and Frieda returning to Italy; at Chesham he first writes 'Study of Thomas Hardy' (1936) and then begins *The Rainbow*; starts important friendships with Ottoline Morrell, Cynthia Asquith, Bertrand Russell and E. M. Forster; grows increasingly desperate and angry about the war.

1915   Finishes *The Rainbow* in Greatham in March; plans lecture course with Russell; they quarrel in June. DHL and Frieda move to Hampstead in August; he and Murry bring out *The Signature* (magazine, three issues only) to which he contributed 'The Crown'. *The Rainbow* published by Methuen in September, suppressed at the end of October, prosecuted and banned in November. DHL meets painters Dorothy Brett and Mark Gertler; he and Frieda plan to leave England for Florida; decide to move to Cornwall instead.

1916   Writes *Women in Love* between April and October; publishes *Twilight in Italy* and *Amores*.

1917   *Women in Love* rejected by publishers; DHL continues to revise it. Makes unsuccessful attempts to go to America. Begins *Studies in Classic American Literature* (1923); publishes *Look! We Have Come Through!* In October he and Frieda evicted from Cornwall on suspicion of spying; in London he begins *Aaron's Rod* (1922).

1918   DHL and Frieda move to Hermitage, Berkshire, then to Middleton-by-Wirksworth; publishes *New Poems*; writes *Movements in European History* (1921), *Touch and Go* (1920) and the first version of 'The Fox' (1920).

1919   Seriously ill with influenza; moves back to Hermitage; publishes *Bay*. In the autumn, Frieda goes to Germany and then joins DHL in Florence; they visit Picinisco and settle in Capri.

1920   Writes *Psychoanalysis and the Unconscious* (1921). He and Frieda move to Taormina, Sicily; DHL writes *The Lost Girl* (1920), *Mr Noon* (1984), continues with *Aaron's Rod*; on summer visit to Florence has affair with Rosalind Baynes; writes many poems from *Birds, Beasts and Flowers* (1923). *Women in Love* published.

1921   DHL and Frieda visit Sardinia and he writes *Sea and Sardinia* (1921); meets Earl and Achsah Brewster; finishes *Aaron's Rod* in the summer and writes *Fantasia of the Unconscious* (1922) and 'The Captain's Doll' (1923); plans to leave Europe and visit USA; puts together collection of stories *England, My England* (1922) and group of short novels *The Ladybird, The Fox* and *The Captain's Doll* (1923).

1922   DHL and Frieda leave for Ceylon, stay with Brewsters, then travel to Australia; he translates Verga. In Western Australia meets Mollie Skinner; at Thirroul, near Sydney, he writes *Kangaroo* (1923) in six weeks. Between August and September, he and Frieda travel to California via South Sea Islands, and meet Witter Bynner and Willard Johnson; settle in Taos, New Mexico, at invitation of Mabel Dodge (later Luhan). In December, move up to Del Monte ranch, near Taos; DHL rewrites *Studies in Classic American Literature* (1923).

1923   Finishes *Birds, Beasts and Flowers*. He and Frieda spend summer at Chapala in Mexico where he writes 'Quetzalcoatl' (first version of *The Plumed Serpent*, 1926). Frieda returns to Europe in August after serious quarrel with DHL; he journeys in USA and Mexico, rewrites Mollie Skinner's 'The House of Ellis' as *The Boy in the Bush* (1924); arrives back in England in December.

1924   At dinner in Café Royal, DHL invites his friends to come to New Mexico; Dorothy Brett accepts and accompanies him and Frieda in March. Mabel Luhan gives Lobo (later renamed Kiowa) Ranch to Frieda; DHL gives her *Sons and Lovers* manuscript in return. During summer on ranch he writes *St. Mawr* (1925), 'The Woman Who Rode Away' (1925) and 'The Princess' (1925); in August, suffers his first bronchial haemorrhage. His father dies in September; in October, he, Frieda and Brett move to Oaxaca, Mexico, where he starts *The Plumed Serpent* and writes most of *Mornings in Mexico* (1927).

1925   Finishes *The Plumed Serpent*, falls ill and almost dies of typhoid and pneumonia in February; in March diagnosed as suffering from tuberculosis. Recuperates at Kiowa Ranch, writes *David* (1926) and compiles *Reflections on the Death of a Porcupine* (1925). He and Frieda return to Europe in September, spend a month in England and settle at Spotorno, Italy; DHL writes first version of *Sun* (1926); Frieda meets Angelo Ravagli.

1926   Writes *The Virgin and the Gypsy* (1930); serious quarrel with Frieda during visit from DHL's sister Ada. DHL visits

Brewsters and Brett; has affair with Brett. Reconciled, DHL and Frieda move to Villa Mirenda, near Florence, in May and visit England (his last visit) in late summer. On return to Italy in October he writes first version of *Lady Chatterley's Lover* (1944); starts second version in November. Friendship with Aldous and Maria Huxley; DHL starts to paint.

1927   Finishes second version of *Lady Chatterley's Lover* (1972); visits Etruscan sites with Earl Brewster; writes *Sketches of Etruscan Places* (1932) and the first part of *The Escaped Cock* (1928). In November, after meetings with Michael Arlen and Norman Douglas, works out scheme for private publication with Pino Orioli, and starts final version of *Lady Chatterley's Lover* (1928).

1928   Finishes *Lady Chatterley's Lover* and arranges for its printing and publication in Florence; fights many battles to ensure its despatch to subscribers in Britain and USA. In June writes second part of *The Escaped Cock* (1929). He and Frieda travel to Switzerland (Gsteig) and the island of Port Cros, then settle in Bandol, in the south of France. He writes many of the poems in *Pansies* (1929); *Lady Chatterley's Lover* pirated in Europe and USA.

1929   Visits Paris to arrange for cheap edition of *Lady Chatterley's Lover* (1929); unexpurgated typescript of *Pansies* seized by police; exhibition of his paintings in London raided by police. He and Frieda visit Majorca, France and Bavaria, returning to Bandol for the winter. He writes *Nettles* (1930), *Apocalypse* (1931) and *Last Poems* (1932); sees much of Brewsters and Huxleys.

1930   Goes into Ad Astra sanatorium in Vence at start of February; discharges himself on 1 March; dies at Villa Robermond, Vence, on Sunday 2 March; buried on 4 March.

1935   Frieda sends Angelo Ravagli (now living with her at Kiowa Ranch – they marry in 1950) to Vence to have DHL exhumed, cremated, and his ashes brought back to the ranch.

1956   Frieda dies and is buried at Kiowa Ranch.

John Worthen, 1994

Introduction

The area around Lake Garda offers the traveller an endless variety of landscapes, from the fairly regular coastline on the southern side, where the towns lie strung out in a row on the edge of the plain surrounding Verona, to the jagged, narrow shoreline around Limone. Towards its northern end, however, the lake seems to squeeze in on itself, pear-like, until the two sides meet in the bay of Riva. The western side of the lake, which became more accessible to tourists after the opening of the new road, the 'Gardesana Occidentale', in 1930–31, is overlooked by massive rocky hills, which seem to rise higher and higher the further one moves inland, till they can deservedly be called mountains north of Limone. This is the part of Lake Garda connected with D. H. Lawrence and Frieda Weekley, the part where they settled[1] for just under seven months, from 18 September 1912 to 3 April 1913, in a villa[2] looking over the lake in Villa di Gargnano. It is a particularly attractive part of the lake, of which local people, even today, are very proud. The land is extremely fertile thanks to the very mild climate which has made it possible to grow fruits usually thought of as exotic, or southern. For hundreds of years, the hills around Gargnano were transformed into a paradise of lemon orchards: an Eden, built in layers on the hillside, surrounded by walls of hard, often irregular stone, with caper bushes dangling from them. The favourable climate and fertile soil made Gargnano a real centre of economic activity, supplying as it did the needs of the Austro-Hungarian Empire and other northern countries.[3] Although the large-scale cultivation of lemons died out at the beginning of the twentieth century, the structures of the lemon houses have left an unmistakable mark on the landscape. These special constructions were not ordinary greenhouses but stony tiers of earth with columns, where the lemon trees grew openly in summer and were covered in winter with wood and glass to protect them from the cold.

The lemon industry, which had originally brought wealth and stability to the region, had already undergone an initial decline at the beginning of the twentieth century, with the building of the railway. This facilitated the importation of lemons from Sicily, which were cheaper since they grew in open orchards and did not require such painstaking care as those cultivated beside Lake Garda.

There is, however, another aspect of the area around the lake which is particularly important in the San Gaudenzio essays of Lawrence's *Twilight in Italy*. As one goes inland from the lake shore, up into the hills, there are villages where time seems to have stopped long ago. These are little more than clusters of stone houses dominated by the bell tower of the local church, all clinging stubbornly to the rock which supports them, a few hundred feet away from the lake. Some of these villages, such as Muslone above San Gaudenzio, whose church is incredibly perched on the very top of a rugged mountain, still retain a simple, agricultural way of life, which enables them to keep in check, to some extent, the invasion of tourism. In each of these small groups of houses there is just one gathering-point, the bar in the main square; but voices can be heard inside the houses at twilight – already dinner-time for these villagers.

San Gaudenzio, which most of Lawrence's readers will at least have heard of, is equally well known – although for other reasons – to the local people, even if it does not always appear on maps. San Gaudenzio is the name of a little church hardly noticeable from the main road, largely hidden by the olive trees and vineyards which protect the small local cemetery.

As is usual in small communities, surnames recur with surprising frequency among the tombs of San Gaudenzio. They are familiar names on the shopfronts of the town of Gargnano: the Feltrinellis, the Samuellis, the Capellis, all of them significant in the Gargnano area and also in this volume. The name Feltrinelli, for example, can be seen on a memorial stone dedicated to the family in the cloister of San Francesco, and in huge letters on façades; Feltrinelli's are also the two villas occupied by Mussolini during the Second World War.[4]

Just opposite the churchyard, the Capelli family has for generations owned a farmhouse with its surrounding land, a habitual stopping-place for people on the way up to Muslone or down to Gargnano, with its front garden facing the road and the back garden (with olive trees, vines and fruit trees) running downhill towards the lake, and ending in a huge lemon house with several tiers.

By 1912, however, when Lawrence used to walk down the slopes of San Gaudenzio and sit at the end of one of the top tiers, where he could write with a wonderful view of the lake and Monte Baldo on the opposite shore, the lemon plants had already been replaced by vines, which would become the real source of wealth for the Capelli family. The lemon houses themselves, a leitmotif of the lake's coastline, were falling into decay, the surviving expression of a prosperous past, and the embodiment of an impressive aspect of the Italian twilight.

Lawrence had come to Lake Garda, where many of the essays are set, after a journey across Germany and the Alps. The essays in this volume can be divided into three main groups: those set in Germany, those describing his crossing the Alps, and those set in Italy. They were all written between 1912 and 1915 when, with a deteriorating international situation, information about neighbouring countries was not only much sought after but was vitally important; knowledge of what and whom England might be opposed to, and with whom she could be allied, offered a kind of reassurance for people at home. As emerges from a letter to Walter de la Mare written in May 1912,[5] Lawrence had originally thought of writing sketches and having them quickly published in magazines – an extremely appealing idea[6] at a time when he very much needed to earn money to support himself and Frieda Weekley, with whom he had come to Germany and who was escaping from her married life. Subsequently he hoped to have the essays published as a book which could sell in both England and America.[7] Two of the essays he wrote in May 1912 were accepted and published by the *Westminster Gazette*,[8] but others were not ('How a Spy is Arrested' was rejected for being 'too violently anti-German').[9]

All the essays in this volume of Lawrence's early travel writing can be read separately, without any need to find links between them, since all of them convey a message (in most cases by telling a story) which is self-sufficient. There is, however, a kind of leitmotif – the threat of an approaching war, the idea of twilight descending on Europe – which runs through them and makes them a sequence. It is, however, important to stress that this volume, compiled in its present form by Paul Eggert for the Cambridge edition,[10] is neither a book which Lawrence himself wrote as a whole, nor the collection which he would have compiled if he had had the chance. The essays nevertheless show his developing insight into a genre he was working with for the first time; and throughout the volume the reader cannot help feeling Europe's passage down the slippery slope towards destruction. This impression actually increases towards the end of the volume, in essays written after the war had already started.

The apparently isolated essay 'With the Guns'[11] takes its place, then, as a link between North and South, Germany and Italy, and the imminent transformation hanging over them. With the alarming tone of a prophetic reflection, it presents the disturbing image of modern man becoming a slave to the machine: the approaching war, Lawrence announces, is bound to be mass suicide, totally blind destruction carried out by guns, in which man, overwhelmed by his own technological sophistication, will tragically be unable to identify or even distinguish his enemy from his own companions.

Another striking element of all the essays in this volume is the preponderance of locations 'on the border'; places where people belonging to different communities come face to face with one another, with different traditions, languages, mentalities, and inevitably with anger and hatred in wartime. The presence of the 'foreigner', of the 'other', is a theme of the collection, since all the essays were written in a critical historical period which happened to coincide with a very difficult period in Lawrence's life. As for Lake Garda, where most of the volume is set, the political situation at the beginning of the century, with the Austro-Hungarian Empire extending as far as Northern Italy, made the presence of foreigners in the area quite common, a part of everyday life, welcomed and resented at the same time.[12] From the very beginning, Lawrence finds himself in the delicate position of observing and being observed at the same time; he tries to analyse the reactions brought about in himself by his interaction with other people, and simultaneously to understand these people's differences. The result is a polyphonic work, with different entities and ethnic multiplicities, speaking a variety of languages, thus recalling Bakhtin's idea of the carnival-like interaction of a variety of voices. Not only does this volume abound in expressions in foreign languages, from German, French and Italian, but there is constant attention to the fact that people are speaking another language, which the author – very English himself – has problems in understanding (especially when they use their dialect), just as he has problems in understanding their mentality, their culture, and the tragedy of their lives. He clearly realizes that, as a foreigner and also as a writer, he is forced to describe their 'foreign reality' while remaining at a distance from it, on the outside, unable fully to penetrate it.

In the impressive essay 'Il Duro' this situation is particularly evident. Lawrence is fascinated by the peculiar aspect of this person, by his tendency to remain isolated, and by the 'strange . . . half-tortured pale gleam' (175:24–5) which Lawrence attributes to his remaining single. When Il Duro reacts to Lawrence's suggestion that he might get married by saying that he has 'seen too much' (176:7), Lawrence insists on carrying on the dialogue, using both languages or variants of them to show the simultaneous existence of two points of view which fail to meet. It is a polyphonic, parallel speaking of two cultures and people which clearly manifests their inability to communicate, which the author contrasts with the silent communication between members of the same culture. The same thing happens in the rather depressing essay 'Italians in Exile', where Lawrence does not dare to delve any deeper into the tragedy of a group of people, isolated in a foreign country, who try to live as a sort of anarchist community.

'In Fortified Germany'

Although only short sketches reflecting Lawrence's first approach to a foreign country, the four essays under the series title 'In Fortified Germany' are full of personal references. In them, Lawrence himself is the protagonist of events which help him focus his attention on the political atmosphere of the time, while also commenting on the landscape, the people, and his impressions of the town of Metz.

In 'The English and the Germans', Lawrence keeps his attention sharply focused on the German soldiers,[13] whose behaviour offers him an opportunity to judge England and the contemporary (partly unjustified) fear of Germany: 'It is our own souls we need to reinforce, not our fleet, to make us safe from any German attack' (9:1–2). His encounter with this German reality – the pride, the fervour of activity of its soldiers – develops into a speculative essay about England seen from another perspective, indicting the English ethos of self-restraint, security and self-preservation which annihilates individual life and dries up individual energies.

The reflectiveness of 'The English and the Germans' develops a somewhat tragicomic tone in 'How a Spy is Arrested', which is a report of an unpleasant personal experience: the arrogant behaviour and (apparently) ridiculous suspicion of a German soldier who rudely asks to see his documents and is about to arrest him because he is sitting on the grass with Anita (modelled on Frieda). The immovable insistence of the soldier, who reacts with insolence to their attempt to defend themselves, reveals the tense atmosphere of this border town, with its lack of freedom and its oppression in everyday life, something confirmed by the serious reaction of the baron, who 'looked worried for a moment, then, after that moment, grew indignant' (15:18–19).

In 'French Sons of Germany', we see how this event has shifted the focus of Lawrence's attention and his sympathy from the Germans towards the French, with whom he feels more comfortable. This essay, together with 'Hail in the Rhine-Land', reflects the same journalistic style as the previous one; critical observations and personal experience are interwoven with amusing and often slightly ironic little incidents, which Lawrence probably thought appropriate for a foreign audience. 'French Sons of Germany' presents the eccentric behaviour of French people, their intimate pride and their hatred of the German occupation. While the tone is very lively at the beginning, with its extraordinarily cheerful and excited barber, who proudly asserts his French identity – 'no Leroy has ever spoken German' (16:23–4) – it becomes grimmer towards the end of the essay, when the owners of the café where Lawrence stops to shelter from the rain show, in words and attitudes, their resentment of foreign domination.

Whereas 'How a Spy is Arrested' records the author's humiliation at being suspected of being an English Officer,[14] and is sarcastic, 'Hail in the Rhine-Land' is amusing, and is related to an extraordinary event also reported in the local newspaper: a huge hailstorm.[15] This situation offers Lawrence the opportunity for some observations on the people and the place (for example, the kindness of the landlord who finds a carriage for him and Johanna), and, consequently, for an ironic comparison with England itself: 'No English landlord could have equalled him' (23:37–8).

What is most striking in these essays is the attention paid by Lawrence to the language. Here, as well as in the section 'By the Lago di Garda', he seems to feel language itself to be an essential part of the flavour of a country. Not only is he very aware of the possibility of an Englishman abroad being misunderstood, but it seems as if he is sounding out the language, or attempting to look for an equivalent in English of the reality he is observing; and, not finding it, he prefers to use the local word in order to keep some of its local character, as, for example, with the Käfer (11:34), Verboten (12:35), Aber (13:12), Streng verboten (22:36), Jawohl (23:11), the Bretzel and Kringel (24:6–7), the Schnapps (25:18, 20) and the Stollwerck chocolate (23:34).

'A Chapel Among the Mountains', 'A Hay-Hut Among the Mountains', 'Christs in the Tyrol'

With a change in focus and style from the previous essays, these three introduce Lawrence's journey southwards, from the Isar valley to the

Italian border near Sterzing (Vipiteno). The type of journalism he experiments with here is neither simply informative, nor (like the essays of 'In Fortified Germany') does it offer large-scale comparisons between peoples and countries; it is rather an attempt to portray his personal experience of an unknown environment, to convey the impressions aroused by the fascinating landscape of the Alps. On a structural level, within this volume, these essays provide the necessary transition from Germany to Italy; taken individually, however, they are interesting for their rendering of a life 'suspended' among the mountains and exposed to an upsetting and impenetrable Nature. Whereas in 'Christs in the Tyrol' Lawrence provides a synthesis of his whole experience in the Alps, the first two essays follow each other in sequence and are rather similar in style.

In 'A Chapel Among the Mountains', the author presents Anita's and his own different reactions to an unfamiliar world, ironically emphasizing the clumsiness of his Englishness, his inability – unlike his exuberant German companion – to face the hostility of the elements when deprived of the trappings of his English routine. Then, when despair is about to overcome them, they suddenly see something they think is a wood-man's hut, but which turns out to be a little chapel, the shrine of isolated people's souls, with impressive ex-voto paintings hanging on the walls. What strikes Lawrence most about these paintings is that they reflect these people's intensely down-to-earth way of living out their religion as a whole, including joy and grief: they thank God even when a misfortune befalls them, and they feel his presence in everyday life.

'A Hay-Hut Among the Mountains', which also deals with a personal experience, is slightly more ironic in the way it presents the unromantic side of sleeping in a hay-hut,[16] emphasizing the dreadful discomfort and the intense cold. The concern with practical details (where to put boots so that they will keep dry, etc.) does not lessen the almost religious feeling of the insignificance of man confronted by an untamed, impervious Nature; on the other hand, it confirms a sympathetic attitude towards the hard, impenetrable life of the people living there, isolated and exposed to the elements.

'Christs in the Tyrol' is particularly interesting, since it describes an aspect of the Alps which can be noticed by a traveller even nowadays: the dissemination of little chapels and crucifixes at almost every corner or crossroads, a kind of leitmotif of the mountains. Protected by their hoods, the crucifixes vary in dimensions, style and expression, from the full-size, beautiful body with hanging, winding curls, 'a pure lady-killer'

(45:18–19), to the painful, suffering figure, tormented by wounds and covered with blood. Scattered all over the area, they are now considered a decorative element of the landscape by tourists, who are unaware of their value as a profound expression of popular religious spirit, and of an ever-present source of fear.

Not only do the Austrian guides ignore the crucifixes, having apparently forgotten their meaning – modern man passes by too quickly to understand them – but Lawrence finds an 'armless Christ, who had tumbled down' (47:2) and who looks horrible and forgotten among the stones. It is not by chance that this fallen image is described at the end of the essay, suggesting the religious sensitivity which once helped keep the inhabitants of the region alive but which is now approaching its twilight, about to be irremediably wiped out by a process of transformation which leaves no space for meditation, awe or reverence.

'By the Lago di Garda'

Lawrence's approach to a foreign country appears to be slightly different in the three essays entitled 'By the Lago di Garda', and is destined to undergo a further change in the essays collected under the title *Twilight in Italy*.

Lawrence's journey across the Alps, his first movement towards the South, seems to follow, at least in part, a tradition of travel writing stemming from Goethe, Byron, Shelley and Stendhal, to Ruskin, Gissing, and E. M. Forster. As his journey moves on, however, he breaks away more and more from this tradition (with its idea of a warm and romantic South); and he stops in isolated places which had not previously been much taken into consideration.[17]

In the three essays 'The Spinner and the Monks', 'The Lemon Gardens of the Signor di P.' and 'The Theatre', vivid descriptions of the landscape combine with a penetrating insight into the traditions and the life of the people, in a medley of observations on history, religion, society and art, thus dismantling certain traditional clichés inherent in the Romantic image of Italy.

In 'The Spinner and the Monks', once Lawrence has reached the church of San Tommaso, stubbornly perched on the top of its hill, his attention zooms in first on a 'big, blue-checked cloth . . . drying in the sunshine' (52:20–1), subsequently passing to the movements of the fingers of an old woman spinning, and finally panning back to take in the whole of her figure. He feels uneasy in front of the woman, who does not care whether or not he understands her rather confused story about the death of a black ewe; this leads him to think – in a romantic but ironic way – of all the men who have kissed her and have been scorned by her, and whimsically to consider himself one of them. The ironic dismantling of Romantic clichés continues at the end of the essay with the two monks walking 'backwards and forwards in their wintry garden' (57:4). Lawrence likes to think of them going into the monastery after twilight to have tea with toast (a nostalgic reminiscence of his own country, now far away), but he ironically concludes with the observation 'I know *they* would not have tea and toast when they went in the monastery, but *my* monks did' (57:31–2).

It is again a human figure who attracts the author's attention in 'The Lemon Gardens of the Signor di P.': his landlord, whom he calls 'signore'. He sees him as a typical representative of the land-owning aristocracy, whose wealth stems mainly from citrus cultivation and who is, like the lemon trees, subject to an uncontrollable decline. Lawrence even perceives a connection between the lemon trees kept in the gloom and darkness of a lemon house – 'an immense, dark, cold place' (65:30) – and prey to a serious disease which makes them sterile, and the sterility of the old padrone, whose social and economic decline – 'His workmen – there are only two – ' (80:5) – is heightened and confirmed by the fact that he has no children (his decision to marry a much younger wife has turned out to be no help). Yet, in this essay, in spite of their decline, the lemon houses are perceived as an essential element of the spirit of the place, where the passage from summer to winter is marked unmistakably by the hammering of men who, in 'their clumsy zoccoli' (64:35), are covering the lemon houses.

From social class, the author's attention moves in 'The Theatre' to art, which is seen partly as the expression of the local environment – 'The theatre is an old church' (69:8–9) – and partly as an example of a polyphonic variety of social reactions in the community, which gathers in the local theatre, especially at Carnival or on the Feast of Epiphany. Lawrence notices that people sit in the audience according to a rigid social hierarchy, and that an archaic relationship survives between the sexes (men and women occupy different rows, as in church). While the 'cream of the village' is seated upstairs (at a higher price) and pay visits to one another between the acts, the 'contadini' sit downstairs, and look up towards the boxes of their 'padroni', very much as 'they look up at the paintings of the Holy Angels in the church' (80:6).

Closely observing the way the audience reacts during and after the performance, Lawrence cannot help comparing it with England, point-ing out that whereas English people, especially in public, are peculiarly stiff in their muscles and try to avoid all physical contact with their neighbours, Italian people commonly lean on each other. At the same time, responding to the Italian performance of Ibsen's *Ghosts*, D'Annunzio's *La fiaccola sotto il moggio*, and Shakespeare's *Hamlet*, he analyses the different effects the plays have on him when he watches them in a foreign language and environment: he stresses the way one's cultural heritage acquires a completely different value outside its usual context. This is particularly evident in the performance of *Hamlet*, which proves to be meaningless in a land where 'the trouble' is more in the soul than in the mind. Realizing the paradox of Italian peasants puzzling their minds over the question of being, Lawrence questions the concept of the universality of any work of art, the validity of which seems limited, to some extent, to the context in which, and for which, it was created.

Twilight in Italy

The essays making up *Twilight in Italy*[18] (published in England by Duckworth in July 1916) begin with 'The Crucifix Among the Moun-tains', followed by the group 'On the Lago di Garda', the four about San Gaudenzio, and finally the two essays 'Italians in Exile' and 'The Return Journey'. The essays 'On the Lago di Garda' partly rewrite the former essays 'By the Lago di Garda', whereas 'The Crucifix Among the Mountains' is the third version of 'Christs in the Tyrol'. The first version of that essay[19] reveals an even more direct response to the place, an immediate, empathic true-to-life portrayal of the crucifixes which Lawrence comes across. He describes their posture and style in detail, finding their strikingly human aspects completely new to an English observer.

The book as a whole reveals a development from the occasional, informative journalism of the original essays to a kind of conscious travel writing, in which the interaction with a foreign environment offers an occasion for philosophical observations on civilization and its present state of corruption and decay.[20] In this connection, we should not forget Lawrence's tendency to rewrite a text every time he revised it, in the light of the new ideas and attitudes he had developed in the meantime.

This blend of conceptual revision with artistic development is clearly visible in *Twilight in Italy*, where the rewritten essays contain intensely meditative passages on the destiny and history of man, which, however, do not appear in the four (almost certainly new) essays about San Gaudenzio. These, by contrast, are short, lively sketches of a foreign environment, where Lawrence portrays either particular situations (as in 'The Dance') or intriguing personalities (as in 'Il Duro' or 'John'). While the rewritten essays are undoubtedly richer in ideas and philosophical insight, they lack, at times, the kind of vivid directness in the presentation of the specific local reality which marks the San Gaudenzio essays. Although original and nicely reasoned, these philosophical observations are, at this early stage of Lawrence's career, still far from constituting an organic system of thought; they thus run the risk of creating an often repetitive digression, distracting attention from the original frame of the essays, and turning the travel writing into a kind of unclassifiable work[21] for which Italy becomes a mere pretext. For this reason, as *Twilight in Italy* is mostly a book about a foreign environment and culture, I shall give relatively little space in this Introduction to such observations which, besides being developed in Lawrence's other philosophical works,[22] have already been widely discussed by critics.[23]

The vivid portrayal of a foreign country is also a characteristic of the last two essays, 'Italians in Exile' and 'The Return Journey', although veiled by sadness and gloom (the impending twilight becomes more threatening towards the end of the book). The leitmotif of the entire book – as in much of Lawrence's fiction written at this time – is a fundamental polarity between North and South, which develops into a variety of chromatic, spatial and ideological polarities: light and dark, day and night, mind and soul, high and low, man and woman, aristocracy and democracy. These oppositions give rise to a continually rediscovered tension in all the essays in the desperate search for a balance, for a point where the two opposites meet in the line of perfection, just as day and night meet harmoniously in the rosy line of twilight.

They seem to illustrate the basic division between the abstraction of the mind (generally identified here with the brooding northern character) and the dark sensual instinct of the blood (seen as still partly surviving in southern countries, and identified with a pagan attitude to life). While in the section 'On the Lago di Garda' Lawrences uses abstract terms, with reference (for example) to the value and function of art in 'The Theatre', the essays about San Gaudenzio offer vivid demonstrations of this 'pagan attitude to life'. He connects this with an aspect of the social behaviour of southern people that fascinates him: the pride of each sex, which creates an element of challenge completely

Introduction

unknown to English people in the relationship between men and women, especially as seen in public.

Thus, while capturing, through observations on Italian life, a turning-point, or rather collapsing-point in the history of Western civilization[24] as it approaches its twilight, Lawrence connects it, characteristically, with the ever-unbalanced polarities of the human soul, as well as with the problematic relationship between the sexes, always one of his main themes. All the essays reflect this dichotomy, as they gradually move from the North towards the South, and then, in a circular way, end up making yet another journey towards the South. Although similar to the journey at the beginning of the book (crossing the Alps towards Italy), this second journey encounters an Italian reality deprived of its pagan soul, and consequently a prey to corruption and mechanization. Paradoxically, what the author indirectly tried to escape from, by setting out for a foreign country, awaits him when he reaches his final destination. Sitting in the Cathedral Square in Milan and sipping Bitter Campari, he also tastes the bitterness of a general European decadence, madly struggling as it is towards 'the perfect mechanising of human life' (226:39).[25]

At the same time, in 'The Return Journey', his first impressions of Italy, with its fruits and its sun-dried places, are belied by the high road heading South, often beside the railway. Crossing the mountains no longer evokes for him the mystery of an untamed Nature, as in the former essays, but instead a sense of horror, of mechanisation scattered everywhere, and a sense of impending doom entrapping man's freedom in quick, mechanical, purposeless activity, apparently just for the pleasure of earning money. And even the 'imperial road to Italy' (91:2) leading southwards is seen by Lawrence as the instrument of a colonisation which, however, does not now proceed northwards but southwards, and whose result is bound to be the same: man's loss of freedom. Thus in spite of the discoveries Italy offers to the writer, he perceives it as a doomed country, in which little islands of hopefulness survive (like the spinner, the little man in 'The Theatre', people like Il Duro). They are, however, inevitably approaching their twilight and, like the Signor di P., they will have no successors in their natural philosophy of life.

The rewritten essays of *Twilight in Italy* clearly reveal Lawrence's attention to the structural unity of his book: thus, for instance, in 'The Theatre', the observation about Enrico Persevalli performing *Hamlet* in a manner 'equivocal as the monks' (149:7) connects this essay with 'The Spinner and the Monks', and an even more explicit link between two essays is established when the little man who, 'like a hawk arching its wings' (150:25), protects his wife and child is seen as belonging to 'the same race as my old woman at San Tommaso' (150:17–18). Another connecting link in the rewritten essays is offered by the opposition between high and low. In 'The Spinner and the Monks' that opposition reflects the contrast between the place of power, suspended in the ethereal sky, and that of common people, down in the shadows; in 'The Lemon Gardens', the higher the author goes up the mountainside, the more profound becomes his perception of the inevitable decline of the place. And in 'The Theatre', the aristocrats sitting in their boxes gain a wide, all-inclusive view of the entire audience, which they sense as part of their property, whereas the people sitting below look up towards them as the embodiment of power.

Another theme which emerges in the rewritten essays, compared with their former versions, is a keener sense of the impending war; it is present in the ominous description of the Imperial road ('The Crucifix Among the Mountains') and the military Strada Nuova, 'winding beautifully and gracefully forward to the Austrian frontier' (110:24–5) ('The Spinner and the Monks'), and again in Lawrence's consideration of the soldier's obedience ('The Lemon Gardens'), and of the Italians' enthusiasm for war, which he sees as a direct consequence of a 'too strong dominion of the blood' (138:15) ('The Theatre'). This essay – not by chance – ends with the description of the bersaglieri going home and the searchlights of the Austrian border the only visible element in the darkness. While in 'Italians in Exile' the Swiss cavalry is welcomed by the entire village on a Sunday morning, the little anarchist community of Italians is opposed to the Italian government, which 'makes [them] soldiers' (201:14). In 'The Return Journey', most people Lawrence meets are about to leave for military service, and the overwhelming presence of soldiers reminds him of the Roman legions with whom, historically and ideologically, the whole history of Western civilization is connected. Their imminent action is confirmed by an event which recalls the atmosphere of 'How a Spy is Arrested': the soldiers – no longer simply 'manoeuvring' – threaten to shoot at him as he is crossing a bridge in Switzerland. This increasing violence is anticipated at the beginning of 'Italians in Exile' by the vivid image of three rapacious birds fighting in the sky above Lake Constance while German travellers watch with pleasure.

Stylistically, these essays reveal a more detached and meditative tone, the result of a different approach to the reality which Lawrence observes;

at the same time, however, he insists on his involvement in the life of the foreign community where he is temporarily living (for example, he says that it was his duty to go to the performance of *Hamlet*, since he would have been expected). Compared with the former versions, these essays reveal a smaller number of foreign words which, when they are used, are not a simple part of the local colour but are functional to the rendering of the reality observed. In 'The Spinner and the Monks', for instance, Lawrence makes the little old woman answer in English (106:28) but then he calls the schoolmistress 'maestra' (141:37), and gives the translation (142:7). He seems to be gaining a deeper linguistic insight into the foreign reality, since he is conscious that the answer 'sì' of the old woman does not lose much if changed into 'yes', whereas 'maestra' semantically identifies this figure and her role in society, not merely as a schoolmistress, but as the centre of basic education for the whole community, a pillar of Gargnano's society.

'The Crucifix Across the Mountains'

'The Crucifix Across the Mountains' performs the important thematic function, in the structure of *Twilight in Italy*, of providing a link between the North and the South, a link which Lawrence helps create in his reference to the Roman Empire, whose policy of expansion and annexation was inherited by 'German kings' (91:6) and transmitted through them to northern countries.

But there is another aspect worth underlining, generally neglected by critics, which is Lawrence's profound, almost religious respect for the peculiarity of the place and for the 'otherness' of the people living there. It is the refusal to accept this 'otherness' which he sees as the main cause of 'a certain Grössenwahn' (91:9), a desire for grandeur which has led some countries to expand,[26] imposing their system of values, power and *Weltanschauung* on the freedom of other peoples.[27] With his reference to the Roman Empire, its German inheritors and their greed for expansion, he seems to indict all forms of imperialism (subtly including, although not overtly, the English variety). At the same time, his condemnation of expansionistic policies (military, economic and political) involves a wider moral, ideological and even epistemological issue: the problematic comprehension (and thus the acceptance) of all kinds of cultural 'otherness'. This, as Lawrence is well aware, is inevitably hindered and deformed by the preconceptions inherent in one's own environment and culture.

Of the three versions of this first essay, the final one suggests in its very title – with the word 'crucifix' used in the singular as a symbol of all the individual ones – a kind of synthesis of the author's experience in a land suspended between the North and the South. It is in this kind of island within Europe that Lawrence finds the only crucifix which he perceives as a real expression of true religious feeling, and which therefore remains 'real and dear to me, among all this violence of representation' (98:37–8). The only other Christ he sees as the embodiment of religious truth is the fallen one at the very end of the essay, forgotten and crumbling to pieces, 'the muscles, carved sparely in the old wood, looking all wrong, upside down' (100:31–3), just like religion itself. This image of the human, emotionally striking Christ leads Lawrence to reflect on the function of art, and the value of institutionalized models: crucifixes 'in the approved Guido Reni fashion' (98:12–13) are nothing but conventional symbols, mainstream ideology commercialized into a multiplicity of identical inexpressive figures.[28]

The intensely pious Bavarian people are therefore the final example of a people isolated and in deep communion with surrounding Nature, whose life is regulated by natural rhythms and events (like the community's religious celebrations): a people approaching their twilight, like the Christs that tumble down, covered by weeds, to be replaced by new ones carved by artists.

At the turn of the imperial road towards Rome, the Christs become 'theatrical', rhetorical and sensational: they oppress the onlooker, and no longer convey any religious feeling, nor do they function as a link between man and transcendence. Their ostentatious display of blood and agony makes them, according to Lawrence, the expression of a kind of morbid, narcissistic indulgence in suffering which arouses in him a feeling of horrified revulsion. Furthermore, the horrible, cruelly tortured Christ in the polished little baroque chapel near St Jakob leads him to reflect on the contrast between the handsome, ornate external shrine and the miserable figure inside. This paradox offers him the opportunity both to expose the falseness and banality of traditional descriptions of the Tyrol (such as that offered by a picture in London of 'Spring in the Austrian Tyrol'), and indirectly to indict all kinds of easy generalizations in one's approach to other countries.

'The Spinner and the Monks'

The spatial opposition between the ethereal mountains,[29] and the lower parts of the earth where people strive for survival, corresponds to the polarity between high and low which becomes a theme of the following essay, 'The Spinner and the Monks'. Here the opposition emerges clearly in Lawrence's dichotomy between the Eagle and the Dove, which correspond to two churches, the embodiment of two opposing streams of sensitivity to Christianity, San Tommaso, high up, ethereal, looking to 'the subservient world below' (103:15), and San Francesco, humble and almost unnoticed among the common people, completely merged into the village, 'offering no resistance to the storming of the traffic' (103:11). Whereas in the earlier version of the essay he had been attracted by the position of San Tommaso and wanted to get to it, here he recalls his attraction and projects into it his past experience in Gargnano: he observes that the church is an inescapable element of the place, not so much because of its exterior aspect as for its presence everywhere when the bells sound, a sound which functions as a distinguishing element of the day.

Almost detached from the earth, like the entrance to an abstract heaven – the way up to it appears a kind of secret passage – the sun-drenched square in front of San Tommaso[30] offers the author a privileged point of observation which allows him to perceive, as he looks across the lake towards the mountains on the opposite shore, the point 'where heaven and earth are divided' (105:21). Compared with the first version of the essay, this clearly shows a shift of attention away from the peculiarity of the place to its symbolic meaning, and consequently away from the individualities of the spinner and the monks (along with what is strange and attractive about them), to what they stand for in the play of oppositions. While Lawrence does not dwell on the spinner's appearance or his conversation with her, he insists on her being 'sun-coloured, sun-discoloured' (108:39), stubbornly clenched to the wall like a 'sun-worn stone' (106:25), solid and self-sufficient, and yet moving her fingers as if unconsciously, spontaneously part of the environment and wholly belonging to the sunshine. He feels overwhelmed by her, almost annihilated by her 'empyrean' transcendence; he is 'a bit of the outside, negligible' (106:29–30), reduced to 'a piece of night and moonshine' (108:40) in front of her.

The author's point of observation within this dichotomy of high and low, dark and light, changes repeatedly in this essay. For example, he associates himself with the *night* when confronting the spinner, and with the *light* when he meets the dark, shadowy glances of Italian people, who seem to live 'hidden in lairs and caves of darkness' (104:13). And again, once the spinner has 'cut off her consciousness' (109:15) from him, he swiftly walks down to a lower level, towards the earth and the darkness, but occasionally looking up towards the shining rocks which make him feel 'uneasy' (109:34); and then, when twilight is about to descend, he runs up again to avoid being trapped in the darkness.

It is once again from a higher level that he perceives the two monks who, in this essay, suggest, in their endless movement backwards and forwards, a kind of 'neutrality' with respect to the opposing principles of light and darkness: 'they paced the narrow path of the twilight, treading in the neutrality of the law' (112:7–8). While day and night are merging in the line of twilight, bringing together their individual completeness, the two monks seem to deny this principle, keeping the two opposites apart and thus preventing the merging of the positive and negative poles.

Another polarity, a historical one, emerges in the essay when Lawrence compares the 'Strada Vecchia' with the 'Strada Nuova': for him, their coexistence marks the 'twilight line' between two ages, one of them on the point of disappearing, swallowed up by darkness, and the other coming into full light: the old road, peaceful and natural, *goes down* towards the plain, while the other one, a 'beautiful, new, military high-road' (110:21–2), *goes up* towards the Austrian frontier.

The oxymoronic quality of this description is also found elsewhere in the essay, in which language itself seems to struggle in search of a meaning as near as possible to the communion of unbalanced opposites. This is, for example, the case with the description of the spinner who disappears at twilight 'like a sleep of wakefulness' (113:1–2), and of the monks who move 'in the neutral, shadowless light of shadow' (112:5).

'The Lemon Gardens'

A similar quality is found in 'The Lemon Gardens', an essay in which the dark fire of the blood of the southern races – opposed to the mystic ecstasy of the mind of the northern countries – is projected into the image of Aphrodite as 'gleaming darkness ... luminous night ... goddess of destruction' (116:28–9). The observation that a 'cold fire' (116:29) consumes the Latin races but 'does not create' (116:30) confirms Lawrence's distance from the enthusiastic Romantic image of Italy; in fact, the attraction which he feels for the country does not prevent him from carrying out an objective analysis of its drawbacks. For him the South and the North correspond respectively – in a kind of Blakean opposition – to the worship of self, the ecstasy of the tiger devouring 'all living flesh' (118:13–14) and pacing – like the monks –

'backwards and forwards in the cage of its own infinite' (118:14–15), and (on the other hand) the worship of the selfless, the ecstasy of the lamb subduing its will to what is outside self, which leads in the opposite direction, to self-destruction through transcendence. Instead of finding a balance, however, these two principles continually gnaw at each other's existence.

Consequently, while the English – and with them all the northern races – have reached 'a perfect and equable human consciousness, selfless' (124:40–125:1) and are attracted by the Italian 'phallic worship' (124:29), the 'padrone' looks greedily towards England and the worship of the machine, the power to subdue nature.[31] Both tendencies are wrong for Lawrence, because while the northern races are destined to be frustrated in their pursuit of phallic worship – 'we do not believe in it' (125:10) – the 'little padrone' is 'too old' (131:39) to achieve his goal.

The consequence of this split between North and South, whose origins Lawrence traces back to the Middle Ages and the Renaissance, is, according to him, a double 'twilight', a twofold decline spreading over both worlds, which will eventually devour each other. To stop the process that makes 'London and the industrial countries [spread] like a blackness over all the world, horrible, in the end destructive' (132:12–14) and which will ultimately lead to the destruction of such natural wonders as Lake Garda, it is necessary to 'turn round' (132:24), that is, to invert this trend. He does not believe, however, that this will happen: as a matter of fact, the end of the essay suggests that, while the old world is approaching its twilight, the new one, in its blind, frantic lust for expansion, is doomed to an even quicker end.

In this essay the 'padrone' is portrayed as 'an ancient, aristocratic monkey' (114:12), with gesticulating, insecure hands, and a furtive, anxious glance; his clown-like mixture of broken French and Italian – without any complete sentences – is matched by his ill-disguised embarrassment at not understanding technical instructions written in 'laconic' American (114:35).

To suggest the doom hanging over the decrepit aristocracy which the 'padrone' represents, Lawrence reintroduces in this essay the dichotomy between inside and outside, darkness and light, in relation to the residence of the little 'padrone', 'a splendid place' (115:17) but only as far as the façade and the hall ('spacious and beautiful', 115:23) are concerned. Once the author enters the house, the rooms are 'dark and ugly' (115:29), 'the carved, cold furniture stands in its tomb' (115:31–2); he feels something deadening in the atmosphere not only of the house (whose inhabitants appear to him like ghosts), but also in the lemon houses, where the trees (once a source of wealth) are deprived of the light coming from the outside and 'look like ghosts in the darkness of the underworld' (129:6).

The more generalizing attitude that characterizes this version of the essay with respect to the former one appears in the title itself, which no longer mentions the Signor di P. Both he and his wife are here given Christian names, *Pietro*[32] and *Gemma*, connoting symbolically their roles in the relationship: Gemma ('gem') suits the wife's function submissively to 'adorn' her husband's life, and her actual ability – as a gemstone – to reflect light on the cold, opaque stone ('pietra' in Italian) he represents.

By emphasizing the woman's submission to her husband, and the latent conflict between the two, who are kept together not by love but by necessity, Lawrence introduces the theme of the 'sex duel' which emerges more fully in 'The Theatre' and in the San Gaudenzio essays. Signora Gemma's verbal exuberance and her somewhat theatrical behaviour are seen as a kind of painful compensation for her subordinate role, as an instinctive reaction to her feeling of 'impotence in her life' (122:25).

Lawrence then links this conflict between man and woman to the split between the mind and the soul, in a kind of digression in which both are seen as the outcome of a Puritan Utopia (the quest for a world of pure democracy) and a yearning for the ideal of a perfect man (120:11–40). It was this inflexible radicalism which led to that unique event in English history, the beheading of Charles the First, which marked the end of the Kings by divine right, but was also the wrong way of passing from aristocracy to democracy (see Explanatory Notes, 120:14). And it must be noted that Lawrence is far from seeing this passage in terms of progress, as he charts its development to a world of 'huge ruins' (132:30), 'quite dead' (132:31).

'The Theatre'

In the final version of 'The Theatre' the transformation of the church into a theatre is seen as the response to 'a new lease of life' (133:16), the result of an attempt to catch up with progress, presented as 'speed, as of flying atoms, chaos' (133:15–16). Noticing how cleverly the church was originally built for 'the dramatic presentation of religious ceremonies' (133:18–19), Lawrence describes – 'looking down on all the world'

(133:29) from his privileged point of view, box number 8 of the Signor di P. – the whole of Gargnano society, in a way that shows how his stay in Italy has endowed him with a penetrating insight into the life of the place[33] and also an emotional involvement in it, exemplified by his instinctive, inexplicable dislike of the village magistrate, who strikes him as 'very republican and self-important' (134:4).

After noticing that even the common people sitting below are arranged according to a social hierarchy, so that 'the more reckless spirits of the village' (134:15) sit at the very back, Lawrence's attention shifts from the class distinctions to the rigid separation between men and women into two groups, each making 'a hard, strong herd' (134:35). This separation seems to intensify what he sees as the natural antagonism between the sexes, leading him to a discussion of their mutual relationship, here seen as an unrelenting fight. The only deep bond between them is the principle of motherhood and fatherhood, the worship of the child, which 'is divine' (135:28). In the 'great reverence for the infant' (135:13), the woman becomes, in the triumph of motherhood, 'the law-giver, the supreme authority' (136:2), a power by which men feel overwhelmed and subjugated. And it is as an escape from the supremacy of maternity that Lawrence explains the Italian men's habit of drinking heavily – making the public house a kind of pseudo-home – and, ultimately, emigrating.[34]

What strikes the author most about this 'sex duel', which he sees as conforming to a very rigid code, is its public performance. Even if the partners feel trapped and uneasy when they have to bear the other's company 'on the public highway' (135:5–6), they walk together affecting a harmony which does not actually exist. This, for Lawrence, is a part of a social comedy which they accept because marriage is the only socially acceptable way of coming together in the creation of a child; that is, doing what the community expects of them, the real *raison d'être*. Unfolding the ritual which regulates the relationships between the sexes, Lawrence also dislodges another Romantic cliché, that of the spontaneous, exuber-ant nature of the Italians, whose reputation as passionate Latin lovers hides (for him) the fact that their real aim is not the bliss of passion but the pride of parenthood, as suggested by the Signor di P.[35]

When he is invited by the latter to see the performance of *Ghosts*,[36] Lawrence observes how, in its pathos and melodrama, it is very different from the production he had 'lately seen in Munich' (136:25–6), with its 'hard, ethical, slightly mechanised characters' (136:27–8). The fact that the Italian performance is 'so different from Ibsen, and so much more moving' (137:34) is due, in his opinion, to a conflict between Ibsen's northern worship of the mind, and the worship of the flesh underlying the way Italian people act; whatever role they perform, their acting appears 'a form of physical gratification' (137:32). From this experience, he proceeds to a discussion of art as an emanation of the spirit of the place, pointing out that transplanting any work of art from one culture to another creates not only a distortion of the original work but often a disturbing effect. After the performance of *Ghosts*, for instance, the barber is left with a sense of 'sterile cold inertia' (138:32), as if he would like to hide himself, whereas D'Annunzio's play fills him with eagerness to communicate his enthusiasm to other people, as if he had 'drunk sweet wine' (138:35–6).[37] Interestingly, Lawrence seems to connect the different effects of the plays with the languages employed in them, which reflect, in turn, the nature of the peoples who use them. Whereas, for example, the English are interested in the objective meaning of words, the Italians are instinctively attracted by rhetoric, 'the physical effect of the language upon the blood' (139:11–12). This, according to Lawrence, accounts for the great popularity of D'Annunzio, whose language – although just 'bosh' – manages to produce a 'sensuous gratification', the pleasure of 'hearing and feeling without understanding' (139:13–16).

But the most important part of the essay (almost half of it) contains an attack on *Hamlet*, in relation to which the other performances mentioned seem to create a frame within the frame. The fact that Enrico Persevalli – the manager of the company, himself of peasant origin – has chosen *Hamlet* for this important last evening is an act of homage to the prestige of wealthy, industrialized, 'modern' England,[38] while he himself is an example of 'the modern Italian, suspicious, isolated, self-nauseated' (144:15). While attending the performance, Lawrence clearly realizes that in this context Hamlet's tragedy turns into a tragic farce,[39] its intellectual sophistication being totally foreign to the down-to-earth peasants performing it; he is relieved when the play is finally over.

From his description of this quaint but disturbing experience, his attention shifts to the value of the play, which leads him to a discussion in abstract terms of the central role of *Hamlet* as a turning-point in the history of Western sensitivity. By admitting that he has 'always felt an aversion from Hamlet' (143:39), Lawrence places himself in the line of a critical tradition (Schlegel, Coleridge, Wilson Knight[40]) which has considered Hamlet as a negative character, as a result of his failure to turn thought into action and his inability to restore order after destroying the old régime. By means of a comparison with Orestes in Greek tragedy, of whom Hamlet is the deformed, modern version, Lawrence makes

Hamlet the embodiment of that negative trend in Western sensitivity which, in its 'convulsed reaction of the mind from the flesh, of the spirit from the self' (144:28–9), leads to the annihilation of Self. And, as such, Hamlet becomes one of the main protagonists of the book's analysis of the way in which European society has plunged itself into the most destructive war of all time.

'San Gaudenzio', 'The Dance', 'Il Duro', 'John'

The four essays about San Gaudenzio are characterized by an increasingly sombre tone which seems to issue from Lawrence's awareness that the uncontaminated nature of the lake and the mountains surrounding it already belongs to the past; what survives is soon to be swallowed up by progress and by the impatience of the new generation with places in which it feels trapped.

At the beginning of 'San Gaudenzio', he presents his move up to the hills as the result of a desire to get closer to the sun,[41] a desire he expresses at the end of a lyrical passage describing the coming of Spring, which suddenly covers the naked branches of trees with almond and apricot blossoms. His need to move towards the sun anticipates the main theme of these essays, the feeling of restlessness and displacement, and the need to escape from a place no longer felt to be 'home'. Lawrence, who was familiar with this feeling, is well aware of the problems involved in this escape, and also with the social and economic problems faced by emigrants.

In 'San Gaudenzio', this theme entwines with that of the 'sex duel' presented through the disputes between Paolo and Maria Fiori;[42] the latter, dark and passionate, comes from the plain, knows what the world is like and is in favour of change and progress; Paolo, fair-haired, blue-eyed and from the high mountains, with a 'curious nobility' and 'something statuesque' (156:26–7) about him, is for tradition and continuity with the past. For Maria, what one has and is in the world depends on one's activity and possessions; for Paolo, it is decided by superior powers which one has to accept unquestioningly.

As an attentive spectator of this verbal 'duel' between a fighter for a better life and emancipation from the old, unchangeable order, and a conservative supporter of life based on the unchangeable rhythms of Nature, Lawrence is ultimately unable to decide the winner. While he does not approve of Maria's greed, he cannot share Paolo's naïve worship of the upper classes (typical of peasants) and his inability to discriminate between the 'accident of riches' and the 'aristocracy of the spirit' (160:26–7).

With her belief in the new order of the rich, and as the supreme authority within the house, Maria has been responsible for her husband's emigration, a destiny which seems inevitably to await their children, who are already learning English. Her ethos of the 'self-made-man' partly derives from her awareness that the old world is collapsing, even at San Gaudenzio, and Lawrence can only agree with her when he watches them 'wringing a little oil and wine out of the rocky soil' (165:37–8) and sees the ruined, empty, ghost-like lemon houses.

But the doom impending on this 'little Garden of Eden' (156:7) had already been found on the way up to San Gaudenzio, anticipated by the colourful sign 'Birra, Verona' – now 'more and more popular' (156:5) – unmistakably betraying a taste for beer (a northern drink infiltrating the reign of southern wine). And no less insidious is the cultural penetration of Italy by the myth of America in the essay 'John', revealed by the village people's admiration for Giovanni, who can speak English and is shabbily dressed in 'American clothes' (186:32).[43]

This infatuation with everything that comes from outside the region is another indication, for Lawrence, of these people's loss of a basically religious way of life; this loss being reflected in the farcical, corrupt figure of the local priest, more interested in drinking than in praying, in Paolo's oaths against Maria, and in Maria's pragmatic attitude to life, which does not accept any higher unquestionable power.

Her materialistic belief that the only 'distinguished' people are those with money leads her, in 'The Dance', to separate the better-off customers coming from the village below, who can pay and who are consequently served food and invited to stay longer, from the peasants, who have to leave when she chooses.[44] A vivid sketch of local life before the First World War, with peasants playing and dances taking place in farmhouses, 'The Dance' prepares for the introduction of the extraordinary figure of Il Duro – analysed in the following essay – and the sinister wood-cutter with a wooden leg, both of them amazing dancers. In a passage where the rhythm of the prose evokes and imitates that of the dance, Lawrence's attention focuses on the 'god-like' nature of the dancers, totally taken by 'the transport of repeated ecstasy' (169:6), and on the almost hypnotic effect which the dance has on the two English-women,[45] 'lifted like a boat on a supreme wave' (168:40), entranced and frightened at the same time by the power these men exert. All the men, in turn, concentrate intensely on the two foreign women, thus revealing once again the tense polarity between the sexes characteristic of Italy. The fact that men love to 'dance with men' (167:29–30) (Maria and the two English Signoras are the only women present) confirms the fact that public places are strictly a male domain, where women are in danger of exposing themselves as 'loose women'[46] and, as a result, of losing their authority within the domestic environment. This is confirmed by the maliciously daring song at the end of the essay, its 'suggestive mockery' undoubtedly addressed to the foreign Signoras, who 'cannot catch the words' (171:28).

In 'Il Duro' and 'John', Lawrence portrays two outstanding characters, closely linked with each other in spite of their profound differences. While the former is a fascinating man, with 'temples . . . distinct and fine as a work of art' (175:22–3), the latter is an 'ingenuous youth, sordidly shabby and dirty' (182:5–6); they embody not only a generation gap, but also two opposing attitudes towards exile, two ways of coming to terms with the inevitable problem of emigration. Self-sufficient and totally isolated, Il Duro, with his swift, easy gestures and his Pan-like, impenetrable 'pale-gleaming eyes' (173:36), appears to Lawrence as the embodiment of the southern worship of the blood, 'a creature in intimate communion with the sensible world' (177:15–16). Like Paolo, he seems to derive his strength from his roots in the place; his stay in America was a sheer necessity and did not touch him deeply. On the contrary, John tried hard to integrate himself into the life of the foreign country, learning its language, adjusting himself to different customs and habits, doing his best to feel part of the foreign culture. As a result, he is now a totally restless soul, uneasy in his home country (his only link with it seems to be his father) and prey to an inexplicable, uncontrollable impulse to emigrate again. Paradoxically, in spite of the humiliation and maltreatment he suffered in America, he – like Paolo and Maria's children – seems to identify the new world with the future, with the promise of life, and his native country with the past, with death. Exile has turned him into a representative of the rootless younger generation, whose destiny – following the restless, changing flux – is to witness the disintegration of 'the old life' and to be precipitated 'into the new chaos' (186:18–19). Both men, however, appear utterly incomprehensible to Lawrence, who is aware that he lacks the capacity to understand both the origins of Il Duro's stubborn decision not to marry, and John's frantic impulse to fly 'away from home . . . to the great, raw America' (186:15–16).

'Italians in Exile', 'The Return Journey'

In these essays, written and revised when the war had already broken out, the author has vastly improved his knowledge of foreign languages; he feels comfortable in a variety of situations, and can even dare to challenge humorously the mocking comment of a French waitress in a Swiss café (220:30–36), to act as an interpreter between a landlord and an Englishman from London (211:16–20), although with the ironic effect of intruding on the Englishman's privacy, and to pretend to be Austrian in front of two old Swiss ladies (208:38–209:12).[47]

And yet, in spite of this confidence, he appears more and more restless; disappointed by the places he comes across, reluctant to stop anywhere unless he has to. In his feverish flight southwards he captures an atmosphere of ruin, madness and death not only in the places, but even in the people he meets on his way, whose neurotic behaviour or physical troubles betray the disease of the world around them. Such a one, for example, is the Englishman who keeps madly walking and walking, like a human machine, taking no heed of the places he goes through (210:17–40), or the landlord just south of Zürich, 'trembling on the edge of delirium tremens' (194:15–16), or the two old Austrian ladies fussing madly over a dog for fear he may go out and wet his feet (208:34–5), or finally the woman in the village at the foot of the Gotthard, 'frightened by her own deafness' (217:32).

To throw off the sense of oppression aroused in him by these encounters, Lawrence tries to escape to the 'Germany of fairy tales and minstrels and craftsmen' (189:18) or to locate 'a warm, ruddy bit of Italy within the cold darkness of Switzerland' (199:22–3), but he cannot entirely dispel his gloomy forebodings.

Another symptom of the disease of Europe is, for Lawrence, the number of uprooted, restless people – Germans, Italians, French, and English – he meets on his way southwards:[48] in a kind of macabre dance preparing for the downward plunge of Europe (as he himself is precipitously plunging down towards the South), people are swarming like parasites in hotels, restlessly walking 'backwards and forwards on the edge of the lake' (225:13–14). Paradoxically, while the author is in search of an old world in the South, many southern people – for example, the Italian community in Switzerland – are looking for a new Utopia in the North. This explains his recoiling away from the community of Italians in exile, who are, like their leader Giuseppino, under the influence of 'a new spirit . . . something strange and pure and slightly frightening' (202:8–9). They are a little community of anarchists who have rebelled against the old order, and consequently against the Italian government, 'an instrument of injustice and of wrong' (201:25–6). They have fled to Switzerland where they are somehow trying to be self-sufficient. In spite of their homesickness (which explodes in the theatrical emphasis with which they talk of Italy, its sunshine and its landscape), they stubbornly endure their disheartening situation, unwilling to give up their belief in 'infinite harmony' (202:16): a belief which the author sadly perceives to be the blind pursuit of an abstract ideal.

As far as Lawrence is concerned, his interaction with a variety of people and places, and his consideration from various angles of the problem of exile, seem to foreshadow his own exile, his long wandering about the world from North to South, from East to West, in search of new beliefs and a new way of life, in order to avoid – like the monks – pacing for ever neutrally in the line of twilight. But in this volume he ends (as always) as one who watches, detached, curious, sceptical, conscious of his own neutrality as a man and as an author. And his personal search, already compellingly presented in these essays, turns out to involve the social and existential problems of contemporary people going far beyond the local specificities which originally prompted them.

This edition of *Twilight in Italy* offers not only a penetrating insight into Lawrence's early travel writing, but also into a critical period of European history. Like a camera moving from one battlefield to the next, it creates an image of Europe coming to terms with the war. What is equally important in this volume, however, is Lawrence's innovatory view of Italy within the English tradition, an Italy which has finally been rescued from its Romantic, but often distorting and patronizing northern European image. This operation is interesting from two points of view: while on the one hand it respects the 'otherness' Italy represents, the English public also becomes informed about aspects of a country unknown to the English, in spite of their traditional relationship with Italy. And this is what Lawrence to some extent continued to do in his subsequent travel books set in Italy, *Sea and Sardinia* and *Sketches of Etruscan Places*. From this perspective, the essays collected in *Twilight in Italy* show Lawrence experimenting for the first time with a new genre and creating, with increasing independence, a new approach to a foreign country particularly suited to the demands of the new age.

NOTES ON THE INTRODUCTION

1. After spending a week in Riva, their first stop on the lake. They stayed at Villa Leonardi, situated in a residential street very close to the centre, where '[they] got a beautiful room, but it [was] too dear'. James T. Boulton, ed., *The Letters of D. H. Lawrence*, volume I (Cambridge University Press, 1979), 448. (Hereafter referred to as *Letters*, i.)

2. The Villa Igea belonged to the family Di Paoli who were living in the majestic neoclassical villa next door, now the centre of the 'Comunità Montana'. Externally the Villa Igea still maintains its original L-shape, with two branches creating an internal garden. Although the inside has been entirely changed, from the window on the side where Lawrence and Frieda lived it is still possible to enjoy the splendid view over the lake.

3. The ledgers of the trading company of Gargnano (the Società Lago di Garda) bear witness to the fact that millions of lemons, as well as a large quantity of olive oil and laurel oil (for medicinal purposes), were exported to Vienna, St Petersburg, the Prussian Empire and England. Lake Garda was the northernmost orchard of Mediterranean fruits.

4. The Italian publishing house Feltrinelli, founded in Milan in 1954, originates from this family, who were once wood-traders from the Tyrol.

5. 'Would you mind offering the articles to somebody you think probable. I am about reduced to my last shilling again . . . so I must work' (*Letters*, i. 405).

6. Lawrence may have developed this idea while travelling, perhaps prompted by the incident of his near-arrest (on 7 May) which became the subject of 'How a Spy is Arrested', or someone else (possibly Edward Garnett or de la Mare) may have given him the idea, as is suggested by George Neville in *A Memoir of D. H. Lawrence: The Betrayal*, ed. Carl Baron (Cambridge University Press, 1981), pp. 155–6. Neville records Lawrence as saying before leaving England that he had had an offer to go abroad and do some descriptive pieces, but there is no other evidence to confirm this.

7. 'I believe my sketches may easily prove good selling stuff, better than a novel. Also they might do very well in America.' George J. Zytaruk and James T. Boulton, *The Letters of D. H. Lawrence*, volume II (Cambridge University Press, 1981), 373. (Hereafter referred to as *Letters*, ii.)

8. 'French Sons of Germany' was published on 3 August in both the *Westminster Gazette* and its special Saturday edition, the *Saturday Westminster*, of the same date. 'Hail in the Rhine-Land' was published in the same manner on 9 and 10 August respectively. Both essays were republished in *Phoenix* in 1936 under the series title, 'German Impressions'. 'Christs in the Tyrol' appeared both in the *Westminster Gazette* and the *Saturday Westminster* on 22 March 1913 and was reprinted in *Phoenix*.

9. Cf. *Letters*, i. 443. The sketch was rejected by J. A. Spender (1862–1942), editor of the *Westminster Gazette*, as noted on the envelope which enclosed the autograph manuscript.

10. It gathers together the essays making up *Twilight in Italy* and their earlier versions (published in the *English Review* in September 1913 under the series title 'By the Lago di Garda'), as well as the essays which Lawrence once conceived as part of a travel book about Germany, which, however, he never completed. Cf. *Letters*, i. 431.

11. The article, signed 'H. D. Lawrence', appeared on the back page of the *Manchester Guardian* on 18 August 1914.

12. 'Riva is fearfully nice . . . It is quite Italian – so is Trient, for that matter – only the Austrians have collared them and stock them with Chocolate Soldiers' (*Letters*, i. 452).

13. The military atmosphere in Germany is expressed also in the stories 'The Prussian Officer' and 'The Thorn in the Flesh', written in June 1913 and published in November 1914. Interestingly, there is a striking difference between the travel essays and the fiction. In the stories, German militarism is really destructive, and obedience to its codes, which are absurd in what they demand, gives rise to different forms of hysteria.

14. Paradoxically, this event was destined to be repeated in Cornwall when Lawrence was suspected of being a German spy and forced to leave the region on 15 October 1917.

15. *Waldbröler Zeitung*, 17 May 1912; Cf. Dieter Mehl, 'D. H. Lawrence in Waldbröl', *Notes & Queries*, xxxi, March 1984, 80. 'When we were driving home . . . the hail came on in immense stones, as big as walnuts' (*Letters*, i. 404).

16. In her unfinished memoirs, Frieda refers to the crossing of the Alps as a very romantic experience: 'we slept very often in haylofts which I thought was wonderful'. They actually slept in hay-huts twice. Cf. John Worthen, *D. H. Lawrence: The Early Years 1885–1912*, Cambridge University Press, 1991, pp. 393–432.

17. He was clearly using Baedeker's guides, such as *Austria-Hungary* (Leipzig 1900), *The Rhine* (Leipzig 1911), *Northern Italy* (Leipzig 1913) and *Switzerland* (Leipzig 1913).

18. In the contract with Duckworth no title had been specified. Lawrence suggested: 'Studies of Restless Italy'; 'An Italian Winter'; 'Uneasy Italy'; 'Studies of Italian Restlessness' – with an explicit preference for the last (*Letters*, ii. 475). As the publisher was trying to avoid any political implications (Italy was an ally), 'Italian Days' was first agreed and then turned into *Twilight in Italy*. Duckworth's title is retained for this edition as there is no record of Lawrence having objected to it.

19. 'Christs in the Tirol', with its German rendering of the place name, can be found in Appendix I.

20. This is confirmed by his letter to Lady Cynthia Asquith of 5 September 1915: 'I am writing a book of sketches, or preparing a book of sketches, about the nations, Italian German and English, full of philosophising and struggling to show things real' (*Letters*, ii. 386).

21. Cf. Michael Black, *D. H. Lawrence: The Early Philosophical Works*, Macmillan, 1991, p. 230.

22. For example, in *Study of Thomas Hardy*, *The Crown*, *Movements in European History* and *Apocalypse*.

23. See, for instance, Michael Black, *op. cit.*; David Ellis and Howard Mills, *D. H. Lawrence's Non-Fiction*, Cambridge University Press, 1988; Del Ivan Janik, 'The Two Infinites: D. H. Lawrence's *Twilight in Italy*', *D. H. Lawrence Review*, 7, 1974, 179–98.

24. In this connection, it is worth considering a near-contemporary philosophical work, Oswald Spengler's *Der Untergang des Abendlands/The Decline of the West* (1918–22), extremely popular in Europe immediately after the First World War.

25. This language recalls Lawrence's ambivalent attitude towards the Italian Futurists, their cult of the machine and their negation of the past and tradition. Cf. his letter to Arthur McLeod of 5 June 1914: 'they want to deny every scrap of tradition and experience, which is silly . . . They will even use their intuition for intellectual and scientific purposes' (*Letters*, ii. 180, 181), and his defence of the innovatory ideas of the movement in a letter of the same day to Edward Garnett: 'it is the inhuman will, call it physiology, or like Marinetti – physiology of matter, that fascinates me' (*Letters*, ii. 183).

26. The basic reason for the war seems to coincide with the inability to understand and respect 'otherness'.

27. Lawrence seems to conceive of the idea of freedom in terms of people's right to their identity: 'If only nations would realise that they have certain natural characteristics, if only they could understand and agree to each other's particular nature, how much simpler it would all be' (91:9–12).

28. The opposition between the Christs carved by peasants imbued with a true religious feeling, and the ones carved by artists conveying a conventional idea, is probably influenced by John Ruskin's ideas about art as an expression of the community, of its ideals and values, in e.g. *Modern Painters* (1843–60) and *The Stones of Venice* (1851–3).

29. The sense of awe created by the mountains, and by radiant snow, cold and divine, timeless and alien to the pains of human life, is a recurrent image in Lawrence's work, from *The Prussian Officer* (the soldier is torn by the dichotomy between his own suffering and the unattainable mountains) to *Women in Love* (Gerald Crich finds death on the snowy mountain tops) and *The Lost Girl*.

30. As in the former version of the essay, the inside of the church is described as dark and oppressive, with its stifling air – the weight of 'centuries of incense' (105:9) – in contrast with the open air outside.

31. This accounts for his gesture of lifting his hand towards the sun, as if trying to encompass it as a source of wealth (131:26).

32. Lawrence recalls the biblical associations of his name to suggest an implicit ironic comparison between the 'stone' on which Christianity is founded, and

this pillar of a declining race.' This reference is highly appropriate in the Italian context since the Catholic church regards Peter as the possessor of the keys of heaven's gate, and Signor Pietro is now the little owner of a declining empire.

33. For example he uses 'francs' instead of 'lire' (see 79:24) to indicate how much the bersaglieri pay for a bunch of cock's plumes on their hats (151:15); 'francs' was (and still is) the word commonly used around Lake Garda to mean 'lire'.

34. They gain 'some dignity . . . as producers' (136:11), not as 're-producers'.

35. 'It was as if his *raison d'être* had been to have a son' (124:24-5).

36. The different effect the play has in that particular environment is anticipated by the observation 'after a few minutes I realised that *I Spettri* was Ibsen's *Ghosts'* (136:17). The Italian title is *Gli Spettri*; a mistake probably due to Lawrence's imperfect Italian.

37. This is also connected with Italian pride in their national writers. D'Annunzio was especially popular on the western shore of Lake Garda. In Gardone Riviera, he built the impressive house-museum known as the 'Vittoriale degli Italiani'; and from there, in 1919-21, he led the nationalist expedition to free Fiume (Istria) from Austro-Hungarian domination. People in Gargnano still remember him as a man of eccentric habits, but nevertheless as a man of 'genius'.

38. It corresponds to the little padrone's admiration for the machines and wealth of England (131:22-38) and to John's inexplicable desire to go back to America in spite of the humiliation he suffered there (186:11-41).

39. This is partly due to its being performed in a foreign language: see, for instance, his remarks about 'Questo cranio, Signore-' (150:1-2), and the incongruity of the word 'signore' in connection with the peasant-actor Enrico Persevalli to whom it is addressed.

40. Cf. G. Wilson Knight, *The Wheel of Fire*, Oxford University Press, 1930, pp. 17-46.

41. 'We could not bear to live down in the village any more . . . It was time to go up, to climb with the sun' (155:33-6).

42. The names Paolo and Maria are taken from real life. Lawrence turned the name of the family from Capelli into Fiori (flowers), thus suggesting a connection with the blossoming flowers at the beginning of the essay which he presents as his very reason for going to San Gaudenzio.

43. The author (thoroughly English) regards them as an expression of 'sordid . . . American respectability' (181:5), ironically pointing out that they cannot hide the fact that he has not washed (182:7).

44. The existence of a plutocratic hierarchy in this society is reflected also in the fact that, in dancing with the two English Signoras, 'the peasants have always to take their turn after the young well-to-do men from the village below' (169:18-20).

45. Frieda and a visitor from England, Tony Cyriax. 'There was a wild and

handsome one-legged man . . . who danced with Frieda, and then Tony, like a wooden-legged angel' (*Letters*, i. 536).

46. See the vivid description in 'The Theatre' (152:22–7).

47. We can observe the difference between the author's first stay in Metz at the beginning of the book, where he could hardly understand the words of the officer, and his confidence in pretending to be a native speaker. By 1913, although his knowledge of German had improved, he was himself far from speaking the language correctly.

48. The title of the last essay, 'The Return Journey', is undoubtedly ambiguous, while in an earlier version (the copy sent to Pinker for the American publication) it was even more ambiguously called 'The Return Home': the English traveller is actually returning to his exile, or rather not returning, but once again departing from his home country.

Note on the Texts

Before a description of how the texts making up this volume have been restored, and the enormous amount of detailed work an editor has to do in getting as close as possible to an author's text, two points should be made clear, as they directly influence the editing of the essays in this volume. First, Lawrence constantly revised his texts, and considered any typescript placed before him an opportunity for further revision, not simply a chance to check for mistakes. Secondly, Lawrence's copyists, typists, copy-editors and printers were in the habit of altering his punctuation, spelling and word use, which was idiosyncratic and expressive. Such alteration included, for example, the reduction of the length of his sentences by the introduction of semicolons – a punctuation mark Lawrence used only rarely – and the insertion of question marks when these were apparently missing, with some change to the meaning as well as an inevitable alteration to the rhythm of his sentences.

Such a tendency to overlay the original punctuation with house-styling particularly influenced these essays; they were, in many cases, meant for magazine publication, and were directly affected by the individual magazine's editorial policy. Norman Douglas's question when working at the *English Review*, 'would Lawrence never learn to be more succinct, and to hold himself in hand a little?' (*Looking Back*, 1934, pp. 345–6), is very revealing. It helps explain the process of making cuts and the variety of emendation the essays went through.

1.   For the essays published under the series title 'In Fortified Germany' and the essay 'Hail in the Rhine-Land', the base-texts are, respectively, the galley proofs of 'French Sons of Germany' and 'Hail in the Rhine-Land'; these are closest to the lost manuscripts. For the two essays unpublished in 1912, 'The English and the Germans' and 'How a Spy is Arrested', the base-texts are the galley proofs and the surviving autograph manuscript.

In these essays, changes in capitalization and house-style significantly altered the printed text from Lawrence's original in ways which effectively diminished Lawrence's knowledge, use of, and confidence with foreign languages. For example, the magazine's tendency to italicize foreign words such as the German 'Kinder, Kuchen, Kirche' (17:26), or the French 'couvre-toi de flannelle' in the first version of 'Christs in the Tirol' (231:30), turned the foreign words into something alien within the text, whereas for Lawrence they were a natural part of it. Magazines also regularized Lawrence's texts: in 'Hail in the Rhine-Land', for example, the precise but surprising adjective 'loopy' (24:6) (to describe the German 'Bretzel') was changed to the dull and conventional 'very'.

2. The base-text of 'A Chapel Among the Mountains' is the 1912 autograph manuscript; the base-text of 'A Hay-Hut Among the Mountains' is the ribbon copy typescript (no manuscript survives).

Paradoxically in these two essays, spellings such as 'squilched' (41:12) and 'towzled' (40:15) were employed by the typist, suggesting that he was following authorial usage rather than normalizing: as a result, although the manuscript is lost, we are probably still fairly close to what Lawrence actually wrote.

In 'A Hay-Hut Among the Mountains', a conclusion deleted by Lawrence in the manuscript, but reproduced by the typist, was printed in the first English edition. It shows that immediate, picturesque, often slightly romanticized response to a foreign reality which characterizes Lawrence's early travel writing (another example is offered by the first version of 'Christs in the Tirol' in Appendix I). The typescript version (here slightly emended) runs:

> We ran ourselves warm, but I felt as if the fires had gone out inside me. Down and down we raced the streams, that fell into beautiful green pools, and fell out again with a roar. Anita actually wanted to bathe, but I forbade it. So, after two hours' running downhill, we came out in the level valley at Glashütte. It was raining now, a thick dree rain. We pushed on to a little Gasthaus, that was really the home of a forester. There the stove was going, so we drank quantities of coffee, ale, and went to bed.
>
> "You spent the night in a hay-hut," said I to Anita. "And the next day in bed."
>
> "But I've done it, and I loved it," said she. "And besides, it's raining."
>
> And it continued to pour. So we stayed in the house of the Jäger who had a good, hard wife. She made us comfortable. But she kept her children in hand. They sat still and good, with their backs against the stove, and watched.
>
> "Your children are good," I said.

"They are wild ones," she answered, shaking her head sternly. And I saw the boy's black eyes sparkle.

"The boy is like his father," I said.

She looked at him.

"Yes—yes! perhaps", she said shortly.

But there was a proud stiffness in her neck, nevertheless. The father was a mark-worthy man, evidently. He was away in the forests now for a day or two. But he had photos of himself everywhere, a good looking, well-made, conceited Jäger, who was photographed standing with his right foot on the shoulder of a slaughtered chamois. And soon his wife had thawed sufficiently to tell me, 'Yes, he had accompanied the Crown Prince to shoot his first chamois.' And finally, she recited to us this letter, from the same Crown Prince:

"Lieber Karl, Ich möchte wissen wie und wann die letzte Gemse geschossen worden—" [Dear Karl, I would like to know how and when the last wild geese were shot—"]

The base-text of 'Christs in the Tyrol' is the *Westminster Gazette* printing of the second version. The autograph manuscript of the first version 'Christs in the Tirol', with the German rendering of the word 'Tyrol', is presented in Appendix I.

3. For the 'By the Lago di Garda' essays of 1913, the autograph manuscript which served as the setting-copy has been chosen as the base-text because it is more reliable than the *English Review* printing.

These essays offer good examples of how Lawrence's texts can be restored after being damaged. This occurs in all three essays. In 'The Spinner and the Monks', the alteration of 'tea and toast' (57:28) into 'a pleasant meal' destroyed on the one hand the nostalgic flavour of the original and, on the other, the author's tendency to interpret foreign reality with material inherited from his own culture. In 'The Lemon Gardens of the Signor di P.', the normalizing of the French word 'vouley' into 'voulez' prevents the reader from perceiving the Signor di P.'s pronunciation, which Lawrence is clearly showing. But the most striking example occurs in 'The Theatre', where the deletion of the sentence 'Hamlet in the book seems to me a very messy person, but the Hamlets I have seen on the stage have been positively nasty' (75:18–20), and the change made from 'that stinking fish, Hamlet' (78:9) to 'the cold Prince of Denmark', both reveal a remarkable toning-down of Lawrence's attack on the play.

4. The base-text of 'With the Guns' is the *Manchester Guardian* printing of 18 August 1914.

5. For most of *Twilight in Italy*, published by Duckworth on 1 June 1916, the base-text is the set of page proofs – Lawrence's duplicate set – in their unrevised state, located at the University of Nottingham. The exception is pages 125:6 to 126:31, where two pages of Lawrence's revised typescript (at Nottingham Archives) are employed. These pages of 'The Lemon Gardens', as explained in a letter from Lawrence to Clayton of 5 September 1915, were meant to be inserted in the final typescript. The typescript text preceding Lawrence's autograph revision shows a still-surviving hope that man may come to terms with the state of cultural crisis hanging over Europe. Lawrence's faith in mankind emerges clearly if we compare what he originally wrote in August 1915, for instance, with his September revision (126:18–29). The August version reads:

> We know that in Eternity exists a great world of truth, which here, in this falsity and confusion, is denied and obscured. And it is our business to set the whole living world into relation to the eternal truth. . . . We can at any rate begin the job. To finish it may be beyond us. But we must make a start, nevertheless. The success will be greater than the failure, however we fail, we shall be in closer relation to the Infinite Truth than we were.

A comparison of the page proofs of *Twilight in Italy* with the first English edition shows, too, how hard it is at times to distinguish the alterations made by publishers and printers from Lawrence's own corrections. Editorial policy has been to retain Lawrence's punctuation and styling in the page proofs and to accept most of the wording changes in the first English edition, eliminating as far as possible the corrections made by others. In the process, some of the revisions made by Lawrence on the proofs may have been lost. Editors have to make choices which – like all textual choices – are open to question. A modern editor can help restore a text, but is also very aware of how problematic the choices involved in the restoration may be, in the attempt to get as near as possible to what Lawrence hoped and expected to get into print.

Advisory Editor's Note

I would like to thank Professor James T. Boulton and Professor Warren Roberts, General Editors of the *Cambridge Edition of the Works of D. H. Lawrence*, and Andrew Brown, of Cambridge University Press, for their help in the preparation of this edition.

John Worthen, 1996

Facsimile of the title page of the first English edition, 1916

TWILIGHT IN ITALY

BY

D. H. LAWRENCE

LONDON: DUCKWORTH AND CO.
3 HENRIETTA STREET, COVENT GARDEN, W.C.

TWILIGHT IN ITALY
AND OTHER ESSAYS

Essays of Germany and the Tyrol, *1912*

In Fortified Germany

I. The English and the Germans.

"Have you," I asked the waiter in the hotel, "any other papers besides German ones?"

He turned round to me swiftly, with the flicker of a smile of triumph.

"No," he said, "only German; Germans to the front, you know."

"Why?" I asked.

"You don't know the saying—from the Chinese war?"

I regretted I neither knew the saying, nor understood its reference to the papers. The waiter smiled. He is very German.

In Metz the Germans *are* German, and the French are French; and I think I am the only Englishman. In Metz there seem to be four soldiers to every civilian. In my hotel seven officers are lodged. Wherever I go to dinner or supper there are officers or soldiers present. I am tired of German soldiers.

They are not like English soldiers. These latter, as a friend of mine said, "feel their bodies." Having no independent spiritual life of their own, they seem to have cultivated a fine flame of physical life. All their soul is in their bodies. As we watch our soldiers go flaunting down the street we feel the pride of the human creature. With the German soldiers it is not so. There marched past me this morning a squad of men with stumpy helmets and trousers bagging over their boots, short, thick men, and they looked for all the world like a division of bears shuffling by. I suppose they are only recruits. But none of the soldiers look, as we should say, military, none of them look martial.

Yet they stare at me aggressively. I am told I look a foreigner in every fibre. I feel it. All the boyish eyes of the private soldiers stare at me from their broad faces, as if to say: "What are *you* doing here?" There is not about them that coldness and indifference one feels in an Englishman's glance. Just as boys, all young things, are "touchy," ready to imagine a slight, are cocky, ready to defend their own manliness, so the German soldiers are "touchy" and "cocky." They impress me remarkably with a feeling of their youngness, an uncouth youngness. They are far more like awkward boys than men.

I am disappointed. I thought they would be warmer than the Englishmen, more generous, more polite. They are warmer, but still less generous in spirit, and not more polite. I am really disappointed.

7

The English have tempered themselves with morality till they are stiff and brittle and unworkable. These men are free of any such excess of moral temper. But that is not because they have lived further than we have. They are fussy; they make as much trouble over a trifle as if it were their whole soul's value; honour consists in the observance of certain rather trifling conventions.

Indeed, the Germans are not as old a nation as we are, as is evident in almost every face. They are not as old in experience. They are more uncouth. And it goes without saying they are not so sad. I, who am accustomed to the miners of the Midlands, feel inclined to wonder at these Germans, so fat and untroubled. They are on the whole much better-looking than our colliers, but I can't find anywhere among them the fine faces of men that are to be seen in the streets at home. It is the lack of wonder that spoils the German. Wonder is the sense of the vastness and terror and consolation of life: life infinitely great beyond our own consciousness. I know dozens of working men in England in whose faces can be seen that selfsame deep sense of wonder, which, unfortunately, owing to the split that exists in the English nature between the senses and the soul, is usually sad almost to despair. I know the colliers of the Midlands best. And I say, look at the best faces among those men, and see if there is not evident a certain desolation. In England we deny ourselves so much that there is scarcely any active living going on among the best people. We are in life, but we do not live. Thence the despair which looks out of so many English eyes. "*Is* there any value in living?" they have asked, and their own souls have been forced to answer "No." The great creed in the English heart to-day is, "Let us forgo the things we want, for we can do without them." It is not money, not position, nor security our souls want; and these are almost the only things the nation lives for. We want freedom to love, freedom to worship the things our deepest nature approves of. And nowadays it is easier not to live than to live. It is easier to suffer than to insist. It is easier to submit than to conquer.

"After all," the Englishman asks of his own soul, "after all, what does it matter, all this fuss about life?" The average Englishman cares vitally for nothing whatsoever, except for his own security in daily life; that is, he hangs on to life by the sheer strength of his instinct of self-preservation. All the rest, the joy, the progressive activity, is missing. As he takes off his clothes for the night, he puts off his show of living, and for a moment or two before he sleeps knows that he calmly and stoically despairs.

8

That is the danger for England. It is our own souls we need to reinforce, not our fleet, to make us safe from any German attack. In Germany there seem very few signs of the mania for self-starvation which is so remarkable in England. These men are healthy and lusty. Each one believes in his right to an individual life, in his right to satisfy his individual desires. He is going to have his own way where he can. Therefore he is effective. The Englishman, older, says, "The Universe is tremendous: I am the smallest atom of one kind of life; there is practically the whole great universe other than I am, and there is the speck of dust that is myself. What do I matter?" So he is ineffective.

If the German, like a lusty, stupid youth, says "I want to give England a licking," he will put his heart and soul into it. The Englishman, defending himself, will be rather bitter at being bothered, like a man who despises dogs when he is attacked by a dog. Why should the more brutal nation in the end always conquer the highly civilised nation? Only because the civilised nation is cynical, despises its own civilisation, and asks to be destroyed. We English are civilised in our very souls, and it makes us beautiful, somewhat noble in ourselves. But we do nothing. What is the good of being noble and of doing nothing! We are like the last members of a noble house of England. Our souls are too civilised to breed.

But why? Why, because we *can* forgo life, why, therefore, should we do so? I know a certain woman wants to love me, I know I want to love her. I can do without loving her, she can do without loving me—just as I can deny myself of something I need. But love is life, both to her and to me. Is it better to live or to forgo life? The English answer is always "to forgo life." But that is a cynicism. A more brutal man will say to me, "It's licence you want, not love nor life." I shall answer, "You are speaking for yourself," and it is he will be ashamed. It is not licence. There is plenty of licence everywhere, for whosoever wants it. There are plenty of well-shaped women in England or in Germany who would love me enough in a licentious fashion. But I don't want them. They are *not* life to me: they would brutalise me. This woman mates my soul. Yet if I love her I shall be no longer respectable, whereas if I loved the other women I should lose no caste. This feeling is stronger in England, I believe, than anywhere else, the insistence on formal respectability. It is most deadly in England, because our souls are refined, civilised, and therefore the brutal way of life is closed to us. Respectability shuts the other door. Hence the atrophy of the souls of many of the best English people, particularly the women. That is why there is a German scare—which seems to me might not be altogether a bogy; because of this strange, perverted will to destroy ourselves, which is common everywhere in England, and which seems comparatively rare here in Germany.

For the German officers are not very much different from the men. See them on Sunday, after service, doing the church parade in the cathedral square, each with his smart lady. The most elegant are slim as wasps, in their frock-tunics of light blue; but these are mostly young. There are three streams of paraders in the cathedral square. The innermost is of the elect. There the officers are perfect dandies; they gaze with perfect vanity through their rimless pince-nez—at nothing. Their ladies have the highest ostrich feathers, of the wildest colours. The second stream is of the second best; the military uniform is still elegant, not barbaric like ours. The ladies are dressed loudly, in slightly worse taste than the first; they are almost frantically dressed. In the last stream there are mostly women. Several are in deep mourning. Two girls of about twenty are armoured in crape, and each has a great length of crape hanging from the back of her hat, something like the worst phase of widow's weeds. This proclaims her sorrow. And so on. It is *not* a civilised nation. Our soldiery is a class apart—barbarous, pagan, curious, and lovable. But in the German soldier the worst national characteristics seem most pronounced—lack of intuition, clumsy sentimentality, affectation; a certain clumsiness of soul, a certain arrogance of stupidity, a certain stupid cleverness.

Nevertheless, the German nation has a warmth and generosity of living, like a full fire roaring, that makes us look very pale. They have none of our wavering, uncertain look about them.

And why we should weaken ourselves, make our wills less strong than those of this people, I do not know. Why we should will to starve ourselves, while these folk—of course masses of English folk are identically the same as the Germans—take their fill, I cannot conceive. Why should the best people leave all the living to the others? Why should so many of our *best* women die of atrophy? Why should our workmen be indifferent, inferior, perhaps, to the German workmen, when they are really superior in soul? If the civilised among us start to live our individual lives intelligently, we are stronger than the whole less-intelligent force. But we do not believe in living; we only believe in going without life, and thus showing our superiority of self-restraint.

II. How a Spy is Arrested.

We went over the bridges under the cathedral, past the old French houses on the quay, to the road lined with trees and dwellings where so many soldiers live. Soldiers on horseback were riding by: soldiers on foot were fetching and carrying: soldiers in their shirt sleeves were busy about the houses. In one barracks they were singing together in their jolly, careless fashion. The Germans have not yet lost the faculty for enjoying themselves simply and happily together.

Anita and I were discussing life very seriously: at least, she was discussing life seriously, and I was burning with a hundred wraths, as soldier after soldier turned and stared at her, and officers, riding by, moved their heads round woodenly upon their very high collars, to take stock.

"She looks so damnably nice," I said in my heart.

She was wearing a dress of red crape, of a coral colour, that suited her fair hair. And, deep in her sad philosophising, she was unconscious of the swarms of men; which made her the more interesting, I suppose. I love the splendid indifference in her bearing.

We crossed the road to avoid the men, and came to a green place arched with trees. The sunlight fell bright in dapplings among the cold shadow on the grass. Two little paths converged from the highway, leading under the trees. It looked mysterious and inviting, so still and green, as if fauns might be near the road.

"Let us go this way," said Anita suddenly.

We went only some two hundred yards from the road where the trams were running, when we saw on our right a clear place all bright with sunshine.

"There!" said Anita. "Let us sit down, I am tired."

A dozen paces from the path, we lay down. It was a quiet spot, sunny, a grassy bank with water below, and trees. The bank was square, the water curved curiously; I thought, vaguely, it must be some system of draining, towards the Mosel. Anita lay down on the grass, red like a fallen poppy. She rested on her elbows, watching a little beetle labouring over the long, warm grass-stalks.

"You nice little Käfer!" she said tenderly, to the beetle. "Stop here and amuse me, with your little legs."

I also lay face down beside her.

"Look at my sister," she continued to me. "She is a Doctor of Political Economy—quite a leading light, she was. And what did she say to me:—'after all, it is nothing to a woman *by itself*, this learning and writing and factory inspecting. It becomes in the end one big dissatisfaction, one big want.'"

"It's like breaking a wild deer into the shafts," I said.

"How?" she asked.

"A deer jumps over the road, four feet together, then stands and looks at me shoulder-deep out of the green corn, its ears lifted. Then something flashes in my heart. I know something. Because I've seen that hind, and she looked at me, I could mend my bicycle better."

"Yes," said Anita doubtfully.

"If we are to *do* anything, our women must keep in direct line with original life, and supply us. But a hind between the shafts! It only makes me want to die."

"To set it free," said Anita.

"Good God, yes!" I said. "But I am only good for *one* woman."

We lay together in the still sunshine. I was twisting Anita's ring, an old square emerald, full of green life.

"But," said Anita, "we keep in direct line with life; we look at our men for them to *see* us, and they *don't*—and it sends us cracked. The thing doesn't go on, from us to the men; the life, or whatever it is."

"You should get hold of the right men."

"How?—the men are afraid of us. They aren't *big* enough for us."

"They are your children."

At this interesting point of the discussion, Anita started, and looked round.

"Oh!" she exclaimed.

I looked over my shoulder. A young fellow in uniform was standing behind us, looking at us from under the ledge of his helmet. He had evidently been listening to, without understanding, our most interesting conversation, which had been carried on in English.

"What are you doing here?" he asked in German.

"Nothing," said Anita. "Why?"

"It is forbidden to come here," he said, with quiet, authoritative tones, almost threatening.

'Verboten!' One is not in Germany five minutes, without seeing or hearing this word: only it is usually, 'Strengstens verboten.'

"Why!" asked Anita, indignant at the interruption.

He did not answer for a moment, then, with quiet insolence:

"Because these are the fortifications."

"Get up," he said to me.

I would not understand.

"He asks you to get up," said Anita to me in English.

I rose and bowed to her. The young policeman looked at me. His anger began to mount. He had dark hazel eyes, rather beautiful, rather furious, rather stupid; the flush was coming under his swarthy skin; he had a petulant mouth, with the soft growth of a young black moustache.

"The Herr is not German?" he asked of Anita.

"No, an Englishman."

"I must arrest any foreigner who comes here," said the man.

"Aber—how absurd!" cried Anita.

The young policeman's eyes opened with wrath.

"We are twenty paces from the path," she cried.

"Yes!" he answered, with his menacing gravity.

"And I believe you have no right to do this," said Anita.

Instantly the revengeful anger hardened on his face.

"Are you also English?" he asked, beginning to bully her. I was furious.

"No, I am German. My father is the Graf zu —. The gentleman is his friend, and is staying with us."

The young, officious fool looked at her with a sneer.

"You *are* English," he said.

My blood boiled. Anita's eyes flashed.

"Do I speak like a foreigner!" she said. "Do you *know* the Herrn Graf —?"

"Yes—!" he said, "and where do you live?"

"Kronprinz-Strasse," she answered, too indignant to think.

"There is no such street."

"Yes!" she cried. "In Montigny."

He shook his head, smiling victoriously, and drew out paper and pencil.

"Kronprinz-Ludwig Strasse," I said. "Number 4."

He looked at me. I met his eyes and shrugged my shoulders. His hand trembled with rage.

"Kronprinz Ludwig Strasse—Number 4," I repeated, and mechanically, he copied it down.

"And your name?" he asked, in calm fury. His official authority was being flouted.

"How ridiculous!" cried Anita. "Would they in England insult a stranger so, and twenty paces from the road? What right have you? There is no notice."

"There *is* a notice," he answered, in his rage. "And I must enter all this. What is your name?"

I left it to Anita to tell him. He copied down many particulars.

"But really!" said Anita, forgetting her anger in amusement. "Really! You don't think the Herr Englishman looks dangerous, do you?"

He glanced at me, still in deep anger and suspicion and resentment. All this was *very* serious to him.

"Have you any papers?" he asked.

I would not understand, so Anita repeated. I had just one letter, stamped and addressed to my innocent old aunt in Lübeck. He looked at the cover as if it were something from a museum. I kept my eye on him all the while, rather amused at his babyish game of authority. He handed me my letter back.

"And I don't know a fortress from a factory," I said in English, laughing, to Anita. "If only the poor creature knew the depths of my ignorance."

She also began to laugh. The young policeman bridled with indignation. One felt the vast, stupid mechanism of German officialdom behind him.

"Come away," he said rudely.

We went side by side, Anita and I, laughing but angry with the youth. It was only a minute's walk to the tramway, down the simple path. We stood on the high-road. Still he looked at me suspiciously, as if he would like to put me in a cage quickly.

"Now," said Anita, "where is the notice! There is none. Why have *you* been overstepping your rights with us!"

"Yes, there *is* a notice—there!" he cried, blazing. On an obscure board, in the trees, it said 'Way for military purposes only.'

"And even so," said Anita, "it gives you no right to behave in the way you have done, interfering with honorable people— — —"

"Moreover, it is forbidden to lie on the grass," he said in wrath.

"That [is] why they never turn their cows out!" I jested to Anita.

Some passers-by collected—some soldiers came up. She, magnificent in her scorn, seemed twice as big as the soldier. He was in a rage. He would have liked to strike her.

"Any foreigner found there I should arrest," he repeated, sticking to the letter of the law—"it is my duty, and—"

I could see he would soon be fulfilling his duty. I lit a cigarette.

"Leave him, Anita," I said, "Leave him."

At the sound of the English he hated me.

"Refer to the Herr Graf zu —," said Anita.

"Yes, we *will* refer to the Herr Graf," replied the man, shutting his lips, putting his note book away, and glaring after us.

"What a fool I am!" said Anita. "I ought to know these German officials—every tiny scrap of a fellow thinks himself as important as the Kaiser."

We went to a friend of Anita's, an officer in the cavalry. He received Anita with great respect, kissing her hands. At home, lacking his sword belt and hat, he was not so impressive. Buttoned up in his pale-blue tunic, with its high pinkish collar, he sat deferentially listening to Anita, who was sitting on the sofa laughing and smoking a cigarette. He also took it seriously, though he politely said, it was nothing.

And even the Graf zu —, Anita's father, looked worried for a moment, then, after that moment, grew indignant. None of them laughed. These fussy little things seem important to them, instead of comic.

Presently came word to my hôtel that still everything was not certain concerning me. It was considered, in official quarters, that I was an English officer. That finished me off. I forgave them everything, stood in front of my long mirror, turning this way and that. An English officer! It was *such* a compliment to my figure, as to feel like a sarcasm.

I looked down at the soldiers drilling in the barracks square, and sighed. Then I packed my bags.

III. French Sons of Germany.

In Metz I prefer the Frenchmen to the Germans. I am more at my ease with them. It is a question of temperament.

From the Cathedral down to the river is all French. The Cathedral seems very German. It is nothing but nave: a tremendous lofty nave, and nothing else; a great jump at heaven, in the conception; a rather pathetic fall to earth, in execution. Still, the splendid conception is there.

So I go down from the Cathedral to the French quarter. It is full of smells, perhaps, but it is purely itself. A Frenchman has the same soul, whether he is eating his dinner or kissing his baby. A German has no soul when he is eating his dinner, and is beautiful when he kisses his baby. So I prefer the Frenchman, who hasn't the tiresome split between his animal nature and his spiritual, in whom the two are fused.

The barber drinks. He has wild hair and bloodshot eyes. Still, I dare trust my throat and chin to him. I address him in German. He dances before me, answering, in mad French, that he speaks no German. Instantly I love him in spite of all.

"You are a foreigner here?" I remark.

He cannot lather me, he is so wildly excited. "No, he was born in Metz, his father was born in Metz, his grandfather was born in Metz. For all he knows, Adam was born in Metz. But no Leroy has ever spoken German; no, not a syllable. It would split his tongue—he could not, you see, Sir, he could not; his construction would not allow of it."

With all of which I agree heartily; whereupon he looks lovingly upon me and continues to lather.

"His wife was a Frenchwoman, born in Paris. I must see his wife." He calls her by some name I do not know, and she appears—fat and tidy.

"You are a subject of France?" my barber demands furiously.

"Certainly," she begins. "I was born in Paris——" As they both talk at once, I can't make out what they say. But they are happy, they continue. At last, with a final flourish of the razor, I am shaved. The barber is very tipsy.

"Monsieur is from Brittany?" he asks me tenderly.

Alas! I am from England.

"But, why?" cries Madame; "you have not an English face; no, never. And a German face—Pah! impossible."

In spite of all I look incurably English. Nevertheless, I start a story about a great-grandfather who was refugeed in England after the revolution. They embrace me, they love me. And I love them.

"Sir," I say, "will you give me a morsel of soap? No, not shaving soap."

"This is French soap, this is German," he says. The French is in a beautiful flowery wrapper, alas! much faded.

"And what is the difference?" I ask.

"The French, of course, is *better*. The German is five pfennigs—one sou, Monsieur—the cheaper."

Of course, I take the French soap. The barber grandly gives my twenty-pfennig tip to the lathering boy, who has just entered, and he bows me to the door. I am in the street, breathless.

A German officer, in a flowing cloak of bluey-grey—like ink and milk—looks at me coldly and inquisitively. I look at him with a "Go to the devil" sort of look, and pass along. I wonder to myself if my dislike of these German officers is racial, or owing to present national feeling, or if it is a temperamental aversion. I decide on the last. A German soldier spills something out of a parcel on to the road and looks round like a frightened boy. I want to shelter him.

I pass along, look at the ridiculous imitation-mediæval church that is built on the islet—or peninsula—in the middle of the river, on the spot that has been called for ages "The Place of Love." I wonder how the Protestant conscience of this ugly church remains easy upon such foundation. I think of the famous "three K's" that are allotted to German women, "Kinder, Kuchen, Kirche," and pity the poor wretches.

Over the river, all is barracks—barracks, and soldiers on foot, and soldiers on horseback. Everywhere these short, baggy German soldiers, with their fair skins and rather stupid blue eyes! I hurry to get away from them. To the right is a steep hill, once, I suppose, the scarp of the river.

At last I found a path, and turned for a little peace to the hillside and the vineyards. The vines are all new young slips, climbing up their sticks. The whole hillside bristles with sticks, like an angry hedgehog. Across lies Montigny; to the right, Metz itself, with its cathedral like a brown rat humped up. I prefer my hillside. In this Mosel valley there is such luxuriance of vegetation. Lilac bushes are only heaps of purple flowers. Some roses are out. Here on the wild hillside there are lovely vetches of all sorts, and white poppies and red; and then the vine shoots, with their tips of most living, sensitive pink and red, just like blood under the skin.

I am happy on the hillside. It is a warm, grey day. The Mosel winds below. The vine sticks bristle against the sky. The little church of the village is in front. I climb the hill, past a Madonna shrine that stands out by the naked path. The faded blue "Lady" is stuck with dying white lilac. She looks rather ugly, but I do not mind. Odd men, and women, are working in the vineyards. They are very swarthy, and they have very small-bladed spades, which glisten in the sun.

At last I come to the cemetery under the church. As I marvel at the bead-work wreaths, with ridiculous little naked china figures of infants floating in the middle, I hear voices, and looking up, see two German soldiers on the natural platform, or terrace, beside the church. Along the vineyard path are squares of yellow and black and white, like notice boards. The two soldiers, in their peculiar caps, almost similar to our round sailors' hats, or blue cooks' caps, are laughing. They watch the squares, then me.

When I go up to the church and round to the terrace, they are gone. The terrace is a natural platform, a fine playground, very dark with great horsechestnuts in flower, and walled up many feet from the hillside, overlooking the far valley of the Mosel. As I sit on a bench, the hens come pecking round me. It is perfectly still and lovely, the only sound being from the boys' school.

Somewhere towards eleven o'clock two more soldiers came. One led his horse, the other was evidently not mounted. They came to the wall, or parapet, to look down the valley at the fort. Meanwhile, to my great joy, the mare belonging to the mounted soldier cocked up her tail and cantered away under the horsechestnuts, down the village. Her owner went racing, shouting after her, making the peculiar *hu-hu*! these Germans use to their horses. She would have been lost had not two men rushed out of the houses, and, shouting in French, stopped her. The soldier jerked her head angrily, and led her back. He was a short, bear-like little German, she was a wicked and delicate mare. He kept her bridle as he returned. Meanwhile, his companion, his hands clasped on his knees, shouted with laughter.

Presently, another, rather taller, rather more manly soldier appeared. He had a sprig of lilac between his teeth. The foot-soldier recounted the escapade with the mare, whereupon the newcomer roared with laughter, and suddenly knocked the horse under the jaw. She reared in terror. He got hold of her by the bridle, teasing her. At last her owner pacified her. Then the newcomer would insist on sticking a piece of lilac in her harness, against her ear. It frightened her, she reared, and she panted, but he would not desist. He teased her, bullied her, coaxed her, took her unawares; she was in torment as he pawed at her head to stick in the flower, she would not allow him. At last, however, he succeeded. She, much discomfited, wore lilac against her ear.

Then the children came out of school—boys, in their quaint pin-afores. It is strange how pleasant, how quaint, and manly these little children are; the tiny boys of six seemed more really manly than the soldiers of twenty-one, more alert to the real things. They cried to each other in their keen, naïf way, discussing the action at the fortress, of which I could make out nothing.

And one of the soldiers asked them, "How old are you, Johnny?" Human nature is very much alike. The boys used French in their play, but they answered the soldiers in German.

As I was going up the hill there came on a heavy shower. I sheltered as much as I could under an apple-tree thick with pink blossom; then I hurried down to the village. "Café—Restauration" was written on one house. I wandered into the living-room beyond the courtyard.

"Where does one drink?" I asked the busy, hard-worked-looking woman. She answered me in French, as she took me in. At once, though she was a drudge, her fine spirit of politeness made me comfortable.

"This is not France?" I asked of her.

"Oh, no—but always the people have been French," and she looked at me quickly from her black eyes. I made my voice tender as I answered her.

Presently I said: "Give me some cigarettes, please."

"French or German?" she asked.

"What's the difference?" I inquired.

"The French, of course, are better."

"Then French," I said, laughing, though I do not really love the black, strong French cigarettes.

"Sit and talk to me a minute," I said to her. "It is so nice not to speak German."

"Ah, Monsieur!" she cried, and she loved me. She could not sit, no. She could only stay a minute. Then she sent her man.

I heard her in the other room bid him come. He was shy—he would not. "Ssh!" I heard her go as she pushed him through the door.

He was very swarthy, burned dark with the sun. His eyes were black and very bright. He was a man of about forty-five. I could not persuade him to sit down or to drink with me; he would accept only a cigarette. Then, laughing, he lighted me my cigarette. He was a gentleman, and he had white teeth.

The village, he told me, was Scy: a French name, but a German village.

"And you are a German subject?" I asked.

He bowed to me. He said he had just come in from the vines, and must go back immediately. Last year they had had a bad disease, so that all the plants I had seen were new. I hoped he would get rich with them. He smiled with a peculiar sad grace.

"Not rich, Monsieur, but not a failure this time."

He had a daughter, Angèle: "In Paris—in *France*."

He bowed and looked at me meaningly. I said I was glad. I said:

"I do not like Metz: too many soldiers. I do not like German soldiers."

"They are scarcely polite," he said quietly.

"You find it?" I asked.

He bowed his acquiescence.

It is a strange thing that these two Frenchmen were the only two men—not acquaintances—whom I felt friendly towards me in the whole of Metz.

Hail in the Rhine-Land.

We were determined to take a long walk this afternoon, in spite of the barometer, which persisted in retreating towards "storm." The morning was warm and mildly sunny. The blossom was still falling from the fruit-trees down the village street, and drifting in pink and white all along the road. The barber was sure it would be fine. But then he'd have sworn to anything I wanted, he liked me so much since I admired, in very bad German, his moustache.

"I may trim your moustache?" he asked.

"You can do what you like with it," I said.

As he was clipping it quite level with my lip he asked:

"You like a short moustache?"

"Ah," I answered, "I could never have anything so beautiful and upstanding as yours."

Whereupon immediately he got excited, and vowed my moustache should stand on end even as Kaiserly as did his own.

"Never," I vowed.

Then he brought me a bottle of mixture, and a gauze bandage, which I was to bind under my nose, and there I should be, in a few weeks, with an upstanding moustache sufficient as a guarantee for any man. But I was modest; I refused even to try.

"No," I said, "I will remember yours." He pitied me, and vowed it would be fine for the afternoon.

I told Johanna so, and she took her parasol. It was really sunny, very hot and pretty, the afternoon. Besides, Johanna's is the only parasol I have seen in Waldbröl, and I am the only Englishman any woman for miles around could boast. So we set off.

We were walking to Nümbrecht, some five or six miles away. Johanna moved with great dignity, and I held the parasol. Every man, even the workmen on the fields, bowed low to us, and every woman looked at us yearningly. And to every woman, and to every man, Johanna gave a bright "Good-day."

"They like it so much," she said. And I believed her.

There was a scent of apple-blossom quite strong on the air. The cottages, set at random and painted white, with their many timbers painted black, have a make-believe, joyful, childish look.

Everywhere the broom was out, great dishevelled blossoms of ruddy gold sticking over the besom strands. The fields were full of dandelion pappus, floating misty bubbles crowded thick, hiding the green grass with their globes. I showed Johanna how to tell the time. "One!" I puffed; "two-three-four-five-six! Six o'clock, my dear."

"Six o'clock what?" she asked.

"Anything you like," I said.

"At six o'clock there will be a storm. The barometer is never wrong," she persisted.

I was disgusted with her. The beech-wood through which we were walking was a vivid flame of green. The sun was warm.

"Johanna," I said. "Seven ladies in England would walk out with me, although they *knew* that at six o'clock a thunder-shower would ruin their blue dresses. Besides, there are two holes in your mittens, and black mittens show so badly."

She quickly hid her arms in the folds of her skirts. "Your English girls have queer taste, to walk out seven at a time with you."

We were arguing the point with some ferocity when, descending a hill in the wood, we came suddenly upon a bullock-wagon. The cows stood like blocks in the harness, though their faces were black with flies. Johanna was very indignant. An old man was on the long, railed wagon, which was piled with last year's brown oak-leaves. A boy was straightening the load, and waiting at the end of the wagon ready to help, a young, strong man, evidently his father, who was struggling uphill with an enormous sack-cloth bundle—enormous, full of dead leaves. The new leaves of the oaks overhead were golden brown, and crinkled with young vigour. The cows stood solid and patient, shutting their eyes, weary of the plague of flies. Johanna flew to their rescue, fanning them with a beech-twig.

"Ah, poor little ones!" she cried. Then, to the old man, in tones of indignation: "These flies will eat up your oxen."

"Yes—their wicked little mouths," he agreed.

"Cannot you prevent them?" she asked.

"They are everywhere," he answered, and he smacked a fly on his hand.

"But you can do something," she persisted.

"You could write a card and stick it between their horns, 'Settling of flies strictly forbidden here,' " I said.

" 'Streng verboten,' " he repeated as he laughed.

Johanna looked daggers at me.

"Thank you, young fellow," she said sarcastically. I stuck leafy branches in the head-harness of the cattle. The old man thanked me with much gratitude.

22

"It is hot weather!" I remarked.

"It will be a thunderstorm, I believe," he answered.

"At six o'clock?" cried Johanna.

But I was along the path.

We went gaily through the woods and open places, and had nearly come to Nümbrecht, when we met a very old man, coming very slowly up the hill with a splendid young bull, of buff-colour and white, which, in its majestic and leisurely way, was dragging a harrow that rode on sledges.

"Fine weather," I remarked, forgetting.

"Jawohl!" he answered. "But there will be a thunderstorm."

"And I knew it," said Johanna.

But we were at Nümbrecht. Johanna drank her mineral water and raspberry juice. It was ten minutes to six.

"It is getting dark," remarked Johanna.

"There is no railway here?" I asked.

"Not for six miles," she replied pointedly.

The landlord was a very handsome man.

"It is getting dark," said Johanna to him.

"There will be a thunderstorm, Madame," he replied with beautiful grace. "Madame is walking?"

"From Waldbröl," she replied. By this time she was statuesque. The landlord went to the door. Girls were leading home the cows.

"It is coming," he said, and immediately there was a rumbling of thunder.

Johanna went to the door.

"An enormous black cloud. The sky is black," she announced. I followed to her side. It was so.

"The barber——" I said.

"Must you live by the word of the barber?" said Johanna.

The landlord retired indoors. He was a very handsome man, but the hair was positively shaved from his head. And I knew Johanna liked the style.

I fled to Stollwerck's chocolate machine, and spent a few anxious moments extracting burnt almonds. The landlord reappeared.

"There is an omnibus goes to Waldbröl for the station and the post. It passes the door in ten minutes," he said gracefully. No English landlord could have equalled him. I thanked him with all my heart.

The omnibus was an old brown cab—a growler. Its only occupant was a brown-paper parcel for Frau ——.

23

"You don't mind riding?" I said tenderly to Johanna.

"I had rather we were at home. I am terribly afraid of thunderstorms," she answered.

We drove on. A young man in black stopped the omnibus. He bowed to us, then mounted the box with the driver.

"It is Thienes, the Bretzel baker," she said. Bretzel is a loopy, twisty little cake like Kringel.

I do not know why, but after this Johanna and I sat side by side in tense silence. I felt very queerly.

"There, the rain!" she suddenly cried.

"Never mind," I pleaded.

"Oh, I like riding in here," she said.

My heart beat, and I put my hand over hers. She pretended not to notice, which made my heart beat more. I don't know how it would have ended. Suddenly there was such a rattle outside, and something pounding on me. Johanna cried out. It was a great hail-storm—the air was a moving white storm—enormous balls of ice, big as marbles, then bigger, like balls of white carbon that housewives use against moths, came striking in. I put up the window. It was immediately cracked, so I put it down again. A hailstone as big as a pigeon-egg struck me on the knee, hurt me, and bounced against Johanna's arm. She cried out with pain. The horses stood still and would not move. There was a roar of hail. All round, on the road balls of ice were bouncing viciously up again. We could not see six yards out of the carriage.

Suddenly the door opened, and Thienes, excusing himself, appeared. I dragged him in. He was a fresh young man, with naïve, wide eyes. And his best suit of lustrous black was shining now with wet.

"Had you no cover?" we said.

He showed his split umbrella, and burst into a torrent of speech. The hail drummed bruisingly outside.

"It had come like horse-chestnuts of ice," he said.

The fury of the storm lasted for five minutes, all of which time the horses stood stock still. The hailstones shot like great white bullets into the carriage. Johanna clung to me in fear. There was a solid sheet of falling ice outside.

At last the horses moved on. I sat eating large balls of ice and realising myself. When at last the fall ceased Thienes *would* get out on to the box again. I liked him; I wanted him to stay. But he would not.

The country was a sight. All over the road, and fallen thick in the ruts, were balls of ice, pure white, as big as very large marbles, and some as big as bantam-eggs. The ditches looked as if stones and stones' weight of loaf sugar had been emptied into them—white balls and cubes of ice everywhere. Then the sun came out, and under the brilliant green birches a thick white mist, only a foot high, sucked at the fall of ice. It was very cold. I shuddered.

"I was only flirting with Johanna," I said to myself. "But, by Jove, I was nearly dished."

The carriage crunched over the hail. All the road was thick with twigs, as green as spring. It made me think of the roads strewed for the Entry to Jerusalem. Here it was cherry boughs and twigs and tiny fruits, a thick carpet; next, brilliant green beech; next, pine-brushes, very beautiful, with their creamy pollen cones, making the road into a green bed; then fir twigs, with pretty emerald new shoots like stars, and dark sprigs over the hailstones. Then we passed two small dead birds, fearfully beaten. Johanna began to cry. But we were near a tiny, lonely inn, where the carriage stopped. I said I *must* give Thienes a Schnapps, and I jumped out. The old lady was sweeping away a thick fall of ice-stones from the doorway.

When I next got into the carriage, I suppose I smelled of Schnapps, and was not lovable. Johanna stared out of the window, away from me. The lovely dandelion bubbles were gone, there was a thicket of stripped stalks, all broken. The corn was broken down, the road was matted with fruit twigs. Over the Rhine-land was a grey, desolate mist, very cold.

At the next stopping place, where the driver had to deliver a parcel, a young man passed with a very gaudily apparelled horse, great red trappings. He was a striking young fellow. Johanna watched him. She was not *really* in earnest with me. We might have both made ourselves unhappy for life, but for this storm. A middle-aged man, very brown and sinewy with work, came to the door. He was rugged, and I liked him. He showed me his hand. The back was bruised, and swollen, and already going discoloured. It made me wince. But he laughed rather winsomely, even as if he were glad.

"A hail-stone!" he said, proudly.

We watched the acres of ice-balls slowly pass by, in silence. Neither of us spoke. At last we came to the tiny station, at home. There was the station-master, and, of all people, the barber.

"I can remember fifty-five years," said the station-master, "but nothing like this."

"Not round, but squares, two inches across, of ice," added the barber, with gusto.

"At the shop they have sold out of tiles, so many smashed," said the station-master.

"And in the green-house roofs, at the Asylum, not a shred of glass," sang the barber.

"The windows at the station smashed——"

"And a man"—I missed the name—"hurt quite badly by——" rattled the barber.

"But," I interrupted, "you said it would be fine."

"And," added Johanna, "we went on the strength of it." It is queer, how sarcastic she can be, without *saying* anything really meaningful.

We were four dumb people. But I had a narrow escape, and Johanna had a narrow escape, and we both know it, and thank the terrific hail-storm, though at present *she* is angry—vanity, I suppose.

A Chapel Among the Mountains

I.

It is all very well trying to wander romantically in the Tyrol. Sadly I sit on the bed, my head and shoulders emerging from the enormous overbolster like a cherub from a cloud, writing out of sheer exasperation; whilst Anita lies on the other bed and is amused.

Two days ago it began to rain. When I think of it I wonder. The gutter of the heavens hangs over the Tyrolese Alps.

We set off with the iridescent cloud of romance ahead, leading us southwards from the Isar towards Italy. We haven't got far. And the iridescent cloud, turned into a column of endless water, still endures around the house.

I omit the pathos of our setting forth, in the dimmery-glimmery light of the Isar valley, before breakfast time, with blue chicory flowers open like wonder on either side the road. Neither will I describe our crawling at dinner-time along the foot of the mountains, the rain running down our necks from the flabby straw hats, and dripping cruelly into one's boots from the pent-house of our Rucksacks. We entered ashamed into a wayside inn, where seven ruddy joyous peasants, three of them handsome, made a bonfire of their hearts in honor of Anita, whilst I sat in a corner and dripped— — —

Yesterday I admit it was fine in the afternoon and evening. We made tea by a waterfall among yellow-dangling noli-me-tangere flowers, whilst an inquisitive lot of mountains poked their heads up to look, and a great green grasshopper, armoured like Ivanhoe, took a flying leap into eternity over a lovely, black-blue gentian: at least I saw him no more.

They had told us there was a foot-path over the mountain, three and a half hours to Glashütte. There *was* a faint track, and myriads of strawberries like ruddy stars below, and a few dark bilberries. We climbed one great steep slope, and scrambled down beyond, into a pine wood. There it was damp and dark and depressing. But one makes the best of things, when one sets out on foot. So we toiled on for an hour, traversing the side of a slope, black, wet, gloomy, looking through the fir-trees across the gulf at another slope, black and gloomy and forbidding, shutting us back. For two hours we slipped and struggled, and still there we were, clamped between these two black slopes,

27

listening to the water that ran uncannily, noisily along the bottom of the trap.

We grew silent and hot with exertion and the dark monotony of the struggle. A Rucksack also has its moments of treachery, close friend though it seems. You are quite certain of a delicate and beautiful balance on a slippery tree-root; you take the leap; then the ironic Rucksack gives you a pull from behind, and you are grovelling.

And the path *had* been a path. The side of the dark slope, steep as a roof, had innumerable little bogs where waters tried to ooze out and call themselves streams, and could not. Across these bogs went an old bed of fir-boughs, dancy and treacherous. So, there was a path! Suddenly there were no more fir-boughs, and one stood lost before the squalor of the slope. I wiped my brow.

"You so soon lose your temper," said Anita.

So I stood aside, and yielded her the lead.

She blundered into another little track lower down.

"You *see!*" she said, turning round.

I did not answer. She began to hum a little tune, because her path descended. We slipped and struggled. Then her path vanished into the loudly-snorting, chuckling stream, and did not emerge.

"Well?" I said.

"But where is it?" she said with vehemence, and pathos.

"You see even *your* road ends in nowhere," I said.

"I *hate* you when you preach," she flashed. "Besides it *doesn't* end in nowhere."

"At any rate," I said, "we can't sleep on the end of it."

I found another track, but I entered on it delicately, without triumph. We went in silence. And it vanished into the same loudly-snorting stream.

"Oh don't look like that!" cried Anita.

So I followed the bedraggled tail of her skirts once more up the wet, dark opposition of the slope. We found another path, and once more we lost the scent in the overjoyed stream.

"Perhaps we're supposed to go across," I said meekly as we stood beside the waters.

"I—*why* did I take a damp match of a man like you!" she cried. "One could scratch you for ever and you wouldn't strike."

I looked at her, wondering, and turned to the stream, which was cunningly bethinking itself. There were chunks of rock, and spouts and combs and rattles of sly water. So I put my rain-coat over my Rucksack and ventured over.

The opposite bank was very steep and high. We were swallowed in this black gorge, swallowed to the bottom, and gazing upwards. I set off on all fours, climbing with my rain-coat over my Rucksack, cloakwise, to leave me free. I scrambled and hauled and struggled.

And from below came shriek upon shriek of laughter. I reached the top, and looked down. I could see nothing, only the whirring of laughter came up.

"What is it?" I called, but the sound was lost amid the cackle of the waters. So I crawled over the edge and sat in the gloomy solitude, extinguished.

Directly I heard a shrill, frightened call:

"Where are you?"

My heart exulted and melted at the same moment.

"Come along," I cried, satisfied that there was one spot in this gloomy solitude to call to.

She arrived, scared with the steep climb, and the fear of loneliness in this place.

"I might never have found you again," she said.

"I don't intend you should lose me," I said.

So she sat down, and presently her head began to nod with laughter, and her bosom shook with laughter, and she was laughing wildly without me.

"Well what?" I said.

"You—you looked like a camel—with your hump—climbing up," she shrieked.

"We'd better be moving," I said.

She slipped and laughed and struggled. At last we came to a beautiful savage road. It was the bed of some stream that came no more this way, a mass of clear boulders leading up the slope through the gloom.

"We are coming out now," said Anita, looking ahead.

I also was quite sure of it. But after an hour of climbing, we were still in the bed of clear boulders, between dark trees, among the toes of the mountains.

Anita spied a hunter's hut, made of bark, and she went to investigate. Night was coming on.

"I can't get in," she called to me, obscurely.

"Then come," I said.

It was too wet and cold to sleep out of doors in the woods. But instead of coming, she stooped in the dark twilight for strawberries. I waited like the shadow of wrath. But she, unconcerned, careless and happy in her contrariety, gathered strawberries among the shadows.

"We *must* find a place to sleep in," I said.

And my utter insistence took effect.

She realised that I was lost among the mountains, as well as she, that the night and the cold and the great dark slopes were close upon us, and we were of no avail, even being two, against the coldness and desolation of the mountains.

So in silence we scrambled upwards, hand in hand. Anita was sure a dozen times that we were coming out. At last even she got dis-heartened.

Then, in the darkness, we spied a hut beside a path among the thinning fir-trees.

"It will be a wood-man's hut," she said.

"A shrine," I answered.

2.

I was right for once. It was a wooden hut just like a model, with a black old wreath hanging on the door. There was a click of the latch in the cold, watchful silence of the upper mountains, and we entered.

By the grey darkness coming in from outside we made out the tiny chapel, candles on the altar and a whole covering of ex-voto pictures on the walls, and four little praying benches. It was all close and snug as a box.

Feeling quite safe, and exalted in this rare, upper shadow, I lit the candles, all. Point after point of flame flowed out on the night. There were six. Then I took off my hat and my Rucksack, and rejoiced, my heart at home.

The walls of the chapel were covered close with naked little pictures, all coloured, painted by the peasants on wood, and framed with little frames. I glanced round, saw the cows and the horses on the green meadows, the men on their knees in their houses, and I was happy as if I had found myself among the angels.

"What wonderful luck!" I said to Anita.

"But what are we going to do?" she asked.

"Sleep on the floor—between the praying desks. There's just room."

"But we *can't* sleep on a wooden floor," she said.

"What better can you find?"

"A hay hut. There must be a hay hut somewhere near. We *can't* sleep here."

"Oh yes," I said.

But I was bound to look at the little pictures. I climbed on to a bench. Anita stood in the open doorway like a disconsolate, eternal angel. The light of the six dusky tapers glimmered on her discontented mouth. Behind her, I could see tips of fir branches just illuminated, and then the night.

She turned and was gone like darkness into the darkness. I heard her boots upon the stones. Then I turned to the little pictures I loved. Perched upon the praying desks, I looked at one, and then another. They were picture-writings that seemed like my own soul talking to me. They were really little pictures for God, because horses and cows and men and women and mountains, they are his own language. How should he read German and English and Russian, like a schoolmaster? The peasants could trust him to understand their pictures: they were not so sure that he would concern himself with their written script.

I was looking at a pale-blue picture. That was a bedroom, where a woman lay in bed, and a baby lay in a cradle not far away. The bed was blue, and it seemed to be falling out of the picture, so it gave me a feeling of fear and insecurity. Also, as the distance receded, the bedstead got wider, uneasily. The woman lay looking straight at me, from under the huge, blue-striped overbolster. Her pink face was round like a penny doll's, with the same round stare. And the baby, like a pink-faced farthing doll, also stared roundly.

"Maria hat geholfen E. G.—1777"

I looked at them. And I knew that I was the husband looking and wondering. G, the husband, did not appear himself. It was from the little picture on his retina that this picture was reproduced. He could not sum it up and explain it, this vision of his wife suffering in child-birth, and then lying still and at peace with the baby in the cradle. He could not make head or tail of it. But at least he could represent it, and hang it up like a mirror before the eyes of God, giving the statement even if he could get no explanation. And he was satisfied.

And so, perforce, was I, though my heart began to knock for knowledge.

The men never actually saw themselves unless in precarious conditions. When their lives were threatened, then they had a fearful flash of self consciousness, which haunted them till they had represented it. They represented themselves in all kinds of ridiculous postures, at the moment when the accident occurred.

Joseph Rieck, for example, was in a toppling-backward attitude rather like a foot-baller giving a very high kick and losing his balance. But on his left ankle had fallen a great grey stone, that might have killed him, squashing out much blood, orange-coloured—or so it looked by the candle light—whilst the Holy Mary stood above in a bolster-frame of clouds, holding up her hands in mild surprise.

"Joseph Rieck
Gott sey Danck gesagt 1834"

It was curious that he thanked God because a stone had fallen on his ankle. But perhaps the thanks was because it had not fallen on his head. Or perhaps because the ankle had got better, though it looked a nasty smash, according to the picture. It didn't occur to him to thank God that all the mountains of the Tyrol had not tumbled on him the first day he was born. It doesn't occur to any of us. We wait till a big stone falls on our ankle. Then we paint a vivid picture, and say "In the midst of life we are in death," and we thank God that we've escaped. All kinds of men were saying "Gott sey Danck": either because big stones had squashed them, or because trees had come down on them whilst they were felling, or else because they'd tumbled over cliffs, or got carried away in streams: all little events which caused them to ejaculate "God be thanked, I'm still alive."

Then some of the women had picture prayers that were touching, because they were prayers for other people, for their children and not for themselves. In a sort of cell kneeled a woman, wearing a Catherine of Russia kind of dress, opposite a kneeling man in Vicar of Wakefield attire. Between them, on the stone wall, hung two long iron chains with iron rings dangling at the end. Above these, framed in an oval of bolster-clouds, Christ on the Cross, and above him, a little Maria, short in stature, something like Queen Victoria, with a very blue cloth over her head, falling down her dumpy figure. She, the Holy Mother of heaven, looked distressed. The woman kneeling in the cell put up her hands, saying:

"O Mutter Gottes von Rerelmos, Ich bitte mach mir mein Kind von

Gefangenschaft los mach im von Eissen und bandten freÿ wansz des
Gottliche willen sey

Susanna Grillen 1783."

I suppose Herr Grillen knew that it was not the affair of the Mutter
Gottes. Poor Susanna Grillen! It was natural and womanly in her to
identify the powers that be with the eternal powers. What I can't see, is
whether the boy had really done anything wrong, or whether he had
merely transgressed some law of some duke or king or community. I
suppose the poor thing did not know herself how to make the distinction. But evidently the father, knowing he was in temporal difficulty,
was not very active in asking help of the eternal.

One must look up the history of the Tyrol for the 1783 period.

A few pictures were family utterances, but the voice which spoke
was always the voice of the mother. Marie Schneeberger thanked God
for healing her son. She kneeled on one side of the bedroom, with her
three daughters behind her; Schneeberger kneeled facing her, with a
space between them, and his one son behind him. The Holy Mary
floated above the space of their thanks. The whole family united this
time to bless the heavenly powers that the bad had not been worse.
And, in the face of the divine power, the man was separate from the
woman, the daughter from the son, the sister from the brother—one
set on one side, one set on the other, separate before the eternal grace,
or the eternal fear.

The last set of pictures thanked God for the salvation of property.
One lady had six cows—all red ones—painted feeding on a meadow
with rocks behind. All the cows I have seen in these parts have been
dun or buff coloured. But these are red. And the goodwife thanks God
very sincerely for restoring to her that which was lost for five days: viz,
her six cows and the little cow-girl Kate. The little girl did not appear
in the picture nor in the thanks: she was only mentioned as having been
lost along with the cows. I do not know what became of her. Cows can
always eat grass. I suppose she milked her beast, and perhaps cranber-
ries were ripe. But five days was a long time for poor Kathel.

There were hundreds of cattle painted standing on meadows like
child's noah's-ark toys arranged in groups: a group of red cows, a
group of brown horses, a group of brown goats, a few grey sheep; as if
they had all been summoned into their classes. Then Maria in her
cloud-frame blessed them. But standing there so hieroglyphic, the
animals had a symbolic power. They did not merely represent property. They were the wonderful animal life which man must take for

food. Arrayed there in their numbers, they were almost frightening, as if they might overthrow us, like an army.

Only one woman had had an accident. She was seen falling downstairs, just landing at the bottom into her peaceful kitchen where the kitten lay asleep by the stove. The kitten slept on, but Mary in a blue mantle appeared through the ceiling, mildly shocked and deprecating.

Alone among all the women, the women who had suffered childbirth or had suffered through some child of their own, was this housewife who had fallen downstairs into the kitchen where the cat slept peacefully. Perhaps she had not any children. However that may be, her position was ignoble, as she bumped on the bottom stair.

There they all were, in their ex-voto pictures that I think the women had ordered and paid for, these peasants of the valley below, pictured in their fear. They lived under the mountains where always was fear. Sometimes they knew it to close on a man or a woman. Then there was no peace in the heart of this man till the fear had been pictured, till he was represented in the grip of terror, and till the picture had been offered to the Deity, the dread, unnamed Deity whose might must be acknowledged; whilst in the same picture the milder divine succour was represented and named and thanked. Deepest of all things, among the mountain darknesses, was the ever-felt fear. First of all gods was the unknown god who crushed life at any moment, and threatened it always. His shadow was over the valleys. And a tacit acknowledgement and propitiation of Him were the ex-voto pictures, painted out of fear and offered to Him unnamed. Whilst upon the face of them all was Mary the divine Succour, She, who had suffered, and knew. And that which had suffered and known, had prevailed, and was openly thanked. But that which had neither known nor suffered, the dread unnamed, which had aimed and missed by a little, this must be acknowledged covertly. For his own soul's sake, man must acknowledge his own fear, acknowledge the power beyond him.

Whilst I was reading the inscriptions high up on the wall, Anita came back. She stood below me in her weather-beaten panama hat, looking up dissatisfied. The light fell warm on her face. She was discontented and excited.

"There's a gorgeous hay-hut a little further on," she said.

"Hold me a candle a minute, will you?" I said.

"A great hay-hut full of hay, in an open space. I climbed in—"

"Do you mind giving me a candle for a moment."

"But no—come along—"

"I just want to read this—give me a candle."

In a silence of impatience, she handed me one of the tapers. I was reading a little inscription.

"Won't you come?" she said.

"We could sleep well here," I said. "It is so dry and secure."

"Why!" she cried irritably. "Come to the hay hut and see."

"In one moment," I said.

She turned away.

"Isn't this altar adorable!" she cried. "Lovely little paper roses, and ornaments."

She was fingering some artificial flowers, thinking to put them in her hair. I jumped down, saying I must finish reading my pictures in the morning. So I gathered the Rucksack and examined the cash-box by the door. It was open and contained six kreutzers. I put in forty pfennigs, out of my poor pocket, to pay for the candles. Then I called Anita away from the altar trinkets, and we closed the door, and were out in the darkness of the mountains.

A Hay-Hut Among the Mountains

I resented being dragged out of my Kapelle, into the black and dismal night. In the Chapel were candles and a boarded floor. And the streams in the mountains refuse to run anywhere but down the paths made by man. Anita said "You cannot imagine how lovely your Chapel looked, as I came on it from the dark, its row of candles shining, and all the inside warm!"

"Then why on earth didn't you stay there?" I said.

"But think of sleeping in a hay-hut," she cried.

"I think a Kapelle is much more soul-stirring," I insisted.

"But much harder to the bones," she replied.

We struggled out onto a small meadow, between the mountain-tops. Anita called it a kettle. I presumed then, that we had come in by the spout and should have to get out by the lid. At any rate, the black heads of the mountains poked up all round, and I felt tiny, like a beetle in a basin.

The hay hut stood big and dark and solid, on the clear grass.

"I know just how to get in," said Anita, who was full of joy now that we were going to be uncomfortably situated. "And now we must eat and drink tea."

"Where's your water?" I asked.

She listened intently. There was a light swishing of pine trees on the mountain side.

"I hear it," she said.

"Somewhere down some horrid chasm," I answered.

"I will go and look," she said.

"Well," I answered, "you needn't go hunting on a hillside where there isn't the faintest sign of a rut or water-course."

We spoke sotto voce, because of the darkness and the stillness. I led down the meadow, nearly breaking my neck over the steepest places. Now I was very thirsty, and we had only a very little Schnapps.

"There is sure to be water in the lowest place," I said.

She followed me stealthily and with glee. Soon we squilched in a soft place.

"A confounded marsh," I said.

"But," she answered, "I hear it trickling."

"What's the good of its trickling, if it's nasty."

"You *are* consoling," she mocked.

36

"I suppose," I said, "it rises here. So if we can get at the Quelle— —"

I don't know why 'Quelle' was necessary, instead of 'source,' but it was. We paddled up the wet place, and in the darkness found where the water welled out. Having filled our can, and our boots by the way, we trudged back. I slipped and spilled half the water.

"This," said Anita, "makes me perfectly happy."

"I wish it did me," I replied.

"Don't you like it dear?" she said, grieved.

My feet were soddened and stone cold. Everywhere was wet, and very dark.

"It's all right," I said. "But the Chapel—"

So we sat at the back of the hut, where the wind didn't blow so badly, and we made tea and ate sausage. The wind wafted the flame of the spirit lamp about, drops of rain began to fall. In the pitch dark, we lost our sausage and the packet of tea among the logs.

"At last I'm perfectly happy," Anita repeated.

I found it irritating to hear her. I was looking for the tea.

Before we had finished this precious meal, the rain came pelting down. We hurried the things into our Rucksacks and bundled into the hut. There was one little bread left for morning.

The hut was as big as a small cottage. It was made of logs laid on top of one another, but they had not been properly notched, so there were stripes of light all round the Egyptian darkness. And in a hay-hut one dares not strike a light.

"There's the ladder to the big part," said Anita.

The front compartment was only one quarter occupied with hay: the back compartment was full nearly to the ceiling. I climbed up the ladder, and felt the hay: putting my hand straight into a nasty messy place where the water had leaked in among the hay from the roof.

"That's all puddly, and the man'll have his whole crop rotten if he doesn't watch it," I said. "It's a stinkingly badly made hay hut."

"Listen to the rain," whispered Anita.

It was rattling on the roof furiously. Then, although there were slots of light, and a hundred horse power draught tearing across the hut, I was glad to be inside the place.

"Hay," I remarked after a while, "has two disadvantages. It tickles like all the creeping insects, and it is porous to the wind."

"'Porous to the wind,'" mocked Anita.

"It is," I said.

There was a great preparation. All valuables, such as hair-pins and garters and pfennigs and hellers and trinkets and collar studs, I carefully collected in my hat. It was pitch dark. I laid the hat somewhere. We took off our soddened shoes and stockings. Imagining they would somehow generate heat and dry better, I pushed the boots into the wall of hay. Then I hung up various draggled garments, hoping they would dry.

"I insist on your tying up your head in a hanky, and on my spreading my waistcoat for a pillow cloth," I said.

Anita humbly submitted. She was too full of joy to refuse. We had no blankets, nothing but a Burberry each.

"A good large hole," I said, "as large as a double grave. And I only hope it won't be one."

"If you catch cold," said Anita, "I shall hate you."

"And if *you* catch cold," I answered, "I s'll nurse you tenderly."

"You dear!" she exclaimed, affectionately.

We dug like two moles at the grave.

"But see the mountains of hay that come out," she said.

"All right," I said, "you can amuse your German fancy by putting them back again, and sleeping underneath them."

"How lovely!" she cried.

"And how much lovelier a German fat bolster would be."

"Don't!" she implored, "Don't spoil it."

"I'd sleep in a lobster-pot to please you," I said.

"I don't want you to please me, I want you to be pleased," she insisted.

"God help me, I *will* be pleased," I promised.

At first it was pretty warm in the trough, but every minute I had to rub my nose or my neck. This hay was the most insidious, persistent stuff. However much I tried to fend it off, one blade tickled my nostrils, a seed fell on my eye-lid, a great stalk went down my neck. I wrestled with it like a Hercules, to keep it at bay, but in vain. And Anita merely laughed at my puffs and snorts.

"Evidently," I said, "you have not so sensitive a skin as I."

"Oh no—not so delicate and fine," she mocked.

"In fact, you can't have," I said, sighing. But presently, she also sighed.

"Why," she said, "did you choose a waistcoat for a pillow, I've always got my face in one of the arm-holes."

38

"You should arrange it better," I said.

We sighed, and suffered the fiendish ticklings of the hay. Then I suppose we slept, in a sort of fitful fever.

I was wakened by the cracks of thunder. Anita clutched me. It was fearfully dark. Like a great whip clacking, the thunder cracked and spattered over our hut, seemed to rattle backwards and forwards from the mountain peaks.

"Something more for your money," I groaned, too sleepy to live.

"Does thunder strike hay-huts?" Anita asked.

"Yes, it makes a dead set at them—simply preys on hay-huts, does thunder," I declared.

"Now you needn't frighten me," she reproached.

"Go to sleep," I commanded.

But she wouldn't. There was Anita, there was thunder, and lightning, then a raging wind and cataracts of rain, and the slow, persistent, evil tickling of the hay seeds, all warring on my sleepiness. Occasionally I got a wink. Then it began to get cold, with the icy wind rushing in through the wide slots between the logs of the walls. The miserable hay couldn't even keep us warm. Through the chinks of it penetrated the vicious wind. And Anita would not consent to be buried, she would have her shoulders and head clear. So of course we had little protection. It grew colder and colder, miserably cold. I burrowed deeper and deeper. Then I felt Anita's bare feet, and they were icy.

"Woman," I said, "poke your wretched head in, and be covered up, and save what modicum of animal heat you can generate."

"I must breathe," she answered crossly.

"The hay is quite well aerated," I assured her.

At last it began to get dawn. Slots of gray came in place of slots of blue-black, all round the walls. There was twilight in the crate of a hay-hut. I could distinguish the ladder and the Rucksacks. Somewhere outside I thought, drowsily, a boy was kicking a salmon-tin down the street; till it struck me as curious, and I remembered it was only the sound of a cow-bell, or a goat-bell.

"It's morning," said Anita.

"Call this morning?" I groaned.

"Are you warm, dear?"

"Baked."

"Shall we get up?"

"Yes. At all events we can be one degree more wretched and cold."

"I'm perfectly happy," she persisted.

"You look it," I said.

Immediately she was full of fear.

"Do I look horrid?" she asked.

She was huddled in her coat: her towzled hair was full of hay.

I pulled on my boots and clambered through the square opening.

"But come and look!" I exclaimed.

It had snowed terrifically during the night; not down at our level, but a little higher up. We were on a grassy place, about half a mile across, and all round us was the blackness of pine-woods, rising up. Then suddenly in the middle air, it changed, and great peaks of snow balanced, intensely white, in the pallid dawn. All the upper world around us belonged to the sky; it was wonderfully white, and fresh, and awake with joy. I felt I had only to run upwards through the pine-trees, then I could tread the slopes that were really sky-slopes, could walk up the sky.

"No!" cried Anita, in protest, her eyes filling with tears. "No!"

We had quite a solemn moment together, all because of that snow. And the fearfully gentle way we talked and moved, as if we were the only two people God had made, touches me to remember.

"Look!" cried Anita.

I thought at least the Archangel Gabriel was standing beside me. But she only meant my breath, that froze while on the air. It reminded me.

"And the cold!" I groaned. "It fairly reduces one to an ash."

"Yes my dear—we must drink tea," she replied solicitously. I took the can for water. Everything looked so different in the morning. I could find the marsh, but not the water bubbling up. Anita came to look for me. She was bare-foot, because her boots were wet. Over the icy mown meadow she came, took the can from me, and found the spring. I went back and prepared breakfast. There was one little roll, some tea, and some Schnapps. Anita came with water, balancing it gingerly. She had a distracted look.

"Oh how it hurt!" she cried. "The ice-cold stubbles, like blunt icy needles, they did hurt!"

I looked at her bare feet and was furious with her.

"No one," I cried, "but a lunatic, would dream of going down there *barefoot* under these conditions—"

"'Under these conditions,'" she mocked.

"It ought to have hurt you *more*," I cried. "There is no crime but stupidity."

"'Crime but stupidity,'" she echoed, laughing at me.

Then I went to look at her feet.

We ate the miserable knob of bread, and swallowed the tea. Then I bullied Anita into coming away. She performed a beautiful toilet that I called the 'brave Tyrolese,' and at last we set out. The snow all above us was laughing with brightness. But the earth, and our boots, were soddened.

"Isn't it wonderful!" cried Anita.

"Yes—with feet of clay," I answered. "Wet, raw clay!"

Sobered, we squilched along an indefinite track. Then we spied a little, dirty farm-house, and saw an uncouth looking man go into the cow-sheds.

"This," I said, "is where the villains and robbers live."

Then we saw the woman. She was wearing the blue linen trousers that peasant women wear at work.

"Go carefully," said Anita. "Perhaps she hasn't performed her toilet."

"I shouldn't think she's got one to perform," I replied.

It was a deadly lonely place, high up, cold, and dirty. Even in such a frost, it stank bravely beneath the snow peaks. But I went softly.

Seeing Anita, the woman came to the door. She was dressed in blue overalls, trousers and bodice, the trousers tight round the ankles, nearly like the old-fashioned leg-of-mutton sleeves. She was pale, seemed rather deadened, as if this continuous silence acted on her like a deadening drug. Anita asked her the way. She came out to show us, as there was no track, walking before us with strides like a man, but in a tired, deadened sort of way. Her figure was not ugly, and the nape of her neck was a woman's, with soft wisps of hair. She pointed us the way down.

"How old was she?" I asked Anita, when she had gone back.

"How old do you think?" replied Anita.

"Forty to forty-five."

"Thirty two or three," answered Anita.

"How do you know, any more than I?"

"I am sure."

I looked back. The woman was going up the steep path in a mechanical, lifeless way. The brilliant snow glistened up above, in peaks. The hollow green cup that formed the farm was utterly still. And the woman seemed infected with all this immobility and silence. It was as if she were gradually going dead, because she had no place there. And I saw the man at the cow shed door. He was thin, with sandy moustaches; and there was about him the same look of distance, as if silence, loneliness, and the mountains deadened him too.

We went down between the rocks, in a cleft where a river rushed. On every side, streams fell and bounded down. Some, coming over the sheer wall of a cliff, drifted dreamily down like a roving rope of mist. All round, so white and candid, were the flowers they call Grass of Parnassus, looking up at us, and the regal, black-blue gentian reared themselves here and there.

Christs in the Tyrol

The real Tyrol does not seem to extend far south of the Brenner, and northward it goes right to the Starnberger See. Even at Sterzing the rather gloomy atmosphere of the Tyrolese Alps is being dispersed by the approach of the South. And, strangely enough, the roadside crucifixes become less and less interesting after Sterzing. Walking down from Munich to Italy, I have stood in front of hundreds of Martertafeln; and now I miss them; these painted shrines by the Garda See are not the same.

I, who see a tragedy in every cow, began by suffering from the Secession pictures in Munich. All these new paintings seemed so shrill and restless. Those that were meant for joy shrieked and pranced for joy, and sorrow was a sensation to be relished, curiously; as if we were epicures in suffering, keen on a new flavour. I thought with kindliness of England, whose artists so often suck their sadness like a lollipop, mournfully, and comfortably.

Then one must walk, as it seems, for miles and endless miles past crucifixes, avenues of them. At first they were mostly factory made, so that I did not notice them, any more than I noticed the boards with warnings, except just to observe they were there. But coming among the Christs carved in wood by the peasant artists, I began to feel them. Now, it seems to me, they create almost an atmosphere over the northern Tyrol, an atmosphere of pain.

I was going along a marshy place at the foot of the mountains, at evening, when the sky was a pale, dead colour and the hills were nearly black. At a meeting of the paths was a crucifix, and between the feet of the Christ a little red patch of dead poppies. So I looked at him. It was an old shrine, and the Christus was nearly like a man. He seemed to me to be real. In front of me hung a Bavarian peasant, a Christus, staring across at the evening and the black hills. He had broad cheek-bones and sturdy limbs, and he hung doggedly on the cross, hating it. He reminded me of a peasant farmer, fighting slowly and meanly, but not giving in. His plain, rudimentary face stared stubbornly at the hills, and his neck was stiffened, as if even yet he were struggling away from the cross he resented. He would not yield to it. I stood in front of him, and realised him. He might have said, "Yes, here I am, and it's bad enough, and it's suffering, and it doesn't come to an end. *Perhaps* something will happen, will help. If it doesn't, I s'll have to go on with it." He seemed stubborn and struggling from the root of his soul, his human soul. No God-ship had been thrust upon him. He was human clay, a peasant Prometheus-Christ, his poor soul bound in him, blind, but struggling stubbornly against the fact of the nails. And I looked across at the tiny square of orange light, the window of a farm-house on the marsh. And, thinking of the other little farms, of how the man and his wife and his children worked on till dark, intent and silent, carrying the hay in their arms out of the streaming thunder-rain which soaked them through, I understood how the Christus was made.

And after him, when I saw the Christs posing on the Cross, à la Guido Reni, I recognised them as the mere conventional symbol, meaning no more Christ than St. George and the Dragon on a five-shilling-piece means England.

There are so many Christs carved by men who have carved to get at the meaning of their own soul's anguish. Often, I can distinguish one man's work in a district. In the Zemm valley, right in the middle of the Tyrol, there are some half-dozen crucifixes by the same worker, who has whittled away in torment to see himself emerge out of the piece of timber, so that he can understand his own suffering, and see it take on itself the distinctness of an eternal thing, so that he can go on further, leaving it. The chief of these crucifixes is a very large one, deep in the Klamm, where it is always gloomy and damp. The river roars below, the rock wall opposite reaches high overhead, pushing back the sky. And by the track where the pack-horses go, in the cold gloom, hangs the large, pale Christ. He has fallen forward, just dead, and the weight of his full-grown, mature body is on the nails of the hands. So he drops, as if his hands would tear away, and he would fall to earth. The face is strangely brutal, and is set with an ache of weariness and pain and bitterness, and his rather ugly, passionate mouth is shut with bitter despair. After all, he had wanted to live and to enjoy his manhood. But fools had ruined his body, and thrown his life away, when he wanted it. No one had helped. His youth and health and vigour, all his life, and himself, were just thrown away as waste. He had died in bitterness. It is sombre and damp, silent save for the roar of water. There hangs the falling body of the man who had died in bitterness of spirit, and the driver of the pack-horses takes off his hat, cringing in his sturdy cheerfulness as he goes beneath.

He is afraid. I think of the carver of the crucifix. He also was more or less afraid. They all, when they carved or erected these crucifixes, had fear at the bottom of their hearts. And so the monuments to physical pain are found everywhere in the mountain gloom. By the same hand that carved the big, pale Christ I found another crucifix, a little one, at the end of a bridge. This Christ had a fair beard instead of a black one, and his body was hanging differently. But there was about him the same bitterness, the same despair, even a touch of cynicism. Evidently the artist could not get beyond the tragedy that tormented him. No wonder the peasants are afraid, as they take off their hats in passing up the valley.

They are afraid of physical pain. It terrifies them. Then they raise, in their startled helplessness of suffering, these Christs, these human attempts at deciphering the riddle of pain. In the same way they paint the humorous little pictures of some calamity—a man drowned in a stream or killed by a falling tree—and nail it up near the scene of the accident. "Memento mori," they say everywhere. And so they try to get used to the idea of death and suffering, to rid themselves of some of the fear thereof. And all tragic art is part of the same attempt.

But some of the Christs are quaint. One I know is very elegant, brushed and combed. "I'm glad I am no lady," I say to him. For he is a pure lady-killer. But he ignores me utterly, the exquisite. The man who made him must have been dying to become a gentleman.

And a fair number are miserable fellows. They put up their eyebrows plaintively, and pull down the corners of their mouths. Sometimes they gaze heavenwards. They are quite sorry for themselves.

"Never mind," I say to them. "It'll be worse yet, before you've done."

Some of them look pale and done-for. They didn't make much fight; they hadn't much pluck in them. They make me sorry.

"It's a pity you hadn't got a bit more kick in you," I say to them. And I wonder why in England one sees always this pale, pitiful Christ with no "go" in him. Is it because our national brutality is so strong and deep that we must create for ourselves an anæmic Christus, forever on the whine; either that, or one of those strange neutrals with long hair, that are supposed to represent to our children the Jesus of the New Testament.

In a tiny glass case beside the high-road, where the Isar is a very small stream, sits another Christ that makes me want to laugh, and makes me want to weep also. His little head rests on his hand, his elbow on his knee, and he meditates, half-wearily. I am strongly reminded of Walther von der Vogelweide and the German mediaeval spirit. Detached, he sits, and dreams, and broods, in his little golden crown of thorns, and his little cloak of red flannel, that some peasant woman has stitched for him.

"Couvre-toi de gloire, Tartarin—couvre-toi de flanelle," I think to myself.

But he sits, a queer little man, fretted, plunged in anxiety of thought, and yet dreaming rather pleasantly at the same time. I think he is the forefather of the warm-hearted German philosopher and professor.

He is the last of the remarkable Christs of the peasants that I have seen. Beyond the Brenner an element of unreality seems to creep in. The Christs are given great gashes in the breast and knees, and from the brow and breast and hands and knees streams of blood trickle down, so that one sees a weird striped thing in red and white that is not at all a Christus. And the same red that is used for the blood serves also to mark the path, so that one comes to associate the Martertafeln and their mess of red stripes with the stones smeared with scarlet paint for guidance. The wayside chapels, going south, become fearfully florid and ornate, though still one finds in them the little wooden limbs, arms and legs and feet, and little wooden cows or horses, hung up by the altar, to signify a cure in these parts. But there is a tendency for the Christs themselves to become either neuter or else sensational. In a chapel near St. Jakob, a long way from the railway, sat the most ghastly Christus I can imagine. He is seated, after the crucifixion. His eyes, which are turned slightly to look at you, are bloodshot till they glisten scarlet, and even the iris seems purpled. And the misery, the almost criminal look of hate and misery on the bloody, disfigured face is shocking. I was amazed at the ghastly thing: moreover, it was fairly new.

South of the Brenner again, in the Austrian Tyrol, I have not seen anyone salute the Christus: not even the guides. As one goes higher the crucifixes get smaller and smaller. The wind blows the snow under the tiny shed of a tiny Christ: the guides tramp stolidly by, ignoring the holy thing. That surprised me. But perhaps these were particularly unholy men. One does not expect a great deal of an Austrian, except real pleasantness.

So, in Austria, I have seen a fallen Christus. It was on the Jaufen, not very far from Meran. I was looking at all the snow-peaks all around, and hurrying downhill, trying to get out of a piercing wind, when I almost ran into a very old Martertafel. The wooden shed was silver-grey with age, and covered on the top with a thicket of lichen, weird, grey-green, sticking up its tufts. But on the rocks at the foot of the cross was the armless Christ, who had tumbled down, and lay on his back, in a weird attitude. It was one of the old, peasant Christs, carved out of wood, and having the long, wedge-shaped shins and thin legs that are almost characteristic. Considering the great sturdiness of a mountaineer's calves, these thin, flat legs are interesting. The arms of the fallen Christ had broken off at the shoulders, and they hung on their nails, as ex voto limbs hang in the shrines. But these arms dangled from their palms, one at each end of the cross, the muscles, carved in wood, looking startling, upside down. And the icy wind blew them backwards and forwards. There, in that bleak place among the stones, they looked horrible. Yet I dared not touch either them or the fallen image. I wish some priest would go along and take the broken thing away.

So many Christs there seem to be: one in rebellion against his cross, to which he was nailed; one bitter with the agony of knowing he must die, his heart-beatings all futile; one who felt sentimental; one who gave in to his misery; one who was a sensationalist; one who dreamed and fretted with thought. Perhaps the peasant carvers of crucifixes are right, and all these were found on the same cross. And perhaps there were others too: one who waited for the end, his soul still with a sense of right and hope; one ashamed to see the crowd make beasts of themselves, ashamed that he should provide for their sport; one who looked at them and thought: "And I am of you. I might be among you, yelling at myself in that way. But I am not, I am here. And so——"

All those Christs, like a populace, hang in the mountains under their little sheds. And perhaps they are falling, one by one. And I suppose we have carved no Christs, afraid lest they should be too like men, too like ourselves. What we worship must have exotic form.

Italian Essays, *1913* and *'With the Guns'*, *1914*

By the Lago di Garda.

I. The Spinner and the Monks.

The church of San Tommaso is not shy, it is *farouche*. I had as lief go looking for Pan among beechwoods, as set out for it. I know well enough if I go out by the back door, I shall find myself in the labyrinth, the catacombs of a village, somewhere over which perches the old church. I don't like these Italian villages. In them, I feel like a beetle crawling in the dark deep in the crevices of some broken pavement. And it was sunny. Overhead was a tantalizing strip of clear blue. And there was I nipped between the high, dark houses, as if I were in some shaft of an underground working. The Italians are supposed to be sunny people. Perhaps the men are, for they are always lounging in the piazza and on the quay. But the houses are forever dark, dank, and sepulchral, and the streets are more horrible than the Valley of the Shadow of Death: for no sun lights upon them, nor any heat, and the inhabitants, small and obscure, slide along by the walls, or stop, half turning, half crouching, to stare.

I know there are not more than a hundred houses in the village. That is what annoys me: that so few should be too many for me. At any rate, I came to the blind, broken end of a street, where the sunshine and the olive trees looked like a mirage seen out of gloom. And there above I saw the thin stiff neck of old San Tommaso, grey in the sun. And in a moment I found a broken staircase, where weeds grew in the gaps the steps had made in falling, and maiden hair fern fringed the darker side of the wall.

I mounted up, saying to myself 'I must go through this decayed Purgatory of a passage, I suppose,' so keeping myself drawn close in, I ran up, and popped out, like a figure on the stage, clear on the platform of my San Tommaso, in the grand sunshine. It is a wonderful position, above the obscure, jumbled tiles of square roofs, high enough over the pale blue lake, opposite the snow of the mountains beyond the water. And the snow glistened white, there was a blood-red sail like a butterfly breathing on the blue water, while the earth on my side gave off a green-silver smoke of olive trees, filming up and around the earth-coloured roofs. So I praised God.

There is no earthly reason why the Church of San Tommaso should be in this position, just where it is most lonely, though so near to the houses. But it is very nice. There is a terrace of cobble pavement, worn, like a great threshold to the ancient grey building. Then the land rises obscurely above, and the land falls somehow below. Yet it always remains in my mind that San Tommaso stands in mid-air by the mountain side. It belongs to nowhere, and has no immediate surroundings. I have only been in the church once. It was very dark, and smelled powerfully of centuries of incense. It reminded me of the lair of some enormous creature, and my senses sprang awake. I expected something, I wanted something, my flesh was alive. And I hurried out again, onto that wonderful table of sunshine outside. And it would cost me a great effort to go inside the church again. But its pavemented threshold is clear as a jewel.

The marvellous clarity of sunshine that becomes blue in the height makes me laugh by myself. Across, the great mountain crouches its length along the lake, and the top half is brilliantly white and skyey, and the lower half is dark, grim. On my side, down sweeps the headland from a great, pale-grey height, in a rush of russet and crimson, to the olive-smoke and the water. And between the two, quaint and naïve, the pale-blue lake goes poking further and further, pushing the mountains aside in its curiosity, inquiring into the Alps.

And then I noticed that a big, blue-checked cloth was drying in the sunshine on the wall of the terrace, just in front of me. So I said 'Whose are you?' And turning round, I saw on the other side of the platform, under a caper-bush that hung like a dark cloud, almost the colour of blood stain, on the grey wall above her, a little old woman, whose fingers were busy. Like the grey church, she made me feel as if I were not in existence. For if I had been a goat walking by the wall, and she a grey old stone, she would have made just as much notice of me.

Her head was tied in a dark-red kerchief, but pieces of hair, like dirty snow, quite short, stuck out over her ears. And—she was spinning! I was so surprised that I dared scarcely cross the terrace to look closer. She was grey, and her apron, and her dress, and her kerchief, and her hands and her face were all sun-bleached or sunstained, greyey, bluey, browny, like stones and half-coloured leaves, sunny in their colourlessness. In my black coat, I felt quite wrong.

But she was spinning! Under her arm she held a distaff of dark, ripe wood: just a plain staff with a clutch at the end, as if someone held up an arm making a basket of brown fingers at the top. And in the grasp of these brown fingers of her distaff was a great fluff of blackish rusty fleece, held up near her shoulder. And her fingers were plucking at the strand of wool drawn down from it; and hanging near her feet, spinning round by a black thread, was her shuttle, her bobbin wound fat with coarse black-brown worsted she was making. All the time, her fingers, so old, but not skinny: thick, brown, sturdy fingers, the thumb having a long grey nail, teased out the fleece to a fairly uniform thickness, and from moment to moment she gave the thread that went down in front of her apron, a new quick rub between her thumb and finger, and the heavy shuttle spun more briskly, and mechanically she felt again at the fleece as she drew it down, and mechanically again she gave a twist to the worsted that issued, and again the bobbin spun swiftly. It was so simple!

"You are spinning!" I said.

She looked at me. Her blue eyes were confident and quite untroubled.

"What?" she said.

"You are spinning," I said.

"Si," she replied, very short.

She was as indifferent to me as if she were the most sought-after young woman of the commune. Yet she must have been more than eighty. She stood short and sturdy, scarcely glancing at her thread, but looking for the most time straight in front, quite satisfied, and her eyes were like two periwinkles in the grey stone. Nothing troubled her, and it was nothing she wanted. Still her fingers went along the strand of fleece near her breast.

"It is an old way of doing it," I said.

"What?"

Again she looked at me with her naïf, untroubled eyes. It was evident my poor Italian roused her. She took no notice of my black coat: I was to her just a man, neither stranger nor gentleman. She looked at me as if to say 'What are you talking about, man?' I repeated.

"Yes, yes," she said, indifferently, "it is an old method—old, yes—" and she looked at me with her wonderful, self-contented eyes, that were not old nor full of dreams, nor yet young and full of flame: just two calm, self-sufficient eyes, extraordinarily like flowers, in that a flower never knows it is lonely, nor cares about the past or future. And to her I was just a man: not a child nor a woman, but a man to whom, after all, it was more interesting, or at least more exciting to talk, than to anyone else. I was an important bit of the landscape to her. She went on talking to me, in her Italian of which I could scarcely understand a syllable, and looking in my eyes. Her shuttle had hung into a dead chicory plant, which stopped its spinning. She did not notice. I stooped and broke off the twigs. There was a glint of blue near their elbows yet. Seeing what I was doing, she merely withdrew a few inches from the plant. Her fingers worked away all the time, in a little, half fretful movement, yet spontaneous as butterflies leaping here and there. She continued to talk to me, never waiting for me to answer. She could not conceive that I did not understand. It was something about a sheep that had died, and her grandson who had eleven children, and what she had said to him 'I will spin out her wool. As well hers as any others. She was a black ewe.' So she went on with the story. Then that she liked to spin: one felt one was doing nothing. She looked into my eyes. So she chuntered rapidly on in her Italian that I could not understand at all, looking meanwhile into my face. Not a feature moved. Her eyes remained candid and open to mine. What did she care about anything! She looked from her spinning to me, telling me more. I could not help wondering how many men had kissed her. She had scorned them all. She scorned them still, old and weathered as she was. But very tolerantly she seemed to admit they could be nice. By this time I could not understand one word. Still we went on with our tête à tête. Her eyes were quite as young as mine, and could *kosen* wonderfully. I knew I was laughing to her. Her thread broke. She seemed to take no notice, but mechanically picked up the shuttle, wound a certain length of worsted, connected the ends from her wool-strand, set it spinning, talking to me in her easy, half intimate, half indifferent fashion all the time. So she stood in the sunshine on the little plateau, erect and aloof, sun-coloured and sun-discoloured, whilst I at her elbow stood deferential, smiling into her eyes, afraid, terribly afraid lest she should think me a fool.

I am sure she did. For at last she stopped talking, did not look at me, went on with her spinning, the brown shuttle twisting gaily. There she stood, belonging to the sunshine and the weather, taking no more notice of me than did the caper-bush hanging like a black blood-stain over her head.

"But you have done a lot," I said.

She waited a minute, glanced at her bobbin.

"Yes," she said scornfully.

"How long has it taken you?" I asked.

She looked at me curiously, as if to say 'What a slow fool you are!' Then quite suddenly she started forward and went across the terrace to the great blue-and-white checked cloth that was drying on the wall.

She glanced round at me as she went. Then I hesitated, and fled up the steps two at a time. In a moment I was between the walls climbing upwards, hidden from her.

They had told me I could find snowdrops behind San Tommaso, and it was for these I had come. The walls broke down suddenly. There was a path went through an olive orchard, over the short grass. I took it, till I came to the brink of the steep valley, or gorge of a little stream. Here I stood to look for my snowdrops. The grassy, rocky bank went down steep from my feet. I heard the water tittle-tattling away in the deep shadow below. There were pale flecks in the dimness, but those, I knew, were primroses, not snowdrops. So I scrambled down. Looking up out of my shadow of water, I could see, right up in the sky, the grey rocks shining. 'Are they so far up, and am I so far down!' I thought to myself.

But it was a lovely place, primroses everywhere in little nests of pale bloom upon the dark, steep face of gully; and tongues of fern hanging out, and here and there under the withies, tufts of wrecked christmas roses, nearly over, but still in the coldest corners, the lovely buds like handfuls of snow. There have been such crowded tufts of christmas roses everywhere in the stream-gullies, that I only give them a nod now. I gathered primroses instead, quite a big handful. They smell so of the weather. I contented myself with them, since I could not find the snowdrops. Yet I had discovered a bank of pale lilac-coloured crocuses, with dark stripes, the day before yesterday. They looked so pretty, under the olive trees near a stream; I thought of thousands of little tongues of lavender flame among the grass. And if one finds crocuses, one may expect snowdrops. When I had got my handful of primroses, I climbed again quickly, for all of a sudden I resented burrowing about down there in the damp and darkness like an otter, when up above I saw the olive trees in their sunny grass, and sunlit grey rocks immensely high. Who should have the sunshine when I did not!

A couple of little birds scudded off in silence from me. 'You needn't be alarmed,' I said, 'I am no bird-devouring Italian.' For here there is scarcely a bird left, and that one so frightened. For they take them in great traps on the mountains, and shoot them among the cliffs. One morning the postman glowed when I opened the door, so I thought it was some proofs that would mean money. But it was eight little birds tied together by the necks: little brown ones, and dark ones with white marks, finches, and larks. The postman likes me, and his eyes shone.

"Ecco signore!" he exclaimed, with gusto.

"But they are *dead*!" I cried.

"Yes, signore, but fresh."

The eyes of the old 'gourmet' shone again, as he offered me the birds. I could more easily have eaten him, than have put my teeth in their little bodies.

I was soon in the sunshine again, on the turf under the olive trees. All the olives are gathered, and the mills go night and day, and there is a great acrid scent of olive oil in preparation, by the lake. The little stream rattled down. A mule driver 'Hued!' to his mules on the *Strada Vecchia*. High up on the *Strada Nuova*—a beautiful wide highway, newly made, that does not *quite* reach the frontier yet—I heard the crack of an oxen whip, and the faint clank of a wagon. And like my old spinning woman, everything was sun-coloured: grey-green olives, tawny grass, clear-grey rocks, browny-green spires of cypresses, with their cones: not a dark shadow or a deep tone anywhere. And all so warm and still, I sat me down under the olives. The four-o'clock steamer was going down the lake, a little thing creeping near under the cliffs. Far away, the Verona side, beyond the Isola, lay fused in dim gold. A cricket hopped. It was Saturday afternoon.

And then just below me I saw two monks walking in their garden between the naked, bony vines. For there is a Franciscan monastery just behind San Tommaso, and sometimes I see a monk looking out of a window. I wonder why it seems queer to think of a monk looking out of his monastery window: almost as queer as to think of a monk in a bathing van. But these two monks were walking in their wintry garden of bony vines and olive trees, their brown cassocks passing between the brown vine-stocks, their heads bare to the sunshine, sometimes a glint of white as their feet strode from under their skirts. It was all so still, that I felt them talking. They marched with the peculiar march of monks, a long, almost loping stride. With their heads together, their skirts swaying, slowly, and with long strides, the two brown monks went down under the bony vines, and lower down, beside the cabbages. I could feel them talking. It was almost as if, like my old woman, they were talking to me. I sat with my primroses saying 'Si'—'si,' as if I understood. And all the time I listened to them, absorbed in their conversation, though I could not hear even the sound of their voices. But I could see the long stride, that has something of a slink in it, because of the almost springless way they slide their feet from the ground, something like a wolf loping along on a quest. And they kept their hands down against the skirts of their robes. And they did not touch each other, or gesticulate as they walked. And yet there was an eagerness in their conversation. Almost like the shy birds they went backwards and forwards in their wintry garden, thinking nobody could see them. And they were so eager, but as if they were frightened. It was like the birds again, as if they dared not enjoy anything, as if there was nothing in that dazzle of snow across—it was faintly, faintly ripening to a glow—for them. But backwards and forwards they walked, talking.

I had not noticed that up above the snow, in the blue sky, was a frail moon, like a piece of ice worn thin to a scalloped film upon the blue surface of water. It had drifted up from behind my snow, upon the slow current of the day. And a bell sounded.

And still my monks were walking, backwards and forwards, pacing, till they seemed like a see-saw. And when it would be night, and that moon's white, splendid body would shine on the dark-fringed olive woods, they would pray, looking forward to the white moonlight of eternity. And this morning, when the dawn had come rippling over the lake filling the sky with this sunlight, they had prayed, looking backward to that frail, white body on the Cross, that was murdered. And always they were not here, they were there: there away back with the murdered body, there away in front with the free white spirit, either in the past or the future, in the death of the tortured body, in the death of the glorified soul, but never here. They were like a bridge that is built from either side of the stream, that leaps out, but does not meet: ends in a gap in mid-air.

They frightened me rather. I saw them turn in to the small monastery. It was tea-time. I hoped they would have toast for tea. I have not had toast for tea since I was in England. I hoped they would have toast for tea, they would seem so real and *present* when they bit it. I know *they* would not have tea and toast when they went in the monastery, but *my* monks did.

The shadows were coming across everything. That is the worst of having mountains even running to the west. The olive wood where I sat was put out. So I got up, climbing after the sunshine. And the moon climbed higher as well. And my primroses looked such a frail, moony little bunch, I put a big, rose-tipped daisy among them. It was just going to sleep between the olive roots, when I took it. And then I saw some little periwinkles, dark blue, like violets, so I put them also, two or three, among my primroses. They reminded me of my old woman's eyes. And they seemed just to make my bunch vital. She is so perfectly the *present*. She certainly does not look before and after, and pine for what is not. Nor do the flowers. And if the birds do, they shouldn't come within reach of these Italian tit-slayers. And as for the monks, I'm so glad I escaped being one myself—after all, it *would* be nice to walk backwards and forwards in the monastery garden, from the past to the future, striding over the present; that I say nothing about them.

And if I were in England—it is Saturday evening—I might avoid all these complexities of old women with distaffs, and monks that 'lope,' and have toast for tea, and go to the theatre—if I had the money.

II. *The Lemon Gardens of the Signor di P.*

The padrone came just when we were drinking coffee after dinner. It was two o'clock, because the steamer going down the lake to Desenzano had bustled through the sunshine, and the rocking of the water still made lights that rose and fell upon the wall, among the shadows by the piano.

The signore was very apologetic. I found him bowing in the hall, a cap in one hand, a slip of paper in the other, and protesting in his broken French against disturbing me. He is a little, shrivelled man, with close cropped grey hair on his skull, and a protruding jaw which, with his gesticulations, always reminds me of a genteel monkey. But the signore is a gentleman, and the last, perishing remnant of his race.

"Mais—mais monsieur—je crains que—que—"

He bows and spreads wide his hands, emphatically. It is a great joy to the signore to speak French. It is less joy to me. He seems to be fetching the words from a long way off. He holds his chin and waits in his anxiety for the phrase to come. Then it filters out grudgingly, ending in Italian. The hall is cold, and he will not come in the dining room. The French language is a wheel upon which so many poor spirits and innocent tongues are broken. Yet he will not speak Italian. It would be beneath his dignity.

I realise that it is an American door-spring that has laid the signore low. I look at the rag of old paper bearing the directions and the picture of the patent.

"Fasten the spring either end up. Wind it up. Never unwind," I read. It is laconic and American. The signore looks at me anxiously and holds his chin. He is afraid he ought to understand my English— Then, with a stuttering equal to his, I translate.

He has not done anything contrary to the directions. He is most distressed.

"La porte—la porte—elle ferme *pas*!—elle s'ouvre—."

He skipped to the door and showed me the whole tragedy. It is shut—Ecco! He lets go, and Pouf!—she flies open. Explain the mystery, monsieur l'Anglais. The honour of the English-speaking world is at stake. I must go and look at this spring. The signore protests, but leaves himself in my hand. I feel I have stepped into the shoes of Sherlock Holmes, and am rather nervous.

Signor di P.'s house is only a stone's throw from this, at the end of our garden. It is quite a magnificent place, cream coloured and pink,

59

with two painted loggias. In the moonlight its noble façade looks more impressive than anything I ever hoped to see. Yet now I am bowed into the hall. I am glad my uncouth appearance can be put down as English eccentricity.

I am sure the signore's house might be called a palazzo. Every consequential-looking establishment is named the villa something, except the great home of the Conte B., which is called the Palazzo B. Now the signore's house has no name, so I am certain that is equivalent to the assumption of the title 'palazzo.'

I entered the palazzo of the Signor di P. The hall is a spacious place, with great glass doors at either end, looking into the courtyard where gold-green bamboos fray out the sunshine. So, with the floor of lovely, soft-red bricks, the gold outside, the neutral of the grey-white walls, and the gaily-painted ceiling, its pink roses and birds fluttering, and the spaces of coloured, tempered air, I was much pleased.

But only the hall pleases me. It is half-way between the open and the interior, and partakes of both. But the interior itself is like an up-holstered tomb. The Italian likes to be impressed. When he enters his drawing-room, he does not want to be left uncertain as to whether this may or may not be a bit of nicely-arranged out-of-doors. It is interior with a vengeance: dark, gloomy, cold, with hearse-like windows, carved, cold furniture, grandeur to inspire awe. Here the red-brick floor seems dreary, like the floor of a vault, and the furniture stands in its grave. The air inside has been starved and darkened to death.

Outside, the sunshine seems to trill like birds singing. God indeed made Italy. But who made the Italian interior? It seems as if all the shadow were cast inside. Poor Hamlet stands with his back to the sun, and his darkness falls on everything he approaches. The Italian is surrounded by sunshine: his very suppleness and ease and grace seem melted in sunshine. But he must be fairly dark inside, or his house could not be as it is. A writer in La Perseveranza says 'noi italiani sopratutto, siamo ancora troppo passionali: allegri più che felici, mentre gli inglesi sono più felici che allegri.' I suppose a passionate people is of necessity unhappy: because passion is an instrument, a means; and to mistake the means for the end is to leave oneself at last empty. And the northern races are the really passionate people, because theirs is the passion that persists and achieves, achieves everything, including that intimacy between a man and a woman which is the fruit of passion, and which is rarely seen here: the love, the knowledge, the simplicity and the absence of shame, that one some-times sees in English eyes, and which is the flower of civilisation.

Signor di P. took me to a small room almost contained in the thickness of the wall. There the signora's dark eyes started into excited surprise at seeing me. She was younger than the signore, below him in station, forsooth!—and childless. It was quite true, the door stood open. Madame put down the screw-driver and drew herself erect. Her eyes were a flame of excitement. The door stood open. The signore never did anything without the assistance of the signora or of the maid, Maria. The signora cleverly makes him believe, poor, decayed, good-natured little gentleman, that he is absolute lord and master. He has the air of a man who rules. But his gentle spirit takes every time her suggestion. He would deny it indignantly. Yet she lives his life for him, utters his words, suggests his movements—and for all that, is afraid of him. For he is a man and she is a woman. So it behoves her in all things to bear herself with meekness. And still she controls him gently.

Now, the signora held the little signore together whilst he undid the screw that fixed the spring. If they had been alone, she would have done it. As a matter of fact, he usually began, and she finished, the task in hand. And his beginning was like the launching of a ship by Lady So-and-so—a mere graceful formality. For she had all the life and vigour. But in my presence, it would have been an abrogation of his dignity if she had driven the screw home. And I dared not offer. So she held him together, watchfully. She was straight and vigorous, he was shaky and grey, though not much more than sixty. She held her hands up as he stood on the chair, afraid lest he should catch her doing it, but more afraid lest he should fall.

They had merely adjusted the strong spring to the shut door, stretching it slightly, so that it drew itself together again the moment the latch was released. It was soon made right. They were delighted. The signora, who gave me the uncomfortable feeling that she might burst into flame at any moment, clasped her hands together in ecstasy as the door swiftly shut itself. 'Ecco—ecco!' she cried. And she ran forward to do it herself. She opened the door expectantly, eagerly. Pouf!—it shut with a bang. 'Ecco!' she cried, her eyes aflame. I felt I must do it also. I opened the door—Pouf!—it shut with a bang. We all exclaimed with joy.

Then the signore, by his tone, dismissed the signora:

"Ah!—Ah!—merci monsieur—mille fois—mille fois merci."

He held his chin, turned to me smiling, turned his back slightly on her. She disappeared. It was a state occasion, and she was in the way. She might want to help him. He chose to have me to himself—'entre hommes' as he said.

He would show me the estate. I had already seen the house. I was quite willing. We went out by the glass doors on the left, into the courtyard. It was lower than the gardens round it, and the sunshine came through the trellised arches, onto the flagstones where the grass grew fine and green in the cracks, where all was wide and still and deserted. In their tubs, one or two fat orange trees squatted. Then I heard a noise, and there in the corner, among all the pink geraniums and the sunshine, the signora sat laughing with a baby. It was a fair, bonny boy of eighteen months. The signora was concentrated upon him as he sat, stolid and handsome in his little white cap, perched on the bench picking at the pink geraniums. She laughed, bent forward her dark face out of the shadow, swift into a glitter of sunshine, near the sunny baby, laughing again, making mother-noises. The child took no notice of her. She caught him swiftly into her shadow, and they were dim; her dark head was against the baby's white wool jacket, she was kissing his neck, under the creeper leaves. The pink geraniums still laughed in the sunshine. The baby had a pink ribbon in the shadow.

I had forgotten the signore. Suddenly I turned to him inquiringly.

"The signora's nephew," he explained briefly, almost coldly.

She had seen us watching and came across the sunshine with the child, laughing, talking to the baby, acknowledging us only as she did the shadow from which she removed him. The signore, queer old horse, began to laugh and neigh at the child, which bent its face to cry. The signora caught it away, dancing off a few yards into the sunshine.

"I am a stranger, he is afraid of me," I said to her across the distance.

"No no," she cried, "you are a man—it is the men—he always cries."

She advanced again, laughing, with the child in her arms. The signore stood aside, almost in the background, shadowed. She and I and the baby, in the sunshine, laughed a moment. Then I heard the neighing laugh of the old signore. He would not be put into the background. But there was something disagreeable about him. His laugh was affected. He felt left out, made nothing. The signora was uncomfortable too. I could tell she wanted to be fleeing with the child, to enjoy him alone. It was her brother's boy. And the signore felt almost as if she insulted him, by being in such an ecstasy with the baby. He held his chin, gloomily, fretful, impotent.

Then I knew what a bitter chagrin it was to him to be childless. He was ashamed. It reminded me of the men in the Old Testament. It was as though his manliness were not proven, until he had a child. And now he would never have one, and the house of di P. would die out.

These Italians, men and women, adore their children, at least while they are little. The man seems not to be able to believe in himself, till he has a child. His whole pride is based in this fact—that he can beget a son. It is his children who justify him. Unless he be an artist, he feels that his only real claim to being a man, is that he has children. That he is himself is nothing. For his soul is nothing to him.

Which is why he can move so gracefully, hang like a bird in the olive trees, row down the lake standing in the boat and swinging forward, rhythmic as the ripples under him. An Englishman walks as if he must brave it out: as if it were a chagrin to him to be forced to acknowledge his legs and arms, in public. For he considers himself partakes of Almighty God, cumbered here in the flesh. But the Italian feels, no matter what he believes, that he is made in the image of God, and in this image of flesh is his godliness, and with its defacement and crumbling, crumbles himself. Which is why he often gives one the feeling that he has nothing inside him.

"Mais," says the signore, starting from this scene of ignominy where his wife plays with another woman's child, "mais—voulez vous vous promener dans mes petites terres?"

It comes out quite rapidly, he is so much roused in self-defence. We walked along the pergola of bony vine-stocks, parallel with the mountains, which stand full of sunshine on our right. I remark how delightful it is in his garden—where does it end? This brought back his pride with a click. He pointed me to the terraces, and the great shut lemon-houses above. They were all his. But—he shrugged his Italian shoulders—it was nothing, just a little garden. I protested that I found it beautiful, as well as extensive. He admitted it was beautiful today: "Perchè—parceque—il fait un temps—così—très bell'—très beau." He alighted on the word 'beau' hurriedly, like a bird that comes to ground with a little bounce, after a flight.

The terraces of the garden have a cosy feel, walled in, and yet leaning at the full sunshine. I move deliciously in heavy sunshine, under the bony avenues of vines, reluctant to go. The signore makes little exclamatory noises that mean nothing, and I learn the names of vegetables. The land is rich and black. We climb one flight of steps, and can see the lake as we walk this next level of garden. We climb again, and come to a great stone building that I take to be a storage house, for open-air storage, because the walls are left open from half way up, so that inside is all dark, and the corner pillar is very clear. Entering carelessly into the dimness, I started, for at my feet was a great floor of water, clear and green in its obscurity, going down between the walls, a reservoir in the gloom. The signore laughed at my surprise. It was for irrigating the land, he said. It stank slightly, with a raw smell, otherwise I said, what a wonderful bath it would make. The old signore gave his little neighing laugh at my eccentricity.

Then we climbed into a great loft of leaves, ruddy brown, stored in a great bank under the roof, seeming to give off a little red heat, as they gave off the lovely perfume of the hills. We passed through, and stood at the foot of the lemon-house. The big, blind building rose high in the sunshine before us.

All summer long, upon the mountain slopes steep by the lake, stand the rows of naked pillars rising out of the green foliage like ruins of temples: white, square pillars of masonry, standing forlorn in their colonnades and squares, rising up the mountain-sides here and there, as if they remained from some great race that had once worshipped here. And still, in the winter, some are seen, standing away in lonely places where the sun streams full, grey rows of pillars rising out of a broken wall, tier above tier, naked to the sky, forsaken.

They are the lemon plantations, and the pillars are to support the heavy branches of the trees, but finally to act as scaffolding of the great wooden houses that stand blind and ugly, covering the lemon-trees in the winter.

In November, when cold winds came down and snow was deep on the mountains, from out of the store-houses the men were carrying timber, and we heard the clank of falling planks. Then, as we walked along the new road on the mountain-side, we saw below, on the top of the lemon gardens, long thin poles laid from pillar to pillar, and we heard the two men talking and singing as they walked across perilously, placing the poles. In their clumsy zoccoli they strode easily across, though they had twenty or thirty feet to fall if they slipped. But the mountain-side, rising steeply, was so near, and above their heads the rocks glowed high into the sky, so that the sense of elevation must have been taken away. At any rate they went easily from pillar-summit to pillar-summit, with a great cave of space below. Then again was the rattle and clang of planks being laid in order, ringing off the mountain-side over the blue lake, till a platform of timber, old and brown, projected from the mountain-side, a floor when seen from above, a hanging roof when seen from below. And we, on the road above, saw the men sitting easily on this flimsy hanging platform, hammering the planks. And all day long the sound of hammering echoed among the rocks and olive woods, and came, a faint quick concussion, to the men on the boats far out. When the roofs were on, they put in the fronts, blocked in between the white pillars with old, dark wood, in roughly made panels. And here and there, at irregular intervals, was a panel of glass, pane overlapping pane in the long strip of narrow window. So that now these enormous, unsightly buildings bulge out on the mountain-sides, rising in two or three tiers, blind, dark, ragged-looking places.

In the morning I often lie in bed and watch the sunrise. The lake lies dim and milky, the mountains are dark-blue at the back, while over them the sky gushes and glistens with light. At a certain place on the mountain ridge the light burns gold, seems to fuse a little groove on the hill's rim. It fuses and fuses at this point, till of a sudden it comes, the intense molten living light. The mountains melt suddenly, the light steps down, there is a glitter, a spangle, a clutch of spangles, a great unbearable sun-track flashing across the milky lake, and the light falls on my face. Then, looking aside, I hear the little slotting noise which tells me they are opening the lemon gardens, a long panel here and there, a long slot of darkness at irregular intervals between the brown wood and the glass stripes.

"Vouley vous"—the signore bows me in with outstretched hand. "Vouley vous entrer, monsieur."

I went into the lemon house, where the poor trees seem to mope in the darkness. It is an immense, dark, cold place. Tall lemon trees, heavy with half-visible fruit, crowd together and rise in the gloom. They look like ghosts in the darkness of the underworld, stately, and as if in life, but only grand shadows of themselves. And lurking here and there, I see one of the pillars. But he too, seems a shadow, not one of the dazzling white fellows I knew. Here we are, trees, men, pillars, the dark earth, the sad black paths, shut in in this enormous box. It is true, there are long slips of window, and slots of space, so that the front is striped, and an occasional beam of light fingers the leaves of an enclosed tree, and the sickly round lemons. But it is nevertheless very gloomy.

"But it is much colder in here than outside," I said.

"Yes," replied the signore, "Now. But at night—I *think*—"

I almost wished it were night, to try. I wanted to imagine the trees cosy. They seemed now in a vault. Between the lemon trees, beside the path, were little orange trees, and dozens of oranges hanging like hot coals in the twilight. When I warm my hands at them, the signore breaks me off one after another, till I have a bunch of glowing oranges among dark leaves, a heavy bouquet. Looking down the lemon house, the many ruddy-clustered oranges beside the path remind me of the lights of a village along the lake at night, while the pale lemons above are the stars. There is a subtle, exquisite scent of lemon flowers. Then I notice a citron. He hangs heavy and bloated upon so small a tree, that he seems a dark-green enormity. There is a great host of lemons overhead, half visible, a swarm of ruddy oranges by the paths, and here and there, a fat citron. It is almost like being under the sea.

At the corners of the path were round little patches of ash, and stumps of charred wood, where fires had been kindled inside the house on cold nights. For during the second and third weeks in January, the snow came down so low on the mountains, that after climbing for an hour, I found myself in a snow lane, and saw olive orchards on lawns of snow.

The signore says that all lemons and sweet oranges are grafted on a bitter-orange stock. The plants raised from seed, lemon and sweet orange, fell prey to disease, so the cultivators found it safe only to raise the native bitter orange, and then to graft upon it.

And the maestra—she is a schoolmistress, and wears black gloves while she teaches us Italian—says that the lemon was introduced by St. Francis of Assisi, who came here, and founded a church and a monastery. Certainly the church of San Francesco is very old and delapidated, and its cloisters have some beautiful and original carvings of leaves and fruit upon the pillars. Which seems to connect San Francesco with the lemon. I imagine him wandering here with a lemon in his pocket. Perhaps he made lemonade in the hot summer. But Bacchus had been before him and cornered the drink trade: and still keeps it.

Looking at his lemons, the signore sighed. I think he hates them. They are leaving him in the lurch. They are sold retail at a halfpenny each, all the year round. "But that is as dear, or dearer, than in England," I say. "Ah but," says the maestra, "that is because your lemons are outdoor fruit from Sicily. Però—one of our lemons is as

66

good as *two* from elsewhere." My mother always said that one of her home-made loaves was as good as two of the baker's. I believe one of my articles is as good as two of anybody else's.—These lemons indeed have an exquisite fragrance and perfume, but whether their force as lemons is double that of an ordinary fruit—. Oranges are sold at fourpence halfpenny the Kilo.—it comes about five for twopence, small ones. The citrons are sold also by weight to Salò, for the making of that liqueur known as 'Cedro.' One citron fetches sometimes a shilling, or more, but then the demand is necessarily small. So that it is evident, from these figures, the Lago di Garda cannot afford to grow its lemons much longer. The gardens are already many of them in ruins, and still more 'Da Vendere.'

We went out of the shadow of the lemon-house, onto the roof of the one below us. When we came to the brink of the roof, I sat down. The signore stood behind me, a shabby, shaky, little figure on his roof against the sky, lifted up like an image of decay. Yet the mountain snow was radiant opposite, and a film of pure blue was on the hills. The water breathed an iridescent dust on the far shore. An orange-sailed boat leaned slim on the dark-blue water, where crisp flecks of foam were fluttering. A woman went down-hill with two goats and two sheep. Among the olives someone was whistling.

"Yes," said the little signore, musing, looking down from his height. "That was once lemon garden down there—you see the stumps of the pillars, between the vines. Twice as much, twice as much lemons, I had. Now it must be vine. And that piece of land brought in two hundred lire a year, from lemons, now from wine, only eighty."

"But wine is a valuable crop," I said.

"Così, così. For a man who grows much. For me, it is not lemons." Suddenly he started into life, an agitated little ruin of a figure against the blue sky. "Perchè—because the lemon is all the year, and the vine—one crop, one harvest."

The last words ring like a knell. I sit and look at the lake. And now the lemon gardens in ruin among the hills, stand out to me. And yet, right up here, I can hear a man singing as he stands rowing down the lake in his boat.

"But it is beautiful!" I protest. "In England—"

"Ah," cries the signore, "in England you have the wealth—les richesses—but here we have the sun—" He waved his hand heavenwards towards the wonderful source of the blue day. But he sounded sadly as if he were making the best of it. If the sun had been a big lemon hanging in his garden, I am afraid he would have sold it by weight.

But when we go down to earth, he gathers me some pink roses, and offers them to me, bowing, as if I were a prince or a lady. Why should he be so anxious to be rich? He has enough. He has more than I am ever likely to have. Yet I wouldn't sell a matchbox-ful of sunshine out of my garden.

III. The Theatre.

During carnival a company is playing in the theatre. On Christmas day the signore came in with the key of his box, and would we care to see the play. The theatre was little, we should find it a nothing in fact, but—and the signore spread out his hands—if it might give us a little diversion—! The key impressed me, with its shield of bronze hanging on the chain and bearing the signore's initials, and the number 8. 'The key of my box at the theatre!'

On the Saturday after Christmas we went to see 'I Spettri.' The theatre is an old church. Since the cinematograph has spread like a conflagration over the world, many old churches burn with new light. But since a chiesa in these parts looks from outside anything but a religious building—a mixture between a malt-house and a town-hall rather; and since the interior is cleverly constructed for the dramatic performance of religious ceremony, the transformation from church to theatre is not very astonishing. No one would recognise our theatre as a cast-off church. The east end was round to begin with, the walls were blind of windows. The entrance hall is, or was, a contiguous building. Now, everything is perfectly in keeping, except the stone floor, and the slightly ecclesiastic seats downstairs.

The box of Signor di P. is one of the best in the place—and there are two tiers of boxes, some forty in all, each lined with dark red, and fringed with velvet, as it should be;—and it just holds three people comfortably. Having paid our entrance fee of threepence, we sat in style. Then I bowed to the barber, seated opposite in an upper box; then to the Signora G., who has the swell box next the stage; then to the chemist, on the same altitude as the barber; then to the padrona of the Hôtel, three boxes away, on my right. So, having made my entry, I arranged the footstool and looked downstairs.

The people were all waiting. On the left, by church instinct, the women sat together, with perhaps a man at the end of the row. On the right were little groups of bersaglieri, in their grey uniforms, then peasants, fishermen, and an odd girl or two, brazen hussies, to be sure, to sit near the men. At the back, under the gallery, stood men in their black-brimmed felt hats, with cloaks flung over their mouths. The theatre is not heated and the floor is of stone. Yet the women sit beneath me without any wraps, their hair dressed with wonderful Italian precision, their bodices very neat, their dark, coloured aprons quite clean. The men are clean, but many are still unshaven. They are shaved once a week, so that their black chins have a disreputable look; but they have dove's eyes, these Italian men. And they lounge with their wonderful ease, unconscious of the patches on their clothes, of their zoccoli, of their collarless throats, of the scarlet rag that is perhaps tied round their neck. Perfectly at their ease, the men lounge and talk, or watch with that wistful sadness one sees in the eyes of a child that is 'glotzend.' The men are together, the women are together. The sexes are always separate. There is very little flirting, even, and it seems, no comradeship between men and women. The two avoid each other. Only a highly civilised man of strong character can bear, or is capable of close intimacy with a woman. One sees very little courting in this part, and no lovers. But on Sunday afternoons and evenings, the woman, accompanied by a child or friend for protection's sake, goes leading home her wine-drunken husband. Otherwise, she is rarely seen at his side. And on Sunday afternoon, an uncomfortable youth walks by the side of his maiden for an hour, in the very public part of the highway. That is all.

The women sit with their perfectly-dressed black hair, and their straight backs, aloof, not very noticeable. They are not particularly graceful, as the men are, nor particularly attractive. For they look hard, and rather soulless. One rarely sees a woman with that beautiful womanly contour of bosom that makes one think her husband is a happy man. But she has often a magnificent straight back, and a regular proportion, which gives one to think her husband should be a satisfied man. Which he seems. But there is nothing winning about these women. They go down the dark streets from their cavernous dark houses, and are silent, unobtrusive, often tired looking, often proud and straight as a cypress, but always cold, without tenderness, capable of heat but not of warmth, passionate perhaps, but not lovable. None of their sons could be a Dickens, with that wonderful warmth and cosy tenderness that makes life rich in an English home.

The company of actors was from a little town beyond the mountains, Brescia way. The curtain rose, everybody was still. And then, after a while, we realised that 'I Spettri' was Ibsen's 'Ghosts.' It was rather startling, and rather stiff fare for the peasants and the fishermen of the Garda. Yet they sat still and absorbed, even the children. The actors are peasants by origin. Signor di P. says, rather disdainfully, that he finds their accent scarcely polished; and he shrugs his shoulders. So Ibsen is translated altogether. The mother is rather a nice woman who feels very harassed by all this bother. The pastor is a stupid, common, affected fellow—a caricature of a protestant parson. The servant is just a pert hussy. And then the son—he is the actor-manager, a man of forty or thereabouts, broad and thickset, ruddy and black—is a very human, decent fellow, not at all like a son of the house of Ghosts, but a convalescent, fretful, fanciful, who doesn't quite know what ails him, and who wants somebody to comfort him, to reassure him, for he is frightened of himself. He is childishly dependent on his mother. To hear him say 'Grazia mamma!' would have touched the mother-soul in any woman living. So forlorn he was, with this trouble that had got him down mysteriously, with such a child's bewildered forlornness, robust, vigorous man that he was, that one could feel and love this childish nation that lives by faith and wants no knowledge. Yet he was not to be trusted. Like a child, he would smash things if he could not have what he wanted, and being a man, his smashing might be more serious than crockery. His flashy, Italian passion for his half sister was real enough to make one uncomfortable: something he wanted, like a child that suddenly goes wild for a desired object. And then he looked frightened. And, frightened, obstinate, bewildered, so he died, leaving one so sorry for him.

Ibsen was translated thus. All the bruised deadness of him was gone. Instead of the characters seeming like indicators registering inevitable records of fate, we had people frightened, obstinate, foolish, passionate, and dead: it was more bearable. Ibsen is the mind, recognising that itself is of no avail against the flesh. Hence his despair. But what was the root of his despair, holds the root of our hope. For of the flesh all things are possible, whereas the mind, being a production, equivalent to shapen carpentry, is finite. And we are of the flesh, which holds all things within itself, both the discovered and that which will be discovered.

At any rate, now I am sorry for the son of Ghosts; I could have sympathy with him: whereas before I had only a horror of him. Before, he was beyond the range of my pity: it was too awful. Now I could put my hand on his hand, and even if I could say nothing, my warm fingers could give him a little love. Which was denied me before, for I couldn't have touched him. For which I hated Ibsen. I believe everybody hates Flaubert and Ibsen. They denied the universality of the blood, of which we are all cups. They owned the universality of the mind, to which we all subscribe, as to the wearing of clothes. Then they showed how the mind is overthrown at any moment by the body. But why shouldn't it be. And if the son of Ghosts must die, still I live, who am the flesh and the blood, the same as he. If I have spilled one cup, many more remain. And if the dream that was in this cup is gone, still it lies somewhere in all the rest of the liquor, and will come again, pieced together. And I am sorry for the son of Ghosts, as if I had lost my left hand. But because I lost my left hand, it is not finished with me. There are many more left hands even within my living flesh: for if I have a son, he will be born with both hands. And if the mind of the son of Ghosts is gone, so is the light of my candle blown out. And yet the bees are carrying their pocketfuls of wax from the flowers, that the flowers got from out of the air and earth whither the light went, and which will make more light, if I like. We are tired of going rigid with grief, or insane, over a little spilt life. The sun will lick it up.

The contadini sat and listened intently, like children who hear and do not understand, and who yet know. For they have flesh and blood too, and it answers, even if the brain is dead. So, even the children sit in the spell, till the play is over. And each drop of blood in them runs hastily with the knowledge that it too may have to suffer as did the blood that ran through the heart of the son of Ghosts.

But they did not care for Ibsen. On the Feast of Epiphany, as a special treat, a poetic drama of D'Annunzio was given: 'La Fiaccola sotto il moggio.' There were several murders, but, like so many murders, they only seemed to be silly showing-off, or bits of extreme mischief. All the terror, all the tragedy, came out of mid-air. The deeds were not exciting, any more than a cook's wringing the neck of a chicken. The people *thought* they ought to cover their ears and shriek and run under the stabbing lightning of heaven's vengeance. And the tragedy was the noise they made because their thoughts told them to do so. But the audience loved it. They got a thrill without a hurt. I loved it myself, for that matter.

"Ah bellissimo, bellissimo!" said the barber, in tones of reverence. After all, the theatre is a church.

"Better than 'I Spettri'!" I said.

"Ah well—it was D'Annunzio!—and the other—who was it, Ibsen?"

"Ibsen," I confirmed.

"Ah well, D'Annunzio—well—"

"But Ibsen is one of the world's greatest dramatists," I said.

"Ah but D'Annunzio—oh, most beautiful, most beautiful!"

It was evident that the name of the Italian was like church bells to the barber, while Ibsen was the scratching of a match on a matchbox.

Yet I thought D'Annunzio's play childish and foolish, as if a party of children had been naughty and expected a whipping. The murders were done as easily, yea with as little heart-beating, as the poisoning of a neighbour's cat.

Carnival ends on the 5th of February, so each Thursday evening there is a Serata d'Onore of one of the actors. The first, and the only one for which prices were raised—fourpence entrance fee instead of threepence—was for the leading lady. Her play 'La Moglie del Dottore,' a modern piece, was sufficiently stupid: the farce that followed it was better. But since it was her evening of honour, she was the most important personage. She is very popular: at least the men often cry 'Beautiful, beautiful!' after her most heart-rending sobs. The women say nothing. I believe, as they sit sternly watching, they quite agree that she represents ill-used, tearstained woman, the bearer of many wrongs; so they would fight for her on principle. But I know they think her much, much too plump.

Yet she is beloved. I wonder why the Gretchen, Dame aux Camélias, Desdemona lady is the beloved of all male audiences, and the appreciated of all female, in all countries, for all time. I am young, and I am inexperienced. Yet I have seen at least a hundred of these pale, tear-stained ladies, white-garbed with their hair down their backs. I loathe them on principle. And yet my bones melt and my heart goes big and loving, each new time I hear her voice, with its faint clang of tears. The last time I saw her—until I went to the theatre here—was in Salò, at the opera. She was the chalked, thin-armed daughter of Rigoletto. I positively hated her. And yet, by the end, I was ready to rush on the stage and slay her recreant lover, take her in my arms, and say: 'Why you poor little thing, don't you fret after that fat clown, he wasn't worth it. You are too loving, you silly little thing: and it's a shame to treat you like it. There, let me dry your little wet face—he wasn't worth a thought, silly deluded little thing. You should fall in love with a *man*—!'

This lady at our theatre—I shall call her Lucia, because it gives me a pleasant sensation, and she will never know—is rather plump, it is true, but she is She, Desdemona, Lucia, Margherita, Gretchen, Ophelia, Iphigenia, Antigone. The moment she looks round—a bit scared—she is recognised. In modern plays She is dressed in black, as in the divorce court, as my lady in 'La Moglie del Dottore.' In the romantic plays, she wears white muslin that trails like a sigh, she has a fillet on her fair hair, whose locks, in touching simplicity, hang below her waist, among the muslin. Lucia always has a handkerchief. It is the last straw: it wrings my heart. She squeezes it up in her poor plump hand, and then she can't help crying, she can't, men are so cruel to her. And there she gives a sob and a cry, and presses her handkerchief and her fist against her eyes, and real tears shake out of her, and it is all so real and natural, I don't know what to do with myself. There I sit in my box, and am saying in my heart all the time, 'What a shame, child, what a shame!' She is twice my age, but what are years! 'Your poor little hanky, why it's sopping wet! There now, you cry yourself better on my chest.' And I cover her in protectively with my arms. I think, in my heat, I might recite to her

> 'Oh wert thou in the cauld blast
> On yonder lea, on yonder lea
> My plaidie to the angry airt
> I'ld shelter thee, I'ld shelter thee.'

I know what sort of a lady Burns wrote that to. And when I came to the line, 'Thy bield should be my bosom,' I should feel the hands of Lucia unfold and creep round my shoulders, and she would cleave to me, and I should know she had confidence in me, and my breast would swell out like a great cuirass, and yet it would be her bield!—Ah, what a divine sensation!

Yet I hate these sad heroines—or don't I? I suppose she knows best. Even Bunty, while she was pulling the strings, had that twang in her voice: something unsatisfied and insidious and feline. And I wonder if there was a man in the Haymarket who did not say in his heart: 'That nice little body is just throwing herself away on that lump of a carpenter—and knows it, too. I wonder why these women do it, when there are real *men* about.' Who the real men are is not defined. They may be married already. But every man has a Doppelgänger, a gay young batchelor 'blood' who has adventures, while the staid reality remains at home. And the business of the leading lady is to have gallant dealings with this Doppelgänger—she can accommodate as many as you like of the dashing sparks—, just as the business of the leading actor is to play cavalier to all the Doppelgängerinnen of the audience.

All these meditations were roused by Lucia, on her Serata D'Onore. During the following week we moved in a storm of little coloured bills 'Great Evening of Honour of Enrico Persevalli.' Now this is the actor-manager. The title of the play was kept dark. I should not have gone, because circumstances were untoward, if the maestra, on the

Thursday evening, had not informed me that certainly I ought to go, the play was Amleto. 'Oh!' I said. 'Sì!' she replied, and her dark eyes were wide with excitement.—The poor maestra, she seems to have been in mourning all her life. She was engaged to a lieutenant in the cavalry, and he went and got drowned, never thinking how he would spoil her life. Then her father died last year. She is nearly fifty, and seems as if she had grown up in perpetual shadow.—'But what's Amleto?' I said, not very interested. Her dark eyes looked rather anxious. 'It is English,' she said. 'Never,' I answered. 'Amleto?' she repeated. The skies seemed to be falling on her. 'Good Lord, it's Hamlet!' I cried. 'Sì!' hissed the signorina, excited as a yellow and black snake, in her relief at not being wrong.

Then, sadly, I felt upon me the burden of honour. I felt like a prince who must attend a performance given in honour of himself. Not for worlds would I have disappointed the Signor Enrico Persevalli. Yet only my consideration for him would have dragged me to the theatre. I knew perfectly well he was performing Hamlet on his evening of honour, for my sake. It seemed rather cruel on him. Hamlet in the book seems to me a very messy person, but the Hamlets I have seen on the stage have been positively nasty.

I was late. The first act was nearly over. I could see—I think I ought to be allowed to say I am sure of it, it is so pleasant to me—that the play was flat in the bosoms of the actors. I closed the door of my box softly. But in a moment the court of Denmark had seen me, and a flash went through the stage. Hamlet's eyes met mine. He looked a sad fool, a sad fool. I stooped down to arrange the footstool, and get the proper gloom onto my countenance.

They are peasants in origin, these actors: so the signore says. They nearly made me weep. I had a cousin, a collier's wife, whom I loved. She had twins when she had already eight children, but she said 'The more the merrier.' Her boast was, 'All my children are named after kings.' She also had a brooch made of a four-shilling piece, so she used to say: 'I've got money when there isn't a penny in my pocket.'

The actors were like Hannah's children—'they were all named after kings.' I sat sadly and looked at their Majesties. The Queen was a burly little body in pink satin. She tried her best to be stately, but she looked anxiously sideways at the audience, to see if she carried conviction. She was rather hoarse with a cold, and her excess of pink satin annoyed her. She dared not for her life move in any direction but straight forward, unless she had savagely kicked and twitched her skirt.

75

I liked her. She was a straightforward woman. She liked being a queen alright while she sat perched on a throne—her figure was something like that of Queen Victoria in later life; but when she must come to earth, she seemed to think that Kind hearts were more than coronets. The King, her noble consort, cleaved not to his garments. He is a man of some sixty years, a born peasant, thin, weedy, very gentle and pathetic. He played the father of the servant maid in Ghosts, and always has such parts. So he felt he was being made a fool of, sitting on a throne, with the other fellows bowing to him. He might have made a good Richard II. He evidently could have said with feeling 'Uneasy lies the head that wears a crown.' Hamlet I loathed. In reality he was a short, broad Italian—a common type—with his black hair cut close. As Amleto, he was a hulking fellow with long hair and black knee-breeches, carrying a long rag of a cloak, and crawling about with his head ducked between his shoulders, reminding me of a black beetle: the more so, as he is always turning up where he shouldn't.

He made me hate Hamlet. Of all the sickly, unnatural beasts, that Prince of Denmark seemed the greatest. When a decent Italian, Enrico Persevalli, put himself through the creepings and twistings of the unwholesome Dane, I revolted. I saw the natural man of hot heart, crawling to an anaemic tune, and it made me sick. Now I know Amleto, the Italian, would have stuck the King who had murdered his father, told the Queen, his mother, to clear out, and would have swept the steps. Or, if the gentle soul who acted King, and who seemed so utterly bewildered with all this nastiness, had been in Hamlet's shoes, he might have wondered what to do: then he would have gone to the priest, or he would have asked his mother. I tried to imagine any Italian in the part: he would not have been a Hamlet. Because every Italian I have seen lives by the human ties which connect him with his neighbour. But Hamlet had no neighbour, and no bond held him to anybody. He could not love, he could only judge. He might well say 'Oh that this too, too solid flesh would melt'—it was dead as half-thawed snow already. It seemed to me Hamlet was not mad, only diseased. He had no feelings. He never had had any. He was a sort of glorified 'Father Time' out of 'Jude the Obscure,' a sort of blind gut, of no use whatsoever except to give trouble. When a living creature begins to question whether man ought to live, or ought not to live, he is like a rotten fungus, giving off light by phosphorescence. And the whole of Hamlet seemed to me like this gleam of decay.

It was curious to see Amleto performing the phosphorescent antics of the Dane. He could not, no he could not work up any hatred of the King and the Queen. He didn't hate them, and yet he had to play tricks on them. It was all to pieces. There was no unity anywhere. Then when he had to recite long speeches, he got passionate.—I am sure, as he stepped forward whispering 'Essere'—took another step 'o non essere'—plunged with his hand—'that is the question,' the contadini thought he was stuck in the back, and they held their breath. But they were had. There was quite a lot of passion in these speeches, so the audience were held. But none of the passion came out of the words. It was all wandering in the blood of Enrico Persevalli, and out it came, like an inarticulate cry shapen to Shakspere's words, the latter having no meaning, only a regulated clatter. Of all the sad performances of Hamlet, this was one of the saddest.

The rôles were naturally condensed. Horatius played the Ghost. I knew him because, when he came in at the Queen-Hamlet scene, he had on Horatius' white trousers and patent slippers. He had a table cloth like a nun's shawl over his head, hanging behind, then another shawl of open-work wool over his face. But the audience took him perfectly seriously. There was even a thrill of fear: and I shared it. That Ghost has been one of my bitterest griefs. A great stain fell on the sky when I knew Punch didn't talk. Then, when I was about seven years old, I went to Teddy Rainer's theatre in the Statutes ground at home: we used to long for the twopence it cost to go in! They played Hamlet once a fortnight. My mother would let me go to see Hamlet, but not 'Maria Martin, or the Murder in the Red Barn.' I hung onto the form when the Ghost said, very deep:

"'Amblet, 'Amblet, I *am* thy father's ghost."

Then a voice from the audience came, cruelly disillusioned:

"Why tha h'arena—I can tell thy voice."

Then I wanted to go dismally home—it was all untrue, and the Ghost wasn't a ghost. Since then, I have seen the spectral form of Hamlet's father both sheeted and cased in tin, and have looked the other way. Now however, I have regained my innocence, and if the Ghost came in a cook's cap and apron, I should shudder. For a ghost may look anything, and still be a ghost. Who am I to say to the spirit—'thus shalt thou be!' And the peasants of the Garda are evidently with me. They sat absorbed and watched.

Ophelia came in white, with her fair hair down her back, and flowers in her hands instead of a hanky. And again I thought, if I'd had a chance, I would have squashed Mr Hamlet like the black-beetle he was, for behaving in his indirect indecent, dirty cockroach fashion to the girl. Poor Ophelia, she laughed and cried in a breath, and threw her flowers away. She at any rate knew what was the matter: he did not love her, never had loved her, could not love anybody. It was enough to send any girl crazy, to have given her love to a phosphorescent fish like Hamlet. What *was* she to do with her poor body, if not deck it with flowers and love it herself, then drown it. The peasants were with her, every man. At the end of her scene was a hoarse roar, half of indignation, half of passion. They evidently loathed that stinking fish, Hamlet.

The grave-yard scene was a great success. It pleased me mightily to see Hamlet looking such a fool, and taken off by the grave digger. It was queer to hear the latter say to the Prince of Denmark, handing him a skull:

"Questo cranio, signore—"

And Amleto, dainty fellow, took the skull in a corner of his black cloak, in order not to soil his hands. That Hamlet is 'signore,' and a skull is a 'cranio,' makes all the difference.

The close fell very flat, as it always does. The contadini applauded the graveyard scene wildly. But at the end of all, they got up and crowded to the doors, unmoved, in spite of the fact that Amleto had achieved a tour de force: he had fallen smack down three steps, in his death drop. But braced muscles will bounce, and Signor Amleto bounced quite high off the stage. 'Good!' I exclaimed, but I was applauding the gymnastic feat, not the death. I have seen Hamlets perish with more vigour, but not with such a bounce.

The people of the audience are a joy for ever. It is free and united as a tea-party downstairs. In English theatres, every man seems to have an abnormal sensitiveness in his knees and his elbows, and he keeps himself contracted as tight as he can, so as not to touch his neighbour. Here, the men lounge and lean on one another, talk and laugh and stroll, or stare in utter childish absorption, so that the place seems full of pleasure for everybody, and everybody shares with everybody else. It gives a warm feeling of life. And at the end of the scenes, the men push their black hats back, rub the hair across their brows, with a pleased, excited movement. And the women stir in their seats.

Just one man is with his wife and child, and he is evidently in love with his wife. He is a fair, handsome, clean fellow, rather queer, in that he seems to have gathered his wife and child into an atmosphere together, so that they are quite separate among the crowd. It reminds me of the Holy Family. I guess Joseph was really like this man; with a keen, abstract look, quite as wild and untamed as a hawk, but like a hawk at its own nest, fierce with love. Why should Joseph always be painted bald and bearded and a muff!—My Joseph buys a tiny, tiny bottle of lemonade, and the mother and child sip it. It is curious how these three are by themselves in the theatre, as much as if they were camping in the desert alone on their way to Egypt.

The bersaglieri sit close together, in groups, with their thick shoulders, their close-cropped, dark heads, their thick brown hands on each other's shoulders. When an act is over, they pick up their cherished hats and fling on their cloaks, and go into the hall. They are like young, half-wild oxen—such strong, healthy, naïve lads. As yet, they are quite womanless. In this they are different from any soldiers I have ever seen. They have no sense of women. Quite free, and fond of each other, almost in love with each other, they put on their beloved hats. These are round, they slant over the left ear, and from them streams a dark-green stream of cock's-plumes. One man is very straight and solid feeling. His cock-feathers slither in a profuse, heavy stream, almost onto his shoulder. He swings round. His feathers slip in a cascade. Then he goes out to the hall, his feathers tossing and falling richly. The last of the bersaglieri walks humbly, as if he wants to escape notice. His poor, thin handful of feathers flutters pitiably. He could not afford any more. These feathers are paid for by the soldiers, and a full plume may cost twenty or thirty lire.

Pietro, who carries from the steamer to the wharf, starts up from sleep like a wild-cat, as somebody claps him on the shoulder. He is young, not more than twenty-three, thin, dark, handsome, but almost ragged, where everybody is so scrupulously tidy, and his black week's beard shows very plainly. He has been flirting with the wife of that stately, gloomy, green-black barber, the Siciliano. For Pietro has a bad character. And he is already married. And in this part, there is very little looseness, very little promiscuity.

The peasants, in their hats and cloaks, crowd the hall. The few women soon slip away home. In the bar, a few are drinking. A glass, that is a tumbler of wine costs a penny. It is horrible new wine. But Hamlet is an expensive play, there are so many intervals. And a man cannot afford to drink so often in one week-day evening. On Sunday it is rather different. The bersaglieri who are well off, drink a glass of vermouth. There is a busy trade, but very little money spent.

Upstairs, the 'quality' has paid its visits and shaken hands. The

Signor di P., our padrone, is one of the gentry, and, next to the magistrate, or judge of the commune, the most important man present. He visits the G. in the box next the stage, and he spends two entre-actes with me. For the rest, he has either a bow or an unseeing eye. His workmen—there are only two—look up at the boxes much as they look up at the paintings of the Holy Angels in the church, with an uncritical, almost unseeing eye. Themselves, poor devils, walk the far earth beneath. The chemist and the grocer and the schoolmistress visit each other. The second grocer and the baker pay calls. The barber goes to see the furniture man, and then downstairs. Class distinctions are cut very fine. As we pass out with the padrona of the Hôtel, who is a German, we stop to speak to our friends, the di P. They have a warm handshake and conversation for us, for the padrona, a distant bow. We realise our mistake, take our leave, and rejoin the padrona.

But I know all about everybody from the barber—not the Siciliano, but the little, flashy barber with the pleasant-sounding voice. He says, in the three performances in Epiphany week, the theatre took two hundred and sixty five lire. The actor-manager pays twenty two lire for every performance given, as rent for the building, including light. The leading lady has thirty lire a week: but then her girl acts too. The King and Queen and four others are all one family, and they have about fifty lire a week. The actor-manager is not married. He once was engaged but—but the barber's tales are too long. He knows everything.

With the Guns.

The Reservists were leaving for London by the nine o'clock train. They were young men, some of them drunk. There was one bawling and brawling before the ticket window; there were two swaying on the steps of the subway shouting, and ending, "Let's go an' have another afore we go." There were a few women seeing off their sweethearts and brothers, but, on the whole, the reservist had been a lodger in the town and had only his own pals. One woman stood before the carriage window. She and her sweetheart were being very matter-of-fact, cheerful, and bumptious over the parting.

"Well, so-long!" she cried as the train began to move. "When you see 'em *let* 'em have it."

"Ay, no fear," shouted the man, and the train was gone, the man grinning.

I thought what it would really be like, "when he saw 'em."

.　　.　　.　　.　　.　　.

Last autumn I followed the Bavarian army down the Isar valley and near the foot of the Alps. Then I could see what war would be like—an affair entirely of machines, with men attached to the machines as the subordinate part thereof, as the butt is the part of a rifle.

I remember standing on a little round hill one August afternoon. There was a beautiful blue sky, and white clouds from the mountains. Away on the right, amid woods and corn-clad hills, lay the big Starnberg lake. This is just a year ago, but it seems to belong to some period outside of time.

On the crown of the little hill were three quick-firing guns, with the gunners behind. At the side, perched up on a tiny platform at the top of a high pair of steps, was an officer looking through a fixed spy-glass. A little further behind, lower down the hill, was a group of horses and soldiers.

Every moment came the hard, tearing, hideous voice of the German command from the officer perched aloft, giving the range to the guns; and then the sharp cry, "Fire!" There was a burst, something in the guns started back, the faintest breath of vapour disappeared. The shots had gone.

I watched, but I could not see where they had gone, nor what had been aimed at. Evidently they were directed against an enemy a mile and a half away, men unseen by any of the soldiers at the guns.

Whether the shot they fired hit or missed, killed or did not touch, I and the gun-party did not know. Only the officer was shouting the range again, the guns were again starting back, we were again staring over the face of the green and dappled, inscrutable country into which the missiles sped unseen.

What work was there to do?—only mechanically to adjust the guns and fire the shot. What was there to feel?—only the unnatural suspense and suppression of serving a machine which, for ought we knew, was killing our fellow-men, whilst we stood there, blind, without knowledge or participation, subordinate to the cold machine. This was the glamour and the glory of the war: blue sky overhead and living green country all around, but we, amid it all, a part in some iron insensate will, our flesh and blood, our soul and intelligence shed away, and all that remained of us a cold, metallic adherence to an iron machine. There was neither ferocity nor joy nor exultation nor exhilaration nor even quick fear: only a mechanical, expressionless movement.

And this is how the gunner would "let 'em have it." He would mechanically move a certain apparatus when he heard a certain shout. Of the result he would see and know nothing. He had nothing to do with it.

Then I remember going at night down a road, whilst the sound of guns thudded continuously. And suddenly I started, seeing the bank of the road stir. It was a mass of scarcely visible forms, lying waiting for a rush. They were lying under fire, silent, scarcely stirring, a mass. If one of the shells that were supposed to be coming had dropped among them it would have burst a hole in the mass. Who would have been torn, killed, no one would have known. There would just have been a hole in the living shadowy mass; that was all. Who it was did not matter. There were no individuals, and every individual soldier knew it. He was a fragment of a mass, and as a fragment of a mass he must live or die or be torn. He had no rights, no self, no being. There was only the mass lying there, solid and obscure along the bank of the road in the night.

This was how the gunner "would let 'em have it." A shell would fall into this mass of vulnerable bodies, there would be a torn hole in the mass. This would be his "letting 'em have it."

And I remember a captain of the bersaglieri who talked to me in the train in Italy when he had come back from Tripoli. The Italian soldier, he said, was the finest soldier in the world at a rush. But—and he spoke with a certain horror that cramped his voice—when it came to lying there under the Snyder fire you had to stand behind them with a revolver. And I saw he could not get beyond the agony of this.

"Well," I said, "that is because they cannot feel themselves parts of a machine. They have all the old natural courage, when one rushes at one's enemy. But it is unnatural to them to lie still under machine-fire. It is unnatural to anybody. War with machines, and the machine predominant, is too unnatural for an Italian. It is a wicked thing, a machine, and your Italians are too naturally good. They will do anything to get away from it. Let us see our enemy and go for him. But we cannot endure this taking death out of machines, and giving death out of machines, our blood cold, without any enemy to rise against."

I remember also standing on a little hill crowned by a white church. This hill was defended, surrounded by a trench half-way down. In this trench stood the soldiers side by side, down there in the earth, a great line of them.

The night came on. Suddenly, on the other side, high up in the darkness, burst a beautiful greenish globe of light, and then came into being a magic circle of countryside set in darkness, a greenish jewel of landscape, splendid bulk of trees, a green meadow, vivid. The ball fell and it was dark, and in one's eye remained treasured the little vision that had appeared far off in the darkness. Then again a light ball burst and sloped down. There was the white farm-house with the wooden, slanting roof, the green apple trees, the orchard paling, a jewel, a landscape set deep in the darkness. It was beautiful beyond belief. Then it was dark. Then the searchlights suddenly sprang upon the countryside, revealing the magic, fingering everything with magic, pushing the darkness aside, showing the lovely hillsides, the noble bulks of trees, the pallor of corn. A searchlight was creeping at us. It slid up our hill. It was upon us; we turned our backs to it, it was unendurable. Then it was gone.

Then out of a little wood at the foot of the hill came the intolerable crackling and bursting of rifles. The men in the trenches returned fire. Nothing could be seen. I thought of the bullets that would find their marks. But whose bullets? And what mark? Why must I fire off my gun in the darkness towards a noise? Why must a bullet come out of the darkness, breaking a hole in me? But better a bullet than the laceration of a shell, if it came to dying. But what is it all about? I cannot understand; I am not to understand. My God, why am I a man at all, when this is all, this machinery piercing and tearing?

It is a war of artillery, a war of machines, and men no more than the subjective material of the machine. It is so unnatural as to be unthinkable. Yet we must think of it.

TWILIGHT IN ITALY
[ITALIAN DAYS]

Contents

The Crucifix Across the Mountains

The Crucifix Across the Mountains

The imperial road to Italy goes from Munich across the Tyrol, through Innsbruck and Bozen to Verona, over the mountains. Here the great processions passed as the emperors went South, or came home again from rosy Italy to their own Germany.

And how much has that old imperial vanity clung to the German soul? Did not the German kings inherit the empire of bygone Rome? It was not a very real empire, perhaps, but the sound was high and splendid.

Maybe a certain Grössenwahn is inherent in the German nature. If only nations would realise that they have certain natural characteristics, if only they could understand and agree to each other's particular nature, how much simpler it would all be.

The imperial procession no longer crosses the mountains, going South. That is almost forgotten, the road has almost passed out of mind. But still it is there, and its signs are standing.

The crucifixes are there, not mere attributes of the road, yet still having something to do with it. The imperial processions, blessed by the Pope and accompanied by the great bishops, must have planted the holy idol like a new plant among the mountains, there where it multiplied and grew according to the soil, and the race that received it.

As one goes among the Bavarian uplands and foothills, soon one realises here is another land, a strange religion. It is a strange country, remote, out of contact. Perhaps it belongs to the forgotten, imperial processions.

Coming along the clear, open roads that lead to the mountains, one scarcely notices the crucifixes and the shrines. Perhaps one's interest is dead. The crucifix itself is nothing, a factory-made piece of sentimentalism. The soul ignores it.

But gradually, one after another looming shadowily under their hoods, the crucifixes seem to create a new atmosphere over the whole of the countryside, a darkness, a weight in the air that is so unnaturally bright and rare with the reflection from the snows above, a darkness hovering just over the earth. So rare and unearthly the light is, from the mountains, full of strange radiance. Then every now and again recurs the crucifix, at the turning of an open, grassy road, holding a shadow and a mystery under its pointed hood.

I was startled into consciousness one evening, going alone over a marshy place at the foot of the mountains, when the sky was pale and unearthly, invisible, and the hills were nearly black. At a meeting of the tracks was a crucifix, and between the feet of the Christ a handful of withered poppies. It was the poppies I saw, then the Christ.

It was an old shrine, the wood-sculpture of a Bavarian peasant. The Christ was a peasant of the foot of the Alps. He had broad cheek-bones and sturdy limbs. His plain, rudimentary face stared fixedly at the hills, his neck was stiffened, as if in resistance to the fact of the nails and the cross, which he could not escape. It was a man nailed down in spirit, but set stubbornly against the bondage and the disgrace. He was a man of middle age, plain, crude, with some of the meanness of the peasant, but also with a kind of dogged nobility that does not yield its soul to the circumstance. Plain, almost blank in his soul, the middle-aged peasant of the crucifix resisted unmoving the misery of his position. He did not yield. His soul was set, his will was fixed. He was himself, let his circumstances be what they would, his life fixed down.

Across the marsh was a tiny square of orange-coloured light, from the farm-house with the low, spreading roof. I remembered how the man and his wife and the children worked on till dark, silent and intent, carrying the hay in their arms out of the streaming thunder-rain into the shed, working silent in the soaking rain.

The body bent forward towards the earth, closing round on itself; the arms clasped full of hay, clasped round the hay that presses soft and close to the breast and the body, that pricks heat into the arms and the skin of the breast, and fills the lungs with the sleepy scent of dried herbs: the rain that falls heavily and wets the shoulders, so that the shirt clings to the hot, firm skin and the rain comes with heavy, pleasant coldness on the active flesh, running in a trickle down towards the loins, secretly; this is the peasant, this hot welter of physical sensation. And it is all intoxicating. It is intoxicating almost like a soporific, like a sensuous drug, to gather the burden to one's body in the rain, to stumble across the living grass to the shed, to relieve one's arms of the weight, to throw down the hay on to the heap, to feel light and free in the dry shed, then to return again into the chill, hard rain, to stoop again under the rain, and rise to return again with the burden.

It is this, this endless heat and rousedness of physical sensation which keeps the body full and potent, and flushes the mind with a blood heat, a blood sleep. And this sleep, this heat of physical experience becomes at length a bondage, at last a crucifixion. It is the life and the fulfilment of the peasant, this flow of sensuous experience. But at last it drives him almost mad, because he cannot escape.

For overhead there is always the strange radiance of the mountains, there is the mystery of the icy river rushing through its pinky shoals into the darkness of the pine-woods, there is always the faint tang of ice on the air, and the rush of hoarse-sounding water.

And the ice and the upper radiance of snow is brilliant with timeless immunity from the flux and the warmth of life. Overhead they transcend all life, all the soft, moist fire of the blood. So that a man must needs live under the radiance of his own negation.

There is a strange, clear beauty of form about the men of the Bavarian highlands, about both men and women. They are large and clear and handsome in form, with blue eyes very keen, the pupil small, tightened, the iris keen, like sharp light shining on blue ice. Their large, full-moulded limbs and erect bodies are distinct, separate, as if they were perfectly chiselled out of the stuff of life, static, cut off. Where they are everything is set back, as in a clear frosty air.

Their beauty is almost this, this strange, clean-cut isolation, as if each one of them would isolate himself still further and for ever from the rest of his fellows.

Yet they are convivial, they are almost the only race with the souls of artists. Still they act the mystery plays with instinctive fulness of interpretation, they sing strangely in the mountain fields, they love make-belief and mummery, their processions and religious festivals are profoundly impressive, solemn, and rapt.

It is a race that moves on the poles of mystic sensual delight. Every gesture is a gesture from the blood, every expression is a symbolic utterance.

For learning there is sensuous experience, for thought there is myth and drama and dancing and singing. Everything is of the blood, of the senses. There is no mind. The mind is a suffusion of physical heat, it is not separated, it is kept submerged.

At the same time, always, overhead, there is the eternal, negative radiance of the snows. Beneath is life, the hot jet of the blood playing elaborately. But above is the radiance of changeless not-being. And life passes away into this changeless radiance. Summer and the prolific, blue-and-white flowering of the earth goes by, with the labour and the ecstasy of man, disappears, and is gone into brilliance that hovers overhead, the radiant cold which waits to receive back again all that which has passed for the moment into being.

The issue is too much revealed. It leaves the peasant no choice. The fate gleams transcendent above him, the brightness of eternal, unthinkable not-being. And this our life, this admixture of labour and of warm experience in the flesh, all the time it is steaming up to the changeless brilliance above, the light of the everlasting snows. This is the eternal issue.

Whether it is singing or dancing or play-acting or physical transport of love, or vengeance or cruelty, or whether it is work or sorrow or religion, the issue is always the same at last, into the radiant negation of eternity. Hence the beauty and completeness, the finality of the highland peasant. His figure, his limbs, his face, his motion, it is all formed in beauty, and it is all completed. There is no flux nor hope nor becoming, all *is*, once and for all. The issue is eternal, timeless, and changeless. All being and all passing away is part of the issue, which is eternal and changeless. Therefore there is no becoming and no passing away. Everything *is*, now and for ever. Hence the strange beauty and finality and isolation of the Bavarian peasant.

It is plain in the crucifixes. Here is the essence rendered in sculpture of wood. The face is blank and stiff, almost expressionless. One realises with a start how unchanging and conventionalised is the face of the living man and woman of these parts, handsome, but motionless as pure form. There is also an underlying meanness, secretive, cruel. It is all part of the beauty, the pure, plastic beauty. The body also of the Christus is stiff and conventionalised, yet curiously beautiful in proportion, and in the static tension which makes it unified into one clear thing. There is no movement, no possible movement. The being is fixed, finally. The whole body is locked in one knowledge, beautiful, complete. It is one with the nails. Not that it is languishing or dead. It is stubborn, knowing its own undeniable being, sure of the absolute reality of the sensuous experience. Though he is nailed down upon an irrevocable fate, yet, within that fate he has the power and the delight of all sensuous experience. So he accepts the fate and the mystic delight of the senses with one will, he is complete and final. His sensuous experience is supreme, a consummation of life and death at once.

It is the same at all times, whether it is the mowing with the scythe on the hill-slopes, or hewing the timber, or steering the raft down the river which is all effervescent with ice; whether it is drinking in the Gasthaus, or making love, or playing some mummer's part, or hating steadily and cruelly, or whether it is kneeling in spell-bound subjection in the incense-filled church, or walking in the strange, dark, subject-procession to bless the fields, or cutting the young birch-trees for the feast of Frohenleichnam, it is always the same, the dark, powerful mystic, sensuous experience is the whole of him, he is mindless and bound within the absoluteness of the issue, the unchangeability of the great icy not-being which holds good for ever, and is supreme.

Passing further away, towards Austria, travelling up the Isar, till the stream becomes smaller and whiter and the air is colder, the full glamour of the northern hills, which are so marvellously luminous and gleaming with flowers, wanes and gives way to a darkness, a sense of ominousness. Up there I saw another little Christ, who seemed the very soul of the place. The road went beside the river, that was seething with snowy ice-bubbles, under the rocks and the high, wolf-like pine-trees, between the pinkish shoals. The air was cold and hard and high, everything was cold and separate. And in a little glass case beside the road sat a small, hewn Christ, the head resting on the hand; and he meditates, half-wearily, doggedly, the eyebrows lifted in strange abstraction, the elbow resting on the knee. Detached, he sits and dreams and broods, wearing his little golden crown of thorns, and his little cloak of red flannel that some peasant woman has stitched for him.

No doubt he still sits there, the small, blank-faced Christ in the cloak of red flannel, dreaming, brooding, enduring, persisting. There is a wistfulness about him, as if he knew that the whole of things was too much for him. There was no solution, either, in death. Death did not give the answer to the soul's anxiety. That which is, is. It does not cease to be when it is cut. Death cannot create nor destroy. What is, is.

The little brooding Christ knows this. What is he brooding, then? His static patience and endurance is wistful. What is it that he secretly yearns for, amid all the placidity of fate? "To be, or not to be," this may be the question, but it is not a question for death to answer. It is not a question of living or not-living. It is a question of being—to be or not to be. To persist or not to persist, that is not the question; neither is it to endure or not to endure. The issue, is it eternal not-being? If not, what, then, is being? For overhead the eternal radiance of the snow gleams unfailing, it receives the efflorescence of all life and is unchanged, the issue is bright and immortal, the snowy not-being. What, then, is being?

As one draws nearer to the turning-point of the Alps, towards the culmination and the southern slope, the influence of the educated world is felt once more. Bavaria is remote in spirit, as yet unattached. Its crucifixes are old and grey and abstract, small like the kernel of the truth. Further into Austria they become new, they are painted white, they are larger, more obtrusive. They are the expressions of a later, newer phase, more introspective and self-conscious. But still they are genuine expressions of the people's soul.

Often, one can distinguish the work of a particular artist here and there in a district. In the Zemm valley, in the heart of the Tyrol, behind Innsbruck, there are five or six crucifixes by one sculptor. He is no longer a peasant working out an idea, conveying a dogma. He is an artist, trained and conscious, probably working in Vienna. He is consciously trying to convey a *feeling*, he is no longer striving awkwardly to render a truth, a religious fact.

The chief of his crucifixes stands deep in the Klamm, in the dank gorge where it is always half-night. The road runs under the rock and the trees, half-way up the one side of the pass. Below, the stream rushes ceaselessly, embroiled among great stones, making an endless loud noise. The rock face opposite rises high overhead, with the sky far up. So that one is walking in a half-night, an underworld. And just below the path, where the pack-horses go climbing to the remote, infolded villages, in the cold gloom of the pass hangs the large, pale Christ. He is larger than life-size. He has fallen forward, just dead, and the weight of the full-grown, mature body hangs on the nails of the hands. So the dead, heavy body drops forward, sags, as if it would tear away and fall under its own weight.

It is the end. The face is barren with a dead expression of weariness, and brutalised with pain and bitterness. The rather ugly, passionate mouth is set for ever in the disillusionment of death. Death is the complete disillusionment, set like a seal over the whole body and being, over the suffering and weariness and the bodily passion.

The pass is gloomy and damp, the water roars unceasingly, till it is almost like a constant pain. The driver of the pack-horses, as he comes up the narrow path in the side of the gorge, cringes his sturdy cheerfulness as if to obliterate himself, drawing near to the large, pale Christ, and he takes his hat off as he passes, though he does not look up, but keeps his face averted from the crucifix. He hurries by in the gloom, climbing the steep path after his horses, and the large white Christ hangs extended above.

The driver of the pack-horses is afraid. The fear is always there in him, in spite of his sturdy, healthy robustness. His soul is not sturdy.

It is blenched and whitened with fear. The mountains are dark overhead, the water roars in the gloom below. His heart is ground between the mill-stones of dread. When he passes the extended body of the dead Christ he takes off his hat to the Lord of Death. Christ is the Deathly One, He is Death incarnate.

And the driver of the pack-horses acknowledges this deathly Christ as supreme Lord. The mountain peasant seems grounded upon fear, the fear of death, of physical death. Beyond this he knows nothing. His supreme sensation is in physical pain, and in its culmination. His great climax, his consummation, is death. Therefore he worships it, bows down before it, and is fascinated by it all the while. It is his fulfilment, death, and his approach to fulfilment is through physical pain.

And so these monuments to physical death are found everywhere in the valleys. By the same hand that carved the big Christ, a little further on, at the end of a bridge, was another crucifix, a small one. This Christ had a fair beard, and was thin, and his body was hanging almost lightly, whereas the other Christ was large and dark and handsome. But in this, as well as in the other, was the same neutral triumph of death, complete, negative death, so complete as to be abstract, beyond cynicism in its completeness of leaving off.

Everywhere is the same obsession with the fact of physical pain, accident, and sudden death. Wherever a misfortune has befallen a man, there is nailed up a little memorial of the event, in propitiation of the God of hurt and death. A man is standing up to his waist in water, drowning in full stream, his arms in the air. The little painting in its wooden frame is nailed to the tree, the spot is sacred to the accident. Again, another little crude picture fastened to a rock: a tree, falling on a man's leg, smashes it like a stalk, while the blood flies up. Always there is the strange ejaculation of anguish and fear, perpetuated in the little paintings nailed up in the place of the disaster.

This is the worship, then, the worship of death and the approaches to death, physical violence, and pain. There is something crude and sinister about it, almost like depravity, a form of reverting, turning back along the course of blood by which we have come.

Turning the ridge on the great road to the south, the imperial road to Rome, a decisive change takes place. The Christs have been taking on various different characters, all of them more or less realistically conveyed. One Christus is very elegant, combed and brushed and foppish on his cross, as Gabriele D'Annunzio's son posing as a martyred saint. The martyrdom of this Christ is according to the most

97

polite convention. The elegance is very important, and very Austrian. One might almost imagine the young man had taken up this striking and original position to create a delightful sensation among the ladies. It is quite in the Viennese spirit. There is something brave and keen in it, too. The individual pride of body triumphs over every difficulty in the situation. The pride and satisfaction in the clean, elegant form, the perfectly trimmed hair, the exquisite bearing, is more important than the fact of death or pain. This may be foolish, it is at the same time admirable.

But the tendency of the crucifix, as it nears the ridge to the south, is to become weak and sentimental. The carved Christs turn up their faces and roll back their eyes very piteously, in the approved Guido Reni fashion. They are overdoing the pathetic turn. They are looking to heaven and thinking about themselves, in self-commiseration. Others again are beautiful as elegies. It is dead Hyacinth lifted and extended to view, in all his beautiful, dead youth. The young, male body droops forward on the cross, like a dead flower. It looks as if its only true nature were to be dead. How lovely is death, how poignant, real, and satisfying! It is the true elegiac spirit.

Then there are the ordinary, factory-made Christs, which are not very significant. They are as null as the Christs we see represented in England, just vulgar nothingness. But these figures have gashes of red, a red paint of blood, which is sensational.

Beyond the Brenner, I have only seen vulgar or sensational cruci-fixes. There are great gashes on the breast and the knees of the Christ-figure, and the scarlet flows out and trickles down, till the crucified body has become a ghastly striped thing of red and white, just a sickly thing of striped red.

They paint the rocks at the corners of the tracks, among the mountains; a blue and white ring for the road to Ginzling, a red smear for the way to St. Jakob. So one follows the blue and white ring, or the three stripes of blue and white, or the red smear, as the case may be. And the red on the rocks, the dabs of red paint, are of just the same colour as the red upon the crucifixes; so that the red upon the crucifixes is paint, and the signs on the rocks are sensational, like blood.

I remember the little brooding Christ of the Isar, in his little cloak of red flannel and his crown of gilded thorns, and he remains real and dear to me, among all this violence of representation.

"Couvre-toi de gloire, Tartarin—couvre-toi de flanelle." Why should it please me so that his cloak is of red flannel?

In a valley near St. Jakob, just over the ridge, a long way from the railway, there is a very big, important shrine by the roadside. It is a chapel built in the baroque manner, florid pink and cream outside, with opulent small arches. And inside is the most startlingly sensational Christus I have ever seen. He is a big, powerful man, seated after the crucifixion, perhaps after the resurrection, sitting by the grave. He sits sideways, as if the extremity were over, finished, the agitation done with, only the result of the experience remaining. There is some blood on his powerful, naked, defeated body, that sits rather hulked. But it is the face which is so terrifying. It is slightly turned over the hulked, crucified shoulder, to look. And the look of this face, of which the body has been killed, is beyond all expectation horrible. The eyes look at one, yet have no seeing in them, they seem to see only their own blood. For they are bloodshot till the whites are scarlet, the iris is purpled. These red, bloody eyes with their stained pupils, glancing awfully at all who enter the shrine, looking as if to see through the blood of the late brutal death, are terrible. The naked, strong body has known death, and sits in utter dejection, finished, hulked, a weight of shame. And what remains of life is in the face, whose expression is sinister and gruesome, like that of an unrelenting criminal violated by torture. The criminal look of misery and hatred on the fixed, violated face and in the bloodshot eyes is almost impossible. He is conquered, beaten, broken, his body is a mass of torture, an unthinkable shame. Yet his will remains obstinate and ugly, integral with utter hatred.

It is a great shock to find this figure sitting in a handsome, baroque, pink-washed shrine in one of those Alpine valleys which to our thinking are all flowers and romance, like the picture in the Tate Gallery. "Spring in the Austrian Tyrol" is to our minds a vision of pristine loveliness. It contains also this Christ of the heavy body defiled by torture and death, the strong, virile life overcome by physical violence, the eyes still looking back bloodshot in consummate hate and misery.

The shrine was well kept and evidently much used. It was hung with ex-voto limbs and with many gifts. It was a centre of worship, of a sort of almost obscene worship. Afterwards the black pine-trees and the river of that valley seemed unclean, as if an unclean spirit lived there. The very flowers seemed unnatural, and the white gleam on the mountain-tops was a glisten of supreme, cynical horror.

After this, in the populous valleys, all the crucifixes were more or less tainted and vulgar. Only high up, where the crucifix becomes smaller and smaller, is there left any of the old beauty and religion. Higher and higher, the monument becomes smaller and smaller, till in the snows it stands out like a post, or a thick arrow stuck barb upwards. The crucifix itself is a small thing under the pointed hood, the barb of the arrow. The snow blows under the tiny shed, upon the little, exposed Christ. All round is the solid whiteness of snow, the awful curves and concaves of pure whiteness of the mountain top, the hollow whiteness between the peaks, where the path crosses the high, extreme ridge of the pass. And here stands the last crucifix, half buried, small and tufted with snow. The guides tramp slowly, heavily past, not observing the presence of the symbol, making no salute. Further down, every mountain peasant lifted his hat. But the guide tramps by without concern. His is a professional importance now.

On a small mountain track on the Jaufen, not far from Meran, was a fallen Christus. I was hurrying downhill to escape from an icy wind which almost took away my consciousness, and I was looking up at the gleaming, unchanging snow-peaks all round. They seemed like blades immortal in the sky. So I almost ran into a very old Martertafel. It leaned on the cold, stony hill-side surrounded by the white peaks in the upper air.

The wooden hood was silver-grey with age, and covered, on the top, with a thicket of lichen, which stuck up in hoary tufts. But on the rock at the foot of the post was the fallen Christ, armless, who had tumbled down and lay in an unnatural posture, the naked, ancient wooden sculpture of the body on the naked, living rock. It was one of the old uncouth Christs hewn out of bare wood, having the long, wedge-shaped limbs and thin flat legs that are significant of the true spirit, the desire to convey a religious truth, not a sensational experience.

The arms of the fallen Christ had broken off at the shoulders, and they hung on their nails, as ex-voto limbs hang in the shrines. But these arms dangled from the palms, one at each end of the cross, the muscles, carved sparely in the old wood, looking all wrong, upside down. And the icy wind blew them backwards and forwards, so that they gave a painful impression, there in the stark, sterile place of rock and cold. Yet I dared not touch the fallen body of the Christ, that lay on its back in so grotesque a posture at the foot of the post. I wondered who would come and take the broken thing away, and for what purpose.

On the Lago di Garda

I. The Spinner and the Monks

The Holy Spirit is a Dove, or an Eagle. In the Old Testament it was an Eagle; in the New Testament it is a Dove.

And there are, standing over the Christian world, the Churches of the Dove and the Churches of the Eagle. There are, moreover, the Churches which do not belong to the Holy Spirit at all, but which are built to pure fancy and logic; such as the Wren Churches in London.

The Churches of the Dove are shy and hidden: they nestle among trees, and their bells sound in the mellowness of Sunday; or they are gathered into a silence of their own in the very midst of the town, so that one passes them by without observing them; they are as if invisible, offering no resistance to the storming of the traffic.

But the Churches of the Eagle stand high, with their heads to the skies, as if they challenged the world below. They are the Churches of the Spirit of David, and their bells ring passionately, imperiously, falling on the subservient world below.

The Church of San Francesco was a Church of the Dove. I passed it several times, in the dark, silent little square, without knowing it was a church. Its pink walls were blind, windowless, unnoticeable, it gave no sign, unless one caught sight of the tan curtain hanging in the door, and the slit of darkness beneath. Yet it was the chief church of the village.

But the Church of San Tommaso perched over the village. Coming down the cobbled, submerged street, many a time I looked up between the houses and saw the thin old church standing above in the light, as if it perched on the house-roofs. Its thin grey neck was held up stiffly, beyond was a vision of dark foliage, and the high hillside.

I saw it often, and yet for a long time it never occurred to me that it actually existed. It was like a vision, a thing one does not expect to come close to. It was there standing away upon the house-tops, against a glamour of foliaged hill-side. I was submerged in the village, on the uneven, cobbled street, between old high walls and cavernous shops and the houses with flights of steps.

For a long time I knew how the day went, by the imperious clangour of midday and evening bells striking down upon the houses and the edge of the lake. Yet it did not occur to me to ask where these bells rang. Till at last my everyday trance was broken in upon, and I knew the ringing of the Church of San Tommaso. The church became a living connection with me.

So I set out to find it, I wanted to go to it. It was very near. I could see it from the piazza by the lake. And the village itself had only a few hundreds of inhabitants. The church must be within a stone's throw.

Yet I could not find it. I went out of the back door of the house, into the narrow gulley of the back street. Women glanced down at me from the top of the flights of steps, old men stood, half-turning, half-crouching under the dark shadow of the walls, to stare. It was as if the strange creatures of the under-shadow were looking at me. I was of another element.

The Italian people are called "Children of the Sun." They might better be called "Children of the Shadow." Their souls are dark and nocturnal. If they are to be easy, they must be able to hide, to be hidden in lairs and caves of darkness. Going through these tiny, chaotic back-ways of the village was like venturing through the labyrinth made by furtive creatures, who watched from out of another element. And I was pale, and clear, and evanescent, like the light, and they were dark, and close, and constant, like the shadow.

So I was quite baffled by the tortuous, tiny, deep passages of the village. I could not find my way. I hurried towards the broken end of a street, where the sunshine and the olive trees looked like a mirage before me. And there above me I saw the thin, stiff neck of old San Tommaso, grey and pale in the sun. Yet I could not get up to the church, I found myself again on the piazza.

Another day, however, I found a broken staircase, where weeds grew in the gaps the steps had made in falling, and maidenhair hung on the darker side of the wall. I went up unwillingly, because the Italians used this old staircase as a privy, as they will any deep side-passage.

But I ran up the broken stairway, and came out suddenly, as by a miracle, clean on the platform of my San Tommaso, in the tremendous sunshine.

It was another world, the world of the eagle, the world of fierce abstraction. It was all clear, overwhelming sunshine, a platform hung in the light. Just below were the confused, tiled roofs of the village, and beyond them the pale blue water, down below; and opposite, opposite my face and breast, the clear, luminous snow of the mountain across the lake, level with me apparently, though really much above.

I was in the skies now, looking down from my square terrace of cobbled pavement, that was worn like the threshold of the ancient church. Round the terrace ran a low, broad wall, the coping of the upper heaven where I had climbed.

There was a blood-red sail like a butterfly breathing down on the blue water, whilst the earth on the near side gave off a green-silver smoke of olive trees, coming up and around the earth-coloured roofs.

It always remains to me that San Tommaso and its terrace hang suspended above the village, like the lowest step of heaven, of Jacob's ladder. Behind, the land rises in a high sweep. But the terrace of San Tommaso is let down from heaven, and does not touch the earth.

I went into the church. It was very dark, and impregnated with centuries of incense. It affected me like the lair of some enormous creature. My senses were roused, they sprang awake in the hot, spiced darkness. My skin was expectant, as if it expected some contact, some embrace, as if it were aware of the contiguity of the physical world, the physical contact with the darkness and the heavy, suggestive substance of the enclosure. It was a thick, fierce darkness of the senses. But my soul shrank.

I went out again. The pavemented threshold was clear as a jewel, the marvellous clarity of sunshine that becomes blue in the height seemed to distil me into itself.

Across, the heavy mountain crouched along the side of the lake, the upper half brilliantly white, belonging to the sky, the lower half dark and grim. So then, that is where heaven and earth are divided. From behind me, on the left, the headland swept down out of a great, pale-grey, arid height, through a rush of russet and crimson, to the olive smoke and the water of the level earth. And between, like a blade of the sky cleaving the earth asunder, went the pale-blue lake, cleaving mountain from mountain with the triumph of the sky.

Then I noticed that a big, blue-checked cloth was spread on the parapet before me, over the parapet of heaven. I wondered why it hung there.

Turning round, on the other side of the terrace, under a caper-bush that hung like a blood-stain from the grey wall above her, stood a little grey woman whose fingers were busy. Like the grey church, she made me feel as if I were not in existence. I was wandering by the parapet of heaven, looking down. But she stood back against the solid wall, under the caper-bush, unobserved and unobserving. She was like a fragment of earth, she was a living stone of the terrace, sun-bleached. She took no notice of me, who was hesitating looking down at the earth beneath. She stood back under the sun-bleached solid wall, like a stone rolled down and stayed in a crevice.

Her head was tied in a dark-red kerchief, but pieces of hair, like dirty snow, quite short, stuck out over her ears. And she was spinning. I wondered so much, that I could not cross towards her. She was grey, and her apron, and her dress, and her kerchief, and her hands and her face were all sun-bleached and sun-stained, greyey, bluey, browny, like stones and half-coloured leaves, sunny in their colourlessness. In my black coat, I felt myself wrong, false, an outsider.

She was spinning, spontaneously, like a little wind. Under her arm she held a distaff of dark, ripe wood, just a straight stick with a clutch at the end, like a grasp of brown fingers full of a fluff of blackish, rusty fleece, held up near her shoulder. And her fingers were plucking spontaneously at the strands of wool drawn down from it. And hanging near her feet, spinning round upon a black thread, spinning busily, like a thing in a gay wind, was her shuttle, her bobbin wound fat with the coarse, blackish worsted she was making.

All the time, like motion without thought her fingers teased out the fleece, drawing it down to a fairly uniform thickness: brown, old, natural fingers that worked as in a sleep, the thumb having a long grey nail; and from moment to moment there was a quick, downward rub, between thumb and forefinger, of the thread that hung in front of her apron, the heavy bobbin spun more briskly, and she felt again at the fleece as she drew it down, and she gave a twist to the thread that issued, and the bobbin spun swiftly.

Her eyes were clear as the sky, blue, empyrean, transcendent. They were clear, but they had no looking in them. Her face was like a sun-worn stone.

"You are spinning," I said to her.

Her eyes glanced over me, making no effort of attention.

"Yes," she said.

She saw merely a man's figure, a stranger, standing near. I was a bit of the outside, negligible. She remained as she was, clear and sustained like an old stone upon the hill-side. She stood short and sturdy, looking for the most part straight in front, unseeing, but glancing from time to time, with a little, unconscious attention, at the thread. She was slightly more animated than the sunshine and the stone and the motionless caper-bush above her. Still her fingers went along the strand of fleece near her breast.

"That is an old way of spinning," I said.

"What?"

She looked up at me with eyes clear and transcendent as the heavens. But she was slightly roused. There was the slight motion of the eagle in her turning to look at me, a faint gleam of rapt light in her eyes. It was my unaccustomed Italian.

"That is an old way of spinning," I repeated.

"Yes—an old way," she repeated, as if to say the words so that they should be natural to her. And I became to her merely a transient circumstance, a man, part of the surroundings. We divided the gift of speech, that was all.

She glanced at me again, with her wonderful, unchanging eyes, that were like the visible heavens, unthinking, or like two flowers that are open in pure clear unconsciousness. To her I was a piece of the environment. That was all. Her world was clear and absolute, without consciousness of self. She was not self-conscious, because she was not aware that there was anything in the universe except *her* universe. In her universe I was a stranger, a foreign *signore*. That I had a world of my own, other than her own, was not conceived by her. She did not care.

So we conceive the stars. We are told that they are other worlds. But the stars are the clustered and single gleaming lights in the night-sky of our world. When I come home at night, there are the stars. When I cease to exist as the microcosm, when I begin to think of the cosmos, then the stars are other worlds. Then the macrocosm absorbs me. But the macrocosm is not me. It is something which I, the microcosm, am not.

So that there is something which is unknown to me and which nevertheless exists. I am finite, and my understanding has limits. The universe is bigger than I shall ever see, in mind or spirit. There is that which is not me.

If I say "The planet Mars is inhabited," I do not know what I mean by "inhabited," with reference to the planet Mars. I can only mean that that world is not my world. I can only know there is that which is not me. I am the microcosm, but the macrocosm is that also which I am not.

The old woman on the terrace in the sun did not know this. She was herself the core and centre to the world, the sun, and the single firmament. She knew that I was an inhabitant of lands which she had never seen. But what of that! There were parts of her own body which she had never seen, which physiologically she could never see. They were none the less her own because she had never seen them. The lands she had not seen were corporate parts of her own living body, the knowledge she had not attained was only the hidden knowledge of her own self. She *was* the substance of the knowledge, whether she had the knowledge in her mind or not. There was nothing which was not herself, ultimately. Even the man, the male, was part of herself. He was the mobile, separate part, but he was none the less herself because he was sometimes severed from her. If every apple in the world were cut in two, the apple would not be changed. The reality is the apple, which is just the same in the half apple as in the whole.

And she, the old spinning-woman, was the apple, eternal, unchangeable, whole even in her partiality. It was this which gave the wonderful clear unconsciousness to her eyes. How could she be conscious of herself, when all was herself?

She was talking to me of a sheep that had died, but I could not understand, because of her dialect. It never occurred to her that I could not understand. She only thought me different, stupid. And she talked on. The ewes had lived under the house, and a part was divided off for the he-goat, because the other people brought their she-goats to be covered by the he-goat. But how the ewe came to die I could not make out.

Her fingers worked away all the time in a little, half-fretful movement, yet spontaneous as butterflies leaping here and there. She chattered rapidly on in her Italian that I could not understand, looking meanwhile into my face, because the story roused her somewhat. Yet not a feature moved. Her eyes remained candid and open and unconscious as the skies. Only a sharp will in them now and then seemed to gleam at me, as if to dominate me.

Her shuttle had caught in a dead chicory plant, and spun no more. She did not notice. I stooped and broke off the twigs. There was a glint of blue on them yet. Seeing what I was doing, she merely withdrew a few inches from the plant. Her bobbin hung free.

She went on with her tale, looking at me wonderfully. She seemed like the Creation, like the beginning of the world, the first morning. Her eyes were like the first morning of the world, so ageless.

Her thread broke. She seemed to take no notice, but mechanically picked up the shuttle, wound up a length of worsted, connected the ends from her wool strand, set the bobbin spinning again, and went on talking, in her half-intimate, half-unconscious fashion, as if she were talking to her own world in me.

So she stood in the sunshine on the little platform, old and yet like the morning, erect and solitary, sun-coloured, sun-discoloured, whilst I at her elbow, like a piece of night and moonshine, stood smiling into her eyes, afraid lest she should deny me existence.

Which she did. She had stopped talking, did not look at me any more, but went on with her spinning, the brown shuttle twisting gaily. So she stood, belonging to the sunshine and the weather, taking no more notice of me than of the dark-stained caper-bush which hung from the wall above her head, whilst I, waiting at her side, was like the moon in the daytime sky, over-shone, obliterated, in spite of my black clothes.

"How long has it taken you to do that much?" I asked.

She waited a minute, glanced at her bobbin.

"This much? I don't know. A day or two."

"But you do it quickly."

She looked at me, as if suspiciously and derisively. Then, quite suddenly, she started forward and went across the terrace to the great blue-and-white checked cloth that was drying on the wall. I hesitated. She had cut off her consciousness from me. So I turned and ran away, taking the steps two at a time, to get away from her. In a moment I was between the walls, climbing upwards, hidden.

The school-mistress had told me I should find snowdrops behind San Tommaso. If she had not asserted such confident knowledge I should have doubted her translation of *perce-neige*. She meant Christmas roses all the while.

However, I went looking for snowdrops. The walls broke down suddenly, and I was out in a grassy olive orchard, following a track beside pieces of fallen overgrown masonry. So I came to skirt the brink of a steep little gorge, at the bottom of which a stream was rushing down its steep slant to the lake. Here I stood to look for my snowdrops. The grassy, rocky bank went down steep from my feet. I heard water tittle-tattling away in deep shadow below. There were pale flecks in the dimness, but these, I knew, were primroses. So I scrambled down.

Looking up, out of the heavy shadow that lay in the cleft, I could see, right in the sky, grey rocks shining transcendent in the pure empyrean. "Are they so far up?" I thought. I did not dare to say, "Am I so far down?" But I was uneasy. Nevertheless it was a lovely place, in the cold shadow, complete; when one forgot the shining rocks far above, it was a complete, shadowless world of shadow. Primroses were everywhere in nests of pale bloom upon the dark, steep face of the cleft, and tongues of fern hanging out, and here and there under the rods and twigs of bushes were tufts of wrecked Christmas roses, nearly over, but still, in the coldest corners, the lovely buds like handfuls of snow. There had been such crowded sumptuous tufts of Christmas roses

everywhere in the stream-gullies, during the shadow of winter, that
these few remaining flowers were hardly noticeable.

I gathered instead the primroses, that smelled of earth and of the
weather. There were no snowdrops. I had found the day before a bank
of crocuses, pale, fragile, lilac-coloured flowers with dark veins, prick-
ing up keenly like myriad little lilac-coloured flames among the grass,
under the olive trees. And I wanted very much to find the snowdrops
hanging in the gloom. But there were not any.

I gathered a handful of primroses, then I climbed suddenly, quickly
out of the deep watercourse, anxious to get back to the sunshine before
the evening fell. Up above I saw the olive trees in their sunny golden
grass, and sunlit grey rocks immensely high up. I was afraid lest the
evening would fall whilst I was groping about like an otter in the damp
and the darkness, that the day of sunshine would be over.

Soon I was up in the sunshine again, on the turf under the olive
trees, reassured. It was the upper world of glowing light, and I was
safe again.

All the olives were gathered, and the mills were going night and day,
making a great, acrid scent of olive oil in preparation, by the lake. The
little stream rattled down. A mule driver "Hued!" to his mules on the
Strada Vecchia. High up, on the Strada Nuova, the beautiful, new,
military high-road, which winds with beautiful curves up the
mountain-side, crossing the same stream several times in clear-leaping
bridges, travelling cut out of sheer slope high above the lake, winding
beautifully and gracefully forward to the Austrian frontier, where it
ends: high up on the lovely swinging road, in the strong evening
sunshine, I saw a bullock wagon moving like a vision, though the
clanking of the wagon and the crack of the bullock whip resounded
close in my ears.

Everything was clear and sun-coloured up there, clear-grey rocks
partaking of the sky, tawny grass and scrub, browny-green spires of
cypresses, and then the mist of grey-green olives fuming down to the
lake-side. There was no shadow, only clear sun-substance built up to
the sky, a bullock wagon moving slowly in the high sunlight, along the
uppermost terrace of the military road. I sat in the warm stillness of
the transcendent afternoon.

The four o'clock steamer was creeping down the lake from the
Austrian end, creeping under the cliffs. Far away, the Verona side,
beyond the Island, lay fused in dim gold. The mountain opposite was
so still, that my heart seemed to fade in its beating, as if it too would be

still. All was perfectly still, pure substance. The little steamer on the floor of the world below, the mules down the road cast no shadow. They too were pure sun-substance travelling on the surface of the sun-made world.

A cricket hopped near me. Then I remembered that it was Saturday afternoon, when a strange suspension comes over the world. And then, just below me, I saw two monks walking in their garden between the naked, bony vines, walking in their wintry garden of bony vines and olive trees, their brown cassocks passing between the brown vine-stocks, their heads bare to the sunshine, sometimes a glint of light as their feet strode from under their skirts.

It was so still, everything so perfectly suspended, that I felt them talking. They marched with the peculiar march of monks, a long, loping stride, their heads together, their skirts swaying slowly, two brown monks with hidden hands, sliding under the bony vines and beside the cabbages, their heads always together in hidden converse. It was as if I were attending with my dark soul to their inaudible undertone. All the time I sat still in silence, I was one with them, a partaker, though I could hear no sound of their voices. I went with the long stride of their skirted feet, that slid springless and noiseless from end to end of the garden, and back again. Their hands were kept down at their sides, hidden in the long sleeves and the skirts of their robes. They did not touch each other, nor gesticulate as they walked. There was no motion save the long, furtive stride and the heads leaning together. Yet there was an eagerness in their conversation. Almost like shadow-creatures ventured out of their cold, obscure element, they went backwards and forwards in their wintry garden, thinking nobody could see them.

Across, above them, was the faint, rousing dazzle of snow. They never looked up. But the dazzle of snow began to glow as they walked, the wonderful, faint, ethereal flush of the long range of snow in the heavens, at evening, began to kindle. Another world was coming to pass, the cold, rare night. It was dawning in exquisite, icy rose upon the long mountain-summit opposite. The monks walked backwards and forwards, talking, in the first undershadow.

And I noticed that up above the snow, frail in the bluish sky, a frail moon had put forth, like a thin, scalloped film of ice floated out on the slow current of the coming night. And a bell sounded.

And still the monks were pacing backwards and forwards, backwards and forwards, with a strange, neutral regularity.

The shadows were coming across everything, because of the mountains in the West. Already the olive wood where I sat was extinguished. This was the world of the monks, the rim of pallor between night and day. Here they paced, backwards and forwards, backwards and forwards, in the neutral, shadowless light of shadow.

Neither the flare of day nor the completeness of night reached them, they paced the narrow path of the twilight, treading in the neutrality of the law. Neither the blood nor the spirit spoke in them, only the law, the abstraction of the average. The infinite is positive and negative. But the average is only neutral. And the monks trod backward and forward down the line of neutrality.

Meanwhile, on the length of mountain-ridge, the snow grew rosy-incandescent, like heaven breaking into blossom. After all, eternal not-being and eternal being are the same. In the rosy snow that shone in heaven over a darkened earth was the ecstasy of consummation. Night and day are one, light and dark are one, both the same in the origin and in the issue, both the same in the moment of ecstasy, light fused in darkness and darkness fused in light, as in the rosy snow above the twilight.

But in the monks it was not ecstasy, in them it was neutrality, the under earth. Transcendent, above the shadowed, twilit earth was the rosy snow of ecstasy. But spreading far over us, down below, was the neutrality of the twilight, of the monks. The flesh neutralising the spirit, the spirit neutralising the flesh, the law of the average asserted, this was the monks as they paced backward and forward.

The moon climbed higher, away from the snowy, fading ridge, she became gradually herself. Between the roots of the olive tree was a rosy-tipped daisy just going to sleep. I gathered it and put it among the frail, moony little bunch of primroses, so that its sleep should warm the rest. Also I put in some little periwinkles, that were very blue, reminding me of the eyes of the old woman.

The day was gone, the twilight was gone, and the snow was invisible as I came down to the side of the lake. Only the moon, white and shining, was in the sky, like a woman glorying in her own loveliness as she loiters superbly to the gaze of all the world, looking sometimes through the fringe of dark olive leaves, sometimes looking at her own superb, quivering body, wholly naked in the water of the lake.

My little old woman was gone. She, all day-sunshine, would have none of the moon. Always she must live like a bird, looking down on all the world at once, so that it lay all subsidiary to herself, herself the wakeful consciousness hovering over the world like a hawk, like a sleep of wakefulness. And, like a bird, she went to sleep as the shadows came.

She did not know the yielding up of the senses and the possession of the unknown, through the senses, which happens under a superb moon. The all-glorious sun knows none of these yieldings up. He takes his way. And the daisies at once go to sleep. And the soul of the old spinning-woman also closed up at sunset, the rest was a sleep, a cessation.

It is all so strange and varied: the dark-skinned Italians ecstatic in the night and the moon, the blue-eyed old woman ecstatic in the busy sunshine, the monks in the garden below, who are supposed to unite both, passing only in the neutrality of the average. Where, then, is the meeting-point: where in mankind is the ecstasy of light and dark together, the supreme transcendence of the afterglow, day hovering in the embrace of the coming night like two angels embracing in the heavens, like Eurydice in the arms of Orpheus, or Persephone embraced by Pluto?

Where is the supreme ecstasy in mankind, which makes day a delight and night a delight, purpose an ecstasy and a concourse in ecstasy, and single abandon of the single body and soul also an ecstasy under the moon? Where is the transcendent knowledge in our hearts, uniting sun and darkness, day and night, spirit and senses? Why do we not know that the two in consummation are one; that each is only part; partial and alone for ever; but that the two in consummation are perfect, beyond the range of loneliness or solitude?

II. The Lemon Gardens

The padrone came just as we were drinking coffee after dinner. It was two o'clock, because the steamer going down the lake to Desenzano had bustled through the sunshine, and the rocking of the water still made lights that danced up and down upon the wall among the shadows by the piano.

The Signore was very apologetic. I found him bowing in the hall, cap in one hand, a slip of paper in the other, protesting eagerly, in broken French, against disturbing me.

He is a little, shrivelled man, with close-cropped grey hair on his skull, and a protruding jaw, which, with his gesticulations, always makes me think of an ancient, aristocratic monkey. The Signore is a gentleman, and the last, shrivelled representative of his race. His only outstanding quality, according to the villagers, is his avarice.

"Mais—mais, monsieur—je crains que—que—que je vous dérange——"

He spreads wide his hands and bows, looking up at me with implicit brown eyes, so ageless in his wrinkled, monkey's face, like onyx. He loves to speak French, because then he feels grand. He has a queer, naïve, ancient passion to be grand. As the remains of an impoverished family, he is not much better than a well-to-do peasant. But the old spirit is eager and pathetic in him.

He loves to speak French to me. He holds his chin and waits, in his anxiety for the phrase to come. Then it stammers forth, a little rush, ending in Italian. But his pride is all on edge: we must continue in French.

The hall is cold, yet he will not come into the large room. This is not a courtesy visit. He is not here in his quality of gentleman. He is only an anxious villager.

"Voyez, monsieur—cet—cet—qu'est-ce que—qu'est-ce que veut dire cet—cela?"

He shows me the paper. It is an old scrap of print, the picture of an American patent door-spring, with directions: "Fasten the spring either end up. Wind it up. Never unwind."

It is laconic and American. The Signore watches me anxiously, waiting, holding his chin. He is afraid he ought to understand my English. I stutter off into French, confounded by the laconic phrases of the directions. Nevertheless, I make it clear what the paper says.

He cannot believe me. It must say something else as well. He has not done anything contrary to these directions. He is most distressed.

"Mais, monsieur, la porte—la porte—elle ferme *pas*—elle s'ouvre——"

He skipped to the door and showed me the whole tragic mystery. The door, it is shut—ecco! He releases the catch, and Pouf!—she flies open. She flies *open*. It is quite final.

The brown, expressionless, ageless eyes, that remind me of a monkey's, or of onyx, wait for me. I feel the responsibility devolve upon me. I am anxious.

"Allow me," I said, "to come and look at the door."

I feel uncomfortably like Sherlock Holmes. The padrone protests—non, monsieur, non, cela vous dérange—that he only wanted me to translate the words, he does not want to disturb me. Nevertheless, we go. I feel I have the honour of mechanical England in my hands.

The Casa di Paoli is quite a splendid place. It is large, pink, and cream, rising up to a square tower in the centre, throwing off a painted loggia at either extreme of the façade. It stands a little way back from the road, just above the lake, and grass grows on the bay of cobbled pavement in front. When at night the moon shines full on this pale façade, the theatre is far outdone in staginess.

The hall is spacious and beautiful, with great glass doors at either end, through which shine the courtyards where bamboos fray the sunlight and geraniums glare red. The floor is of soft red tiles, oiled and polished like glass, the walls are washed grey-white, the ceiling is painted with pink roses and birds. This is half-way between the outer world and the interior world, it partakes of both.

The other rooms are dark and ugly. There is no mistake about their being interior. They are like furnished vaults. The red-tiled, polished floor in the drawing-room seems cold and clammy, the carved, cold furniture stands in its tomb, the air has been darkened and starved to death, it is perished.

Outside the sunshine runs like birds singing. Up above, the grey rocks build the sun-substance in heaven, San Tommaso guards the terrace. But inside here is the immemorial shadow.

Again I had to think of the Italian soul, how it is dark, cleaving to the eternal night. It seems to have become so, at the Renaissance, after the Renaissance.

In the Middle Ages Christian Europe seems to have been striving, out of a strong, primitive, animal nature, towards the self-abnegation and the abstraction of Christ. This brought about by itself a great sense of completeness. The two halves were joined by the effort towards the one as yet unrealised. There was a triumphant joy in the Whole.

But the movement all the time was in one direction, towards the elimination of the flesh. Man wanted more and more to become purely free and abstract. Pure freedom was in pure abstraction. The Word was absolute. When man became as the Word, a pure law, then he was free.

But when this conclusion was reached, the movement broke. Already Botticelli painted Aphrodite, queen of the senses, supreme along with Mary, Queen of Heaven. And Michael Angelo suddenly turned back on the whole Christian movement, back to the flesh. The flesh was supreme and god-like, in the oneness of the flesh, in the oneness of our physical being, we are one with God, with the Father. God the Father created man in the flesh, in His own image. Michael Angelo swung right back to the old Mosaic position. Christ did not exist. To Michael Angelo there was no salvation in the spirit. There was God the Father, the Begetter, the Author of all flesh. And there was the inexorable law of the flesh, the Last Judgment, the fall of the immortal flesh into Hell.

This has been the Italian position ever since. The mind, that is the Light; the senses, they are the Darkness. Aphrodite, the queen of the senses, she, born of the sea-foam, is the luminousness of the gleaming senses, the phosphorescence of the sea, the senses become a conscious aim unto themselves; she is the gleaming darkness, she is the luminous night, she is goddess of destruction, her white, cold fire consumes and does not create.

This is the soul of the Italian since the Renaissance. In the sunshine he basks asleep, gathering up a vintage into his veins which in the night-time he will distil into ecstatic sensual delight, the intense, white-cold ecstasy of darkness and moonlight, the raucous, cat-like, destructive enjoyment, the senses conscious and crying out in their consciousness in the pangs of the enjoyment, which has consumed the Southern nation, perhaps all the Latin races, since the Renaissance.

It is a lapse back, back to the original position, the Mosaic position, of the divinity of the flesh, and the absoluteness of its laws. But also there is the Aphrodite-worship. The flesh, the senses, are now self-conscious. They know their aim. Their aim is in supreme sensation. They seek the maximum of sensation. They seek the reduction of the flesh, the flesh reacting upon itself, to a crisis, an ecstasy, a phosphorescent transfiguration in ecstasy.

The mind, all the time, subserves the senses. As in a cat, there is subtlety and beauty and the dignity of the darkness. But the fire is cold, as in the eyes of a cat, it is a green fire. It is fluid, electric. At its maximum it is the white ecstasy of phosphorescence, in the darkness, always amid the darkness, as under the black fur of a cat. Like the feline fire, it is destructive, always consuming and reducing to the ecstasy of sensation, which is the end in itself.

There is the I, always the I. And the mind is submerged, overcome. But the senses are superbly arrogant. The senses are the absolute, the god-like. For I can never have another man's senses. These are me, my senses absolutely me. And all that is can only come to me through my senses. So that all is me, and is administered unto me. The rest, that is not me, is nothing, it is something which is nothing. So the Italian, through centuries, has avoided our Northern purposive industry, because it has seemed to him a form of nothingness.

It is the spirit of the tiger. The tiger is the supreme manifestation of the senses made absolute. This is the

Tiger, tiger, burning bright,
In the forests of the night

of Blake. It does indeed burn within the darkness. But the *essential* fire of the tiger is cold and white, a white ecstasy. It is seen in the white eyes of the blazing cat. This is the supremacy of the flesh, which devours all, and becomes transfigured into a magnificent brindled flame, a burning bush indeed.

This is one way of transfiguration into the eternal flame, the transfiguration through ecstasy in the flesh. Like the tiger in the night, I devour all flesh, I drink all blood, until this fuel blazes up in me to the consummate fire of the Infinite. In the ecstasy I am Infinite, I become again the great Whole, I am a flame of the One White Flame which is the Infinite, the Eternal, the Originator, the Creator, the Everlasting God. In the sensual ecstasy, having drunk all blood and devoured all flesh, I am become again the eternal Fire, I am infinite.

This is the way of the tiger; the tiger is supreme. His head is flattened as if there were some great weight on the hard skull, pressing, pressing, pressing the mind into a stone, pressing it down under the blood, to serve the blood. It is the subjugate instrument of the blood. The will lies above the loins, as it were at the base of the spinal column, there is the living will, the living mind of the tiger, there in the slender loins. That is the node, there in the spinal cord.

So the Italian, so the soldier. This is the spirit of the soldier. He, too, walks with his consciousness concentrated at the base of the spine, his mind subjugated, submerged. The will of the soldier is the will of the great cats, the will to ecstasy in destruction, in absorbing life into his own life, always his own life supreme, till the ecstasy burst into the white, eternal flame, the Infinite, the Flame of the Infinite. Then he is satisfied, he has been consummated in the Infinite.

This is the true soldier, this is the immortal climax of the senses. This is the acme of the flesh, the one superb tiger who has devoured all living flesh, and now paces backwards and forwards in the cage of its own infinite, glaring with blind, fierce, absorbed eyes at that which is nothingness to it.

The eyes of the tiger cannot see, except with the light from within itself, by the light of its own desire. Its own white, cold light is so fierce that the other warm light of day is outshone, it is not, it does not exist. So the white eyes of the tiger gleam to a point of concentrated vision, upon that which does not exist. Hence its terrifying sightlessness. The something which I know I am is hollow space to its vision, offers no resistance to the tiger's looking. It can only see of me that which it knows I am, a scent, a resistance, a voluptuous solid, a struggling warm violence that it holds overcome, a running of hot blood between its jaws, a delicious pang of live flesh in the mouth. This it sees. The rest is not.

And what is the rest, that which is-not the tiger, that which the tiger is-not? What is this?

What is that which parted ways with the terrific eagle-like angel of the senses at the Renaissance? The Italians said, "We are one in the Father: we will go back." The Northern races said, "We are one in Christ: we will go on."

What *is* the consummation in Christ? Man knows satisfaction when he surpasses all conditions and becomes, to himself, consummate in the Infinite, when he reaches a state of infinity. In the supreme ecstasy of the flesh, the Dionysic ecstasy, he reaches this state. But how does it come to pass in Christ?

It is not the mystic ecstasy. The mystic ecstasy is a special sensual ecstasy, it is the senses satisfying themselves with a self-created object.

It is self-projection into the self, the sensuous self satisfied in a projected self.

Blessed are the poor in spirit, for theirs is the kingdom of heaven.
Blessed are they which are persecuted for righteousness sake, for theirs is the kingdom of heaven.

The kingdom of heaven is this Infinite into which we may be consummated, then, if we are poor in spirit or persecuted for righteousness sake.

Whosoever shall smite thee on the right cheek, turn to him the other also.
Love your enemies, bless them that curse you, do good to them that hate you, and pray for them which despitefully use you, and persecute you.
Be ye therefore perfect, even as your Father which is in heaven is perfect.

To be perfect, to be one with God, to be infinite and eternal, what shall we do? We must turn the other cheek, and love our enemies.

Christ is the lamb which the eagle swoops down upon, the dove taken by the hawk, the deer which the tiger devours.

What then, if a man come to me with a sword, to kill me, and I do not resist him, but suffer his sword and the death from his sword, what am I? Am I greater than he, am I stronger than he? Do I know a consummation in the Infinite, I, the prey, beyond the tiger who devours me? By my non-resistance I have robbed him of his consummation. For a tiger knows no consummation unless he kill a violated and struggling prey. There is no consummation merely for the butcher, nor for a hyena. I can rob the tiger of his ecstasy, his consummation, his very *raison d'être* by my non-resistance. In my non-resistance the tiger is infinitely destroyed.

But I, what am I? "Be ye therefore perfect." Wherein am I perfect in this submission? Is there an affirmation, behind my negation, other than the tiger's affirmation of his own glorious infinity?

What is the Oneness to which I subscribe, I who offer no resistance in the flesh?

Have I only the negative ecstasy of being devoured, of becoming thus part of the Lord, the Great Moloch, the superb and terrible God? I have this also, this subject ecstasy of consummation. But is there nothing else?

The Word of the tiger is: my senses are supremely Me, and my senses are God in me. But Christ said: God is in the others, who are not-me. In all the multitude of the others is God, and this is the great God, greater than the God which is Me. God is that which is Not-Me.

And this is the Christian truth, a truth complementary to the pagan affirmation: "God is that which is Me."

God is that which is Not-Me. In realising the Not-Me I am consummated, I become infinite. In turning the other cheek I submit to God who is greater than I am, other than I am, who is in that which is not me. This is the supreme consummation. To achieve this consummation I love my neighbour as myself. My neighbour is all that is not me. And if I love all this, have I not become one with the Whole, is not my consummation complete, am I not one with God, have I not achieved the Infinite?

After the Renaissance the Northern races continued forward, to put into practice this religious belief in the God which is Not-Me. Even the idea of the saving of the soul was really negative: it was a question of escaping damnation. The Puritans made the last great attack on the God who is Me. When they beheaded Charles the First, the king by Divine Right, they destroyed, symbolically, for ever, the supremacy of the Me who am the image of God, the Me of the flesh, of the senses, Me, the tiger burning bright, me the king, the Lord, the aristocrat, me who am divine because I am the body of God.

After the Puritans, we have been gathering data for the God who is not-me. When Pope said, "Know then thyself, presume not God to scan, The proper study of mankind is Man," he was stating the proposition: A man is right, he is consummated, when he is seeking to know Man, the great abstract; and the method of knowledge is by the analysis, which is the destruction, of the Self. The proposition up to that time was, a man is the epitome of the universe. He has only to express himself, to fulfil his desires, to satisfy his supreme senses.

Now the change has come to pass. The individual man is a limited being, finite in himself. Yet he is capable of apprehending that which is not himself. "The proper study of mankind is Man." This is another way of saying, "Thou shalt love thy neighbour as thyself." Which means, a man is consummated in his knowledge of that which is not himself, the abstract Man. Therefore the consummation lies in seeking that other, in knowing that other. Whereas the Stuart proposition was: "A man is consummated in expressing his own Self."

The new spirit developed into the empirical and ideal systems of philosophy. Everything that is, is consciousness. And in every man's consciousness, Man is great and illimitable, whilst the individual is small and fragmentary. Therefore the individual must sink himself in the great whole of Mankind.

This is the spirituality of Shelley, the perfectibility of man. This is the way in which we fulfil the commandment, "Be ye therefore perfect, even as your Father which is in heaven is perfect." This is Saint Paul's, "Now I know in part; but then shall I know even as I am known."

When a man knows everything and understands everything, then he will be perfect, and life will be blessed. He is capable of knowing everything and understanding everything. Hence he is justified in his hope of infinite freedom and blessedness.

The great inspiration of the new religion was the inspiration of freedom. When I have submerged or distilled away my concrete body and my limited desires, when I am like the skylark dissolved in the sky yet filling heaven and earth with song, then I am perfect, consummated in the Infinite. When I am all that is not-me, then I have perfect liberty, I know no limitation. Only I must eliminate the Self.

It was this religious belief which expressed itself in science. Science was the analysis of the outer self, the elementary substance of the self, the outer world. And the machine is the great reconstructed selfless power. Hence the active worship to which we were given at the end of the last century, the worship of mechanised force.

Still we continue to worship that which is not-me, the Selfless world, though we would fain bring in the Self to help us. We are shouting the Shakspearean advice to warriors, "Then simulate the action of the tiger." We are trying to become again the tiger, the supreme, imperial, warlike Self. At the same time our ideal is the selfless world of equity.

We continue to give service to the Selfless God, we worship the great selfless oneness in the spirit, oneness in service of the great humanity, that which is Not-Me. This selfless God is He Who works for all alike, without consideration. And His image is the machine which dominates and cows us, we cower before it, we run to serve it. For it works for all humanity alike.

At the same time, we want to be warlike tigers. That is the horror: the confusing of the two ends. We warlike tigers fit ourselves out with machinery, and our blazing tiger wrath is emitted through a machine. It is a horrible thing to see machines hauled about by tigers, at the mercy of tigers, forced to express the tiger. It is a still more horrible thing to see tigers caught up and entangled and torn in machinery. It is horrible, a chaos beyond chaos, an unthinkable hell.

The tiger is not wrong, the machine is not wrong, but we, liars, lip-servers, duplicate fools, we are unforgivably wrong. We say: "I will be a tiger because I love mankind; out of love for other people, out of selfless service to that which is not me, I will even become a tiger." Which is absurd. A tiger devours because it is consummated in devouring, it achieves its absolute self in devouring. It does not devour because its unselfish conscience bids it do so, for the sake of the other deer and doves or the other tigers.

Having arrived at the one extreme of mechanical selflessness, we immediately embrace the other extreme of the transcendent Self. But we try to be both at once. We do not cease to be the one before we become the other. We do not even play the rôles in turn. We want to be the tiger and the deer both in one. Which is just ghastly nothingness. We try to say, "The tiger is the lamb and the lamb is the tiger." Which is nil, nihil, nought.

The padrone took me into a small room almost contained in the thickness of the wall. There the Signora's dark eyes glared with surprise and agitation, seeing me intrude. She is younger than the Signore, a mere village tradesman's daughter, and, alas, childless.

It was quite true, the door stood open. Madame put down the screw-driver and drew herself erect. Her eyes were a flame of excitement. This question of a door-spring that made the door fly open when it should make it close roused a vivid spark in her soul. It was she who was wrestling with the angel of mechanism.

She was about forty years old, and flame-like and fierily sad. I think she did not know she was sad. But her heart was eaten by some impotence in her life.

She subdued her flame of life to the little padrone. He was strange and static, scarcely human, ageless, like a monkey. She supported him with her flame, supported his static, ancient, beautiful form, kept it intact. But she did not believe in him.

Now, the Signora Gemma held her husband together whilst he undid the screw that fixed the spring. If they had been alone, she would have done it, pretending to be under his direction. But since I was there, he did it himself; a grey, shaky, highly-bred little gentleman, standing on a chair with a long screw-driver, whilst his wife stood behind him, her hands half-raised to catch him if he should fall. Yet he was strangely absolute, with a strange, intact force in his breeding.

They had merely adjusted the strong spring to the shut door, and stretched it slightly in fastening it to the door-jamb, so that it drew together the moment the latch was released, and the door flew open.

We soon made it right. There was a moment of anxiety, the screw was fixed. And the door swung to. They were delighted. The Signora Gemma, who roused in me an electric kind of melancholy, clasped her hands together in ecstasy as the door swiftly shut itself.

"Ecco!" she cried, in her vibrating, almost warlike woman's voice: "Ecco!"

Her eyes were a-flame as they looked at the door. She ran forward to try it herself. She opened the door expectantly, eagerly. Pouf!—it shut with a bang.

"Ecco!" she cried, her voice quivering like bronze, overwrought but triumphant.

I must try also. I opened the door. Pouf! It shut with a bang. We all exclaimed with joy.

Then the Signor di Paoli turned to me, with a gracious, bland, formal grin. He turned his back slightly on the woman, and stood holding his chin, his strange horse-mouth grinning almost pompously at me. It was an affair of gentlemen. His wife disappeared as if dismissed. Then the padrone broke into cordial motion. We must drink.

He would show me the estate. I had already seen the house. We went out by the glass doors on the left, into the domestic courtyard.

It was lower than the gardens round it, and the sunshine came through the trellised arches on to the flagstones, where the grass grew fine and green in the cracks, and all was deserted and spacious and still. There were one or two orange-tubs in the light.

Then I heard a noise, and there in the corner, among all the pink geraniums and the sunshine, the Signora Gemma sat laughing with a baby. It was a fair, bonny thing of eighteen months. The Signora was concentrated upon the child as he sat, stolid and handsome, in his little white cap, perched on a bench picking at the pink geraniums.

She laughed, bent forward her dark face out of the shadow, swift into a glitter of sunshine near the sunny baby, laughing again excitedly, making mother-noises. The child took no notice of her. She caught him swiftly into the shadow, and they were obscured; her dark head was against the baby's wool jacket, she was kissing his neck, avidly, under the creeper leaves. The pink geraniums still frilled joyously in the sunshine.

I had forgotten the padrone. Suddenly I turned to him enquiringly.

"The Signora's nephew," he explained, briefly, curtly, in a small voice. It was as if he were ashamed, or too deeply chagrined.

The woman had seen us watching, so she came across the sunshine with the child, laughing, talking to the baby, not coming out of her own world to us, not acknowledging us, except formally.

The Signor Pietro, queer old horse, began to laugh and neigh at the child, with strange, rancorous envy. The child twisted its face to cry. The Signora caught it away, dancing back a few yards from her old husband.

"I am a stranger," I said to her across the distance. "He is afraid of a stranger."

"No, no," she cried back, her eyes flaring up. "It is the man. He always cries at the men."

She advanced again, laughing and roused, with the child in her arms. Her husband stood as if overcast, obliterated. She and I and the baby, in the sunshine, laughed a moment. Then I heard the neighing, forced laugh of the old man. He would not be left out. He seemed to force himself forward. He was bitter, acrid with chagrin and obliteration, struggling as if to assert his own existence. He was nullified.

The woman also was uncomfortable. I could see she wanted to go away with the child, to enjoy him alone, with palpitating, pained enjoyment. It was her brother's boy. And the old padrone was as if nullified by her ecstasy over the baby. He held his chin, gloomy, fretful, unimportant.

He was annulled. I was startled when I realised it. It was as though his reality were not attested till he had a child. It was as if his *raison d'être* had been to have a son. And he had no children. Therefore he had no *raison d'être*. He was nothing, a shadow that vanishes into nothing. And he was ashamed, consumed by his own nothingness.

I was startled. This, then, is the secret of Italy's attraction for us, this phallic worship. To the Italian the phallus is the symbol of individual creative immortality, to each man his own Godhead. The child is but the evidence of the Godhead.

And this is why the Italian is attractive, supple, and beautiful, because he worships the Godhead in the flesh. We envy him, we feel pale and insignificant beside him. Yet at the same time we feel superior to him, as if he were a child and we adult.

Wherein are we superior? Only because we went beyond the phallus in the search of the Godhead, the creative origin. And we found the physical forces and the secrets of science.

We have exalted Man far above the man who is in each one of us. Our aim is a perfect humanity, a perfect and equable human consciousness, selfless. And we obtain it in the subjection, reduction, analysis, and destruction of the Self. So on we go, active in science and mechanics, and social reform.

But we have exhausted ourselves in the process. We have found great treasures, and we are now impotent to use them. So we have said: "What good are these treasures, they are vulgar nothings." We have said: "Let us go back from this adventuring, let us enjoy our own flesh, like the Italian." But our habit of life, our very constitution, prevents our being quite like the Italian. The phallus will never serve us as a Godhead, because we do not believe in it: no northern race does. Therefore, either we set ourselves to serve our children, calling them "the future," or else we turn perverse and destructive, give ourselves joy in the destruction of the flesh.

The children are not the future. The living truth is the future. Time and people do not make the future. Retrogression is not the future. Fifty million children growing up purposeless, with no purpose save the attainment of their own individual desires, these are not the future, they are only a disintegration of the past. The future is in living, growing truth, in advancing fulfilment.

But it is no good. Whatever we do, it is within the greater will towards self-reduction and a perfect society, analysis on the one hand, and mechanical construction on the other. This will dominates us as a whole, and until the whole breaks down, the will must persist. So that now, continuing in the old, splendid will for a perfect selfless humanity, we have become inhuman and unable to help ourselves, we are but attributes of the great mechanised society we have created on our way to perfection. And this great mechanised society, being selfless, is pitiless. It works on mechanically and destroys us, it is our master and our God.

It is past the time to leave off, to cease entirely from what we are doing, and from what we have been doing for hundreds of years. It is past the time to cease seeking one Infinite, ignoring, trying to eliminate the other. The Infinite is two-fold: the Father and the Son, the Dark and the Light, the Senses and the Mind, the Soul and the Spirit, the self and the not-self, the Eagle and the Dove, the Tiger and the Lamb. The consummation of Man is twofold, in the Self and in Selflessness. By great retrogression back to the source of darkness in me, the Self, deep in the senses, I arrive at the Original Creative Infinite. By projection forth from myself, by the elimination of my absolute sensual Self, I arrive at the Ultimate Infinite, Oneness in the

Spirit. They are two Infinites, twofold approach to God. And man must know both.

But he must never confuse them. They are eternally separate. The lion shall never lie down with the lamb. The lion eternally shall devour the lamb, the lamb eternally shall be devoured of the lion. Man knows the great consummation in the flesh, the sensual ecstasy, and that is eternal. Also the spiritual ecstasy of unanimity, that is eternal. But the two are separate and never to be confused. To neutralise the one with the other is unthinkable, an abomination. Confusion is horror and nothingness.

The two Infinites, negative and positive, they are always related, but they are never identical. They are always opposite, but there is a relation between them. This is the Holy Ghost of the Christian Trinity. And it is this, the relation which is established between the two Infinites, the two Natures of God, which we have transgressed, forgotten, sinned against. The Father is the Father, and the Son is the Son. I may know the Son and deny the Father, or I may know the Father and deny the Son. But that which I may never deny, and which I have denied, is the Holy Ghost which relates the dual Infinites into One Whole, which relates and keeps distinct the dual natures of God. To say that the Two are One, this is the inadmissible lie. The Two are related, by the intervention of the Third, into a Oneness.

There are two ways, there is not only One. There are two opposite ways to consummation. But that which relates them, like the base of a triangle, this is constant and absolute, this makes the Ultimate Whole. And in the Holy Spirit, I know the Two Ways, the two Infinites, the two Consummations. And knowing the Two, I admit the Whole. But excluding One, I exclude the Whole. And confusing the Two, I make nullity, nihil.

"Mais," said the Signore, starting from his scene of ignominy, where his wife played with another man's child, "mais—voulez-vous vous promener dans mes petites terres?"

It came out fluently, he was so much roused in self-defence and self-assertion.

We walked under the pergola of bony vine-stocks, secure in the sunshine within the walls, only the long mountain, parallel with us, looking in.

I said how I liked the big vine-garden, I asked when it ended. The pride of the padrone came back with a click. He pointed me to the terrace, to the great shut lemon-houses above. They were all his. But—he shrugged his Italian shoulders—it was nothing, just a little garden, vous savez, monsieur. I protested it was beautiful, that I loved it, and that it seemed to me *very* large indeed. He admitted that to-day, perhaps, it was beautiful.

"Perchè—parceque—il fait un tempo—così—très bell'—très beau, ecco!"

He alighted on the word "beau" hurriedly, like a bird coming to ground with a little bounce.

The terraces of the garden are held up to the sun, the sun falls full upon them, they are like a vessel slanted up, to catch the superb, heavy light. Within the walls we are remote, perfect, moving in heavy spring sunshine, under the bony avenue of vines. The padrone makes little exclamatory noises that mean nothing, and teaches me the names of vegetables. The land is rich and black.

Opposite us, looking down on our security, is the long, arched mountain of snow. We climbed one flight of steps, and we could see the little villages on the opposite side of the lake. We climbed again, and could see the water rippling.

We came to a great stone building that I had thought was a storehouse, for open-air storage, because the walls are open half-way up, showing the darkness inside and the corner pillar very white and square and distinct in front of it.

Entering carelessly into the dimness, I started, for at my feet was a great floor of water, clear and green in its obscurity, going down between the walls, a reservoir in the gloom. The Signore laughed at my surprise. It was for irrigating the land, he said. It stank slightly, with a raw smell, otherwise I said, what a wonderful bath it would make. The old Signore gave his little neighing laugh at the idea.

Then we climbed into a great loft of leaves, ruddy brown, stored in a great bank under the roof, seeming to give off a little red heat, as they gave off the lovely perfume of the hills. We passed through, and stood at the foot of the lemon-house. The big, blind building rose high in the sunshine before us.

All summer long, upon the mountain slopes steep by the lake, stand the rows of naked pillars rising out of the green foliage like ruins of temples: white, square pillars of masonry, standing forlorn in their colonnades and squares, rising up the mountain-sides here and there, as if they remained from some great race that had once worshipped here. And still, in the winter, some are seen, standing away in lonely places where the sun streams full, grey rows of pillars rising out of a broken wall, tier above tier, naked to the sky, forsaken.

They are the lemon plantations, and the pillars are to support the heavy branches of the trees, but finally to act as scaffolding of the great wooden houses that stand blind and ugly, covering the lemon-trees in the winter.

In November, when cold winds came down and snow had fallen on the mountains, from out of the store-houses the men were carrying timber, and we heard the clank of falling planks. Then, as we walked along the military road on the mountain-side, we saw below, on the top of the lemon gardens, long thin poles laid from pillar to pillar, and we heard the two men talking and singing as they walked across perilously, placing the poles. In their clumsy zoccoli they strode easily across, though they had twenty or thirty feet to fall if they slipped. But the mountain-side, rising steeply, seemed near, and above their heads the rocks glowed high into the sky, so that the sense of elevation must have been taken away. At any rate they went easily from pillar-summit to pillar-summit, with a great cave of space below. Then again was the rattle and clang of planks being laid in order, ringing from the mountain-side over the blue lake, till a platform of timber, old and brown, projected from the mountain-side, a floor when seen from above, a hanging roof when seen from below. And we, on the road above, saw the men sitting easily on this flimsy hanging platform, hammering the planks. And all day long the sound of hammering echoed among the rocks and olive-woods, and came, a faint quick concussion, to the men on the boats far out. When the roofs were on, they put in the fronts, blocked in between the white pillars with old, dark wood, in roughly made panels. And here and there, at irregular intervals, was a panel of glass, pane overlapping pane in the long strip of narrow window. So that now these enormous, unsightly buildings bulge out on the mountain-sides, rising in two or three receding tiers, blind, dark, sordid-looking places.

In the morning I often lie in bed and watch the sunrise. The lake lies dim and milky, the mountains are dark-blue at the back, while over them the sky gushes and glistens with light. At a certain place on the mountain ridge the light burns gold, seems to fuse a little groove on the hill's rim. It fuses and fuses at this point, till of a sudden it comes, the intense molten living light. The mountains melt suddenly, the light steps down, there is a glitter, a spangle, a clutch of spangles, a great unbearable sun-track flashing across the milky lake, and the light falls on my face. Then, looking aside, I hear the little slotting noise which tells me they are opening the lemon gardens, a long panel here and there, a long slot of darkness at irregular intervals between the brown wood and the glass stripes.

"Vouley vous"—the Signore bows me in with outstretched hand. "Vouley vous entrer, monsieur."

I went into the lemon house, where the poor trees seem to mope in the darkness. It is an immense, dark, cold place. Tall lemon trees, heavy with half-visible fruit, crowd together and rise in the gloom. They look like ghosts in the darkness of the underworld, stately, and as if in life, but only grand shadows of themselves. And lurking here and there, I see one of the pillars. But he too, seems a shadow, not one of the dazzling white fellows I knew. Here we are, trees, men, pillars, the dark earth, the sad black paths, shut in in this enormous box. It is true, there are long slips of window, and slots of space, so that the front is striped, and an occasional beam of light fingers the leaves of an enclosed tree, and the sickly round lemons. But it is nevertheless very gloomy.

"But it is much colder in here than outside," I said.

"Yes," replied the Signore, "Now. But at night—I *think*—"

I almost wished it were night, to try. I wanted to imagine the trees cosy. They seemed now in the underworld. Between the lemon trees, beside the path, were little orange trees, and dozens of oranges hanging like hot coals in the twilight. When I warm my hands at them, the Signore breaks me off one twig after another, till I have a bunch of burning oranges among dark leaves, a heavy bouquet. Looking down the Hades of the lemon house, the many ruddy-clustered oranges beside the path remind me of the lights of a village along the lake at night, while the pale lemons above are the stars. There is a subtle, exquisite scent of lemon flowers. Then I notice a citron. He hangs heavy and bloated upon so small a tree, that he seems a dark-green enormity. There is a great host of lemons overhead, half visible, a swarm of ruddy oranges by the paths, and here and there, a fat citron. It is almost like being under the sea.

At the corners of the path were round little patches of ash, and stumps of charred wood, where fires had been kindled inside the house on cold nights. For during the second and third weeks in January, the snow came down so low on the mountains, that after climbing for an hour, I found myself in a snow lane, and saw olive orchards on lawns of snow.

The padrone says that all lemons and sweet oranges are grafted on a bitter-orange stock. The plants raised from seed, lemon and sweet orange, fell prey to disease, so the cultivators found it safe only to raise the native bitter orange, and then to graft upon it.

And the maestra—she is the schoolmistress, who wears black gloves while she teaches us Italian—says that the lemon was brought by St. Francis of Assisi, who came to the Garda here, and founded a church and a monastery. Certainly the church of San Francesco is very old and dilapidated, and its cloisters have some beautiful and original carvings of leaves and fruit upon the pillars. Which seems to connect San Francesco with the lemon. I imagine him wandering here with a lemon in his pocket. Perhaps he made lemonade in the hot summer. But Bacchus had been before him in the drink trade.

Looking at his lemons, the Signore sighed. I think he hates them. They are leaving him in the lurch. They are sold retail at a halfpenny each, all the year round. "But that is as dear, or dearer, than in England," I say. "Ah but," says the maestra, "that is because your lemons are outdoor fruit from Sicily. Però—one of our lemons is as good as *two* from elsewhere."

It is true these lemons have an exquisite fragrance and perfume, but whether their force as lemons is double that of an ordinary fruit is a question. Oranges are sold at fourpence halfpenny the Kilo.—it comes about five for twopence, small ones. The citrons are sold also by weight in Salò, for the making of that liqueur known as "Cedro." One citron fetches sometimes a shilling, or more, but then the demand is necessarily small. So that it is evident, from these figures, the Lago di Garda cannot afford to grow its lemons much longer. The gardens are already many of them in ruins, and still more "Da Vendere."

We went out of the shadow of the lemon-house, onto the roof of the section below us. When we came to the brink of the roof, I sat down. The padrone stood behind me, a shabby, shaky, little figure on his roof in the sky, a little figure of dilapidation, dilapidated as the lemon-houses themselves.

We were always level with the mountain-snow opposite. A film of pure blue was on the hills to the right and the left. There had been a wind, but it was still now. The water breathed an iridescent dust on the far shore, where the villages were groups of specks.

On the low level of the world, on the lake, an orange-sailed boat leaned slim to the dark-blue water, which had flecks of foam. A woman went down-hill quickly, with two goats and a sheep. Among the olives a man was whistling.

"Voyez," said the padrone, with distant, perfect melancholy. "There was once a lemon garden also there—you see the short pillars, cut off to make a pergola for the vine. Once there were twice as many lemons as now. Now we must have vine instead. From that piece of land I had two hundred lire a year, in lemons. From the vine I have only eighty."

"But wine is a valuable crop," I said.

"Ah—così-così! For a man who grows much. For me—poco, poco—peu."

Suddenly his face broke into a smile of profound melancholy, almost a grin, like a gargoyle. It was the real Italian melancholy, very deep, static.

"Vous voyez, monsieur—the lemon, it is all the year, all the year. But the vine—one crop——?"

He lifts his shoulders and spreads his hands with that gesture of finality and fatality, while his face takes the blank, ageless look of misery, like a monkey's. There is no hope. There is the present. Either that is enough, the present, or there is nothing.

I sat and looked at the lake. It was beautiful as paradise, as the first creation. On the shores were the ruined lemon-pillars standing out in melancholy, the clumsy, enclosed lemon-houses seemed ramshackle, bulging among vine stocks and olive trees. The villages, too, clustered upon their churches, seemed to belong to the past. They seemed to be lingering in bygone centuries.

"But it is very beautiful," I protested. "In England——"

"Ah, in England," exclaimed the padrone, the same ageless, monkey-like grin of fatality, tempered by cunning, coming on his face, "in England you have the wealth—les richesses—you have the mineral coal and the machines, vous savez. Here, we have the sun——"

He lifted his withered hand to the sky, to the wonderful source of that blue day, and he smiled, in histrionic triumph. But his triumph was only histrionic. The machines were more to his soul than the sun. He did not know these mechanisms, their great, human-contrived, inhuman power, and he wanted to know them. As for the sun, that is common property, and no man is distinguished by it. He wanted machines, machine-production, money, and human power. He wanted to know the joy of man who has got the earth in his grip, bound it up with railways, burrowed it with iron fingers, subdued it. He wanted this last triumph of the ego, this last reduction. He wanted to go where the English have gone, beyond the Self, into the great inhuman Not-Self, to create the great unliving creators, the machines, out of the active forces of nature that existed before flesh.

But he is too old. It remains for the young Italian to embrace his mistress, the machine.

I sat on the roof of the lemon-house, with the lake below and the snowy mountain opposite, and looked at the ruins on the old, olive-fuming shores, at all the peace of the ancient world still covered in sunshine, and the past seemed to me so lovely that one must look towards it, backwards, only backwards, where there is peace and beauty and no more dissonance.

I thought of England, the great mass of London, and the black, fuming, laborious Midlands and north-country. It seemed horrible. And yet, it was better than the padrone, this old, monkey-like cunning of fatality. It is better to go forward into error than to stay fixed inextricably in the past.

Yet what should become of the world? There was London and the industrial counties spreading like a blackness over all the world, horrible, in the end destructive. And the Garda was so lovely under the sky of sunshine, it was intolerable. For away, beyond, beyond all the snowy Alps, with the iridescence of eternal ice above them, was this England, black and foul and dry, with her soul worn down, almost worn away. And England was conquering the world with her machines and her horrible destruction of natural life. She was conquering the whole world.

And yet, was she not herself finished in this work. She had had enough. She had conquered the natural life to the end: she was replete with the conquest of the outer world, satisfied with the destruction of the Self. She would cease, she would turn round; or else expire.

If she still lived, she would begin to build her knowledge into a great structure of truth. There it lay, vast masses of rough-hewn knowledge, vast masses of machines and appliances, vast masses of ideas and methods, and nothing done with it, only teeming swarms of disinte-grated human beings seething and perishing rapidly away amongst it, till it seems as if a world will be left covered with huge ruins, and scored by strange devices of industry, and quite dead, the people disappeared, swallowed up in the last efforts towards a perfect, selfless, society.

III. The Theatre

During carnival a company is playing in the theatre. On Christmas Day the padrone came in with the key of his box, and would we care to see the drama? The theatre was small, a mere nothing, in fact; a mere affair of peasants, you understand; and the Signor di Paoli spread his hands and put his head on one side, parrot-wise; but we might find a little diversion—*un peu de divertiment*. With this he handed me the key.

I made suitable acknowledgments, and was really impressed. To be handed the key of a box at the theatre, so simply and pleasantly, in the large sitting-room looking over the grey lake of Christmas Day; it seemed to me a very graceful event. The key had a chain and a little shield of bronze, on which was beaten out a large figure 8.

So the next day we went to see *I Spettri*, expecting some good, crude melodrama. The theatre is an old church. Since that triumph of the deaf and dumb, the cinematograph, has come to give us the nervous excitement of speed, grimace, agitation, and speed, as of flying atoms, chaos, many an old church in Italy has taken a new lease of life.

This cast-off church made a good theatre. I realised how cleverly it had been constructed for the dramatic presentation of religious ceremonies. The east end is round, the walls are windowless, sound is well distributed. Now everything is theatrical, except the stone floor and two pillars at the back of the auditorium, and the slightly ecclesiastical seats below.

There are two tiers of little boxes in the theatre, some forty in all, with fringe and red velvet, and lined with dark red paper, quite like real boxes in a real theatre. And the padrone's is one of the best. It just holds three people.

We paid our threepence entrance fee in the stone hall and went upstairs. I opened the door of Number 8, and we were shut in our little cabin, looking down on all the world. Then I found the barber, Luigi, bowing profusely in a box opposite. It was necessary to make bows all round: ah, the chemist, on the upper tier, near the barber; how-do-you-do to the padrona of the hotel, who is our good friend, and who sits, wearing a little beaver shoulder-cape, a few boxes off; very cold salutation to the stout village magistrate with the long brown beard, who leans forward in the box facing the stage, while a grouping of faces look out from behind him; a warm smile to the family of the Signora Gemma, across next to the stage. Then we are settled.

I cannot tell why I hate the village magistrate. He looks like a family portrait by a Flemish artist, he himself weighing down the front of the picture with his portliness and his long brown beard, whilst the faces of his family are arranged in two groups for the background. I think he is angry at our intrusion. He is very republican and self-important. But we eclipse him easily, with the aid of a large black velvet hat, and black furs, and our Sunday clothes.

Downstairs the villagers are crowding, drifting like a heavy current. The women are seated, by church instinct, all together on the left, with perhaps an odd man at the end of a row, beside his wife. On the right, sprawling in the benches, are several groups of bersaglieri, in grey uniforms and slanting, cock's-feather hats; then peasants, fishermen, and an odd couple or so of brazen girls taking their places on the men's side.

At the back, lounging against the pillars or standing very dark and sombre, are the more reckless spirits of the village. Their black felt hats are pulled down, their cloaks are thrown over their mouths, they stand very dark and isolated in their moments of stillness, they shout and wave to each other when anything occurs.

The men are clean, their clothes are all clean washed. The rags of the poorest porter are always well washed. But it is Sunday to-morrow, and they are shaved only on a Sunday. So that they have a week's black growth on their chins. But they have dark, soft eyes, unconscious and vulnerable. They move and balance with loose, heedless motion upon their clattering zoccoli, they lounge with wonderful ease against the wall at the back, or against the two pillars, unconscious of the patches on their clothes or of their bare throats, that are knotted perhaps with a scarlet rag. Loose and abandoned, they lounge and talk, or they watch with wistful absorption the play that is going on.

They are strangely isolated in their own atmosphere, and as if revealed. It is as if their vulnerable being was exposed and they have not the wit to cover it. There is a pathos of physical sensibility and mental inadequacy. Their mind is not sufficiently alert to run with their quick, warm senses.

The men keep together, as if to support each other; the women also are together, in a hard, strong herd. It is as if the power, the hardness, the triumph, even in this Italian village, were with the women in their relentless, vindictive unity.

That which drives men and women together, the indomitable necessity, is like a bondage upon the people. They submit as under compulsion, under constraint. They come together mostly in anger

and in violence of destructive passion. There is no comradeship
between men and women, none whatsoever, but rather a condition of
battle, reserve, hostility.

On Sundays the uncomfortable, excited, unwilling youth walks for
an hour with his sweetheart, at a little distance from her, on the public
highway in the afternoon. This is a concession to the necessity for
marriage. There is no real courting, no happiness of being together,
only the roused excitement which is based on a fundamental hostility.
There is very little flirting, and what there is is of the subtle, cruel
kind, like a sex duel. On the whole, the men and women avoid each
other, almost shun each other. Husband and wife are brought together
in a child, which they both worship. But in each of them there is only
the great reverence for the infant, and the reverence for fatherhood or
motherhood, as the case may be, there is no spiritual love.

In marriage, husband and wife wage the subtle, satisfying war of sex
upon each other. It gives a profound satisfaction, a profound intimacy.
But it destroys all joy, all unanimity in action.

On Sunday afternoons the uncomfortable youth walks by the side of
his maiden for an hour in the public highway. Then he escapes, as
from a bondage he goes back to his men companions. On Sunday
afternoons and evenings the married woman, accompanied by a friend
or by a child—she dare not go alone, afraid of the strange, terrible
sex-war between her and the drunken man—is seen leading home the
wine-drunken, liberated husband. Sometimes she is beaten when she
gets home. It is part of the process. But there is no synthetic love
between men and women, there is only passion, and passion is fundamental hatred, the act of love is a fight.

The child, the outcome, is divine. Here the union, the oneness, is
manifest. Though spirit strove with spirit, in mortal conflict, during
the sex-passion, yet the flesh united with flesh in oneness. The phallus
is still divine. But the spirit, the mind of man, this has become nothing.

So the women triumph. They sit down below in the theatre, their
perfectly dressed hair gleaming, their backs very straight, their heads
carried tensely. They are not very noticeable. They seem held in
reserve. They are just as tense and stiff as the men are slack and
abandoned. Some strange will holds the women taut. They seem like
weapons, dangerous. There is nothing charming nor winning about
them; at the best, a full, prolific maternity, at the worst a yellow,
poisonous bitterness of the flesh that is like a narcotic. But they are too
strong for the men. The male spirit, which would subdue the immedi-

ate flesh to some conscious or social purpose, is overthrown. The woman in her maternity is the law-giver, the supreme authority. The authority of the man, in work, in public affairs, is something trivial in comparison. The pathetic ignominy of the village male is complete on Sunday afternoon, on his great day of liberation, when he is accompanied home, drunk but sinister, by the erect, unswerving, slightly cowed woman. His drunken terrorising is only pitiable, she is so obviously the more constant power.

And this is why the men must go away to America. It is not the money. It is the profound desire to rehabilitate themselves, to recover some dignity as men, as producers, as workers, as creators from the spirit, not only from the flesh. It is a profound desire to get away from women altogether, the terrible subjugation to sex, the phallic worship.

The company of actors in the little theatre was from a small town away on the plain, beyond Brescia. The curtain rose, everybody was still, with that profound, naïve attention which children give. And after a few minutes I realised that *I Spettri* was Ibsen's *Ghosts*. The peasants and fishermen of the Garda, even the rows of ungovernable children, sat absorbed in watching as the Norwegian drama unfolded itself.

The actors are peasants. The leader is the son of a peasant proprietor. He is qualified as a chemist, but is unsettled, vagrant, prefers play-acting. The Signor Pietro di Paoli shrugs his shoulders and apologises for their vulgar accent. It is all the same to me. I am trying to get myself to rights with the play, which I have just lately seen in Munich, perfectly produced and detestable.

It was such a change from the hard, ethical, slightly mechanised characters in the German play, which was as perfect an interpretation as I can imagine, to the rather pathetic notion of the Italian peasants, that I had to wait to adjust myself.

The mother was a pleasant, comfortable woman harassed by something, she did not quite know what. The pastor was a ginger-haired caricature imitated from the northern stage, quite a lay figure. The peasants never laughed, they watched solemnly and absorbedly, like children. The servant was just a slim, pert, forward hussy, much too flagrant. And then the son, the actor-manager: he was a dark, ruddy man, broad and thick-set, evidently of peasant origin, but with some education now; he was the important figure, the play was his.

And he was strangely disturbing. Dark, ruddy, and powerful, he could not be the blighted son of *Ghosts*, the hectic, unsound, northern issue of a diseased father. His flashy, Italian passion for his half-sister was real enough to make one uncomfortable: something he wanted and would have in spite of his own soul, something which fundamentally he did not want.

It was this contradiction within the man that made the play so interesting. A robust, vigorous man of thirty-eight, flaunting and florid as a rather successful Italian can be, there was yet a secret sickness which oppressed him. But it was no taint in the blood, it was rather a kind of debility in the soul. That which he wanted and would have, the sensual excitement, in his soul he did not want it, no, not at all. And yet he must act from his physical desires, his physical will.

His true being, his real self, was impotent. In his soul, he was dependent, forlorn. He was childish and dependent on the mother. To hear him say, "Grazia, mamma!" would have tormented the mother-soul in any woman living. Such a child crying in the night! And for what?

For he was hot-blooded, healthy, almost in his prime, and free as a man can be in his circumstances. He had his own way, he admitted no thwarting. He governed his circumstances pretty much, coming to our village with his little company, playing the plays he chose himself. And yet, that which he would have he did not vitally want, it was only a sort of inflamed obstinacy that made him so insistent, in the masculine way. He was not going to be governed by women, he was not going to be dictated to in the least by any one. And this because he was beaten by his own flesh.

His real man's soul, the soul that goes forth and builds up a new world out of the void, was ineffectual. It could only revert to the senses. His divinity was the phallic divinity. The other male divinity, which is the spirit that fulfils in the world the new germ of an idea, this was denied and obscured in him, unused. And it was this spirit which cried out helplessly in him through the insistent, inflammable flesh. Even this play-acting was a form of physical gratification for him, it had in it neither real mind nor spirit.

It was so different from Ibsen, and so much more moving. Ibsen is exciting, nervously sensational. But this was really moving, a real crying in the night. One loved the Italian nation, and wanted to help it with all one's soul. But when one sees the perfect Ibsen, how one hates the Norwegian and Swedish nations! They are detestable.

They seem to be fingering with the mind the secret places and sources of the blood, impertinent, irreverent, nasty. There is a certain intolerable nastiness about the real Ibsen: the same thing is in Strindberg and in most of the Norwegian and Swedish writings. It is with them a sort of phallic worship also, but now the worship is mental and perverted: the phallus is the real fetish, but it is the source of uncleanliness and corruption and death, it is the Moloch, worshipped in obscenity.

Which is unbearable. The phallus is a symbol of creative divinity. But it represents only part of creative divinity. The Italian has made it represent the whole. Which is now his misery, for he has to destroy his symbol in himself.

Which is why the Italian men have the enthusiasm for war, unashamed. Partly it is the true phallic worship, for the phallic principle is to absorb and dominate all life. But also it is a desire to expose themselves to death, to know death, that death may destroy in them this too strong dominion of the blood, may once more liberate the spirit of outgoing, of uniting, of making order out of chaos, in the outer world, as the flesh makes a new order from chaos in begetting a new life, set them free to know and serve a greater idea.

The peasants below sat and listened intently, like children who hear and do not understand, yet who are spellbound. The children themselves sit spellbound on the benches till the play is over. They do not fidget or lose interest. They watch with wide, absorbed eyes at the mystery, held in thrall by the sound of emotion.

But the villagers do not really care for Ibsen. They let it go. On the feast of Epiphany, as a special treat, was given a poetic drama by D'Annunzio, *La Fiaccola sotto il Moggio—The Light under the Bushel*.

It is a foolish romantic play of no real significance. There are several murders and a good deal of artificial horror. But it is all a very nice romantic piece of make-believe, like a charade.

So the audience loved it. After the performance of *Ghosts* I saw the barber, and he had the curious grey, clayey look of an Italian who is cold and depressed. The sterile cold inertia, which the so-called passionate nations know so well, had settled on him, and he went obliterating himself in the street, as if he were cold, dead.

But after the D'Annunzio play he was like a man who has drunk sweet wine and is warm.

"Ah, bellissimo, bellissimo!" he said, in tones of intoxicated reverence, when he saw me.

"Better than *I Spettri*?" I said.

He half-raised his hands, as if to imply the fatuity of the question.

"Ah, but——" he said, "it was D'Annunzio. The other ..."

"That was Ibsen—a great Norwegian," I said, "famous all over the world."

"But, you know—D'Annunzio is a poet—oh, beautiful, beautiful!" There was no going beyond this "bello—bellissimo."

It was the language which did it. It was the Italian passion for rhetoric, for the speech which appeals to the senses and makes no demand on the mind. When an Englishman listens to a speech he wants at least to imagine that he understands thoroughly and impersonally what is meant. But an Italian only cares about the emotion. It is the movement, the physical effect of the language upon the blood which gives him supreme satisfaction. His mind is scarcely engaged at all. He is like a child, hearing and feeling without understanding. It is the sensuous gratification he asks for. Which is why D'Annunzio is a god in Italy. He can control the current of the blood with his words, and although much of what he says is bosh, yet the hearer is satisfied, fulfilled.

Carnival ends on the 5th of February, so each Thursday there is a Serata d'Onore of one of the actors. The first, and the only one for which prices were raised—to a fourpence entrance fee instead of threepence—was for the leading lady. The play was *The Wife of the Doctor*, a modern piece, sufficiently uninteresting; the farce that followed made me laugh.

Since it was her Evening of Honour, Adelaida was the person to see. She is very popular, though she is no longer young. In fact, she is the mother of the young, pert person of *Ghosts*.

Nevertheless, Adelaida, stout and blonde and soft and pathetic, is the real heroine of the theatre, the prima. She is very good at sobbing; and afterwards the men exclaim, involuntarily, out of their strong emotion, "bella, bella!" The women say nothing. They sit stiffly and dangerously as ever. But no doubt they quite agree, this is the true picture of ill-used, tear-stained woman, the bearer of many wrongs. Therefore they take unto themselves the homage of the men's "bella, bella!" that follows the sobs: it is due recognition of their hard wrongs: "the woman pays." Nevertheless, they despise in their souls the plump, soft Adelaida.

Dear Adelaida, she is irreproachable. In every age, in every clime, she is dear, at any rate to the masculine soul, this soft, tear-blenched, blonde, ill-used thing. She must be ill-used and unfortunate. Dear Gretchen, dear Desdemona, dear Iphigenia, dear Dame aux Camélias, dear Lucy of Lammermoor, dear Mary Magdalene, dear, pathetic, unfortunate soul, in all ages and lands, how we love you. In the theatre she blossoms forth, she is the lily of the stage. Young and inexperienced as I am, I have broken my heart over her several times. I could write a sonnet-sequence to her, yes, the fair, pale, tear-stained thing, white-robed, with her hair down her back; I could call her by a hundred names, in a hundred languages, Mélisande, Elizabeth, Juliet, Butterfly, Phèdre, Minnehaha, etc. Each new time I hear her voice, with its faint clang of tears, my heart grows big and hot, and my bones melt. I detest her, but it is no good. My heart begins to swell like a bud under the plangent rain.

The last time I saw her was here, on the Garda, at Salò. She was the chalked, thin-armed daughter of Rigoletto. I detested her, her voice had a chalky squeak in it. And yet, by the end, my heart was over-ripe in my breast, ready to burst with loving affection. I was ready to walk on to the stage, to wipe out the odious, miscreant lover, and to offer her all myself, saying, "I can see it is real *love* you want, and you shall have it: *I* will give it to you."

Of course I know the secret of the Gretchen magic; it is all in the "Save me, Mr. Hercules!" phrase. Her shyness, her timidity, her trustfulness, her tears foster my own strength and grandeur. I am the positive half of the universe. But so I am, if it comes to that, just as positive as the other half.

Adelaida is plump, and her voice has just that moist, plangent strength which gives one a real, voluptuous thrill. The moment she comes on the stage and looks round—a bit scared—she is *she*, Electra, Isolde, Sieglinde, Marguèrite. She wears a dress of black voile, like the lady who weeps at the trial in the police-court. This is her modern uniform. Her antique garment is of trailing white, with a blonde pigtail and a flower. Realistically, it is black voile and a handkerchief.

Adelaida always has a handkerchief. And still I cannot resist it. I say, "There's the hanky!" Nevertheless, in two minutes it has worked its way with me. She squeezes it in her poor, plump hand, as the tears begin to rise; Fate, or man, is inexorable, so cruel. There is a sob, a cry, she presses the fist and the hanky to her eyes, one eye, then the other. She weeps real tears, tears shaken from the depths of her soft, vulnerable, victimised female self. I cannot stand it. There I sit in the padrone's little red box and stifle my emotion, whilst I repeat in my heart: "What a shame, child, what a shame!" She is twice my age, but what is age in such a circumstance? "Your poor little hanky, it's sopping. There, then, don't cry. It'll be all right. *I'll* see you're all right. *All* men are not beasts, you know." So I cover her protectively in my arms, and soon I shall be kissing her, for comfort, in the heat and prowess of my compassion, kissing her soft, plump cheek and neck, closely, bringing my comfort nearer and nearer.

It is a pleasant and exciting rôle for me to play. Robert Burns did the part to perfection:

> O wert thou in the cauld blast
> On yonder lea, on yonder lea.

How many times does one recite that, to all the Ophelias and Gretchens in the world:

> Thy bield should be my bosom.

How one admires one's bosom in that capacity! Looking down at one's shirt-front, one is filled with strength and pride.

Why are the women so bad at playing this part in real life, this Ophelia-Gretchen rôle? Why are they so unwilling to go mad and die for our sakes? They do it regularly on the stage.

But perhaps, after all, we write the plays. What a villain I am, what a black-browed, passionate, ruthless, masculine villain I am, to the leading lady on the stage; and, on the other hand, dear heart, what a hero, what a fount of chivalrous generosity and faith! I am *anything* but a dull and law-abiding citizen. I am a Galahad, full of purity and spirituality, I am the Lancelot of valour and lust; I fold my hands, or I cock my hat on one side, as the case may be; I am *myself*. Only, I am not a respectable citizen, not that, in this hour of my glory and my escape.

Dear Heaven, how Adelaida wept, her voice plashing like violin music, at my ruthless, masculine cruelty. Dear heart, how she sighed to rest on my sheltering bosom! And how I enjoyed my dual nature! How I admired myself!

Adelaida chose *La Moglie del Dottore* for her Evening of Honour. During the following week came a little storm of coloured bills: "Great Evening of Honour of Enrico Persevalli."

This is the leader, the actor-manager. What should he choose for his great occasion, this broad, thick-set, ruddy descendant of the peasant proprietors of the plain? No one knew. The title of the play was not revealed.

So we were staying at home, it was cold and wet. But the maestra came inflammably on that Thursday evening, and were we not going to the theatre, to see *Amleto*?

Poor maestra, she is yellow and bitter-skinned, near fifty, but her dark eyes are still corrosively inflammable. She was engaged to a lieutenant in the cavalry, who got drowned when she was twenty-one. Since then she has hung on the tree unripe, growing yellow and bitter-skinned, never developing.

"*Amleto!*" I say. "Non lo conosco."

A certain fear comes into her eyes. She is schoolmistress, and has a mortal dread of being wrong.

"Si," she cries, wavering, appealing, "una dramma inglese."

"English!" I repeated.

"Yes, an English drama."

"How do you write it?"

Anxiously, she gets a pencil from her reticule, and, with black-gloved scrupulousness, writes *Amleto*.

"*Hamlet!*" I exclaim, wonderingly.

"Ecco, *Amleto!*" cries the maestra, her eyes aflame with thankful justification.

Then I knew that Signor Enrico Persevalli was looking to me for an audience. His Evening of Honour would be a bitter occasion to him if the English were not there to see his performance.

I hurried to get ready, I ran through the rain. I knew he would take it badly that it rained on his Evening of Honour. He counted himself a man who had fate against him.

"Sono un disgraziato, io."

I was late. The first act was nearly over. The play was not yet alive, neither in the bosoms of the actors nor in the audience. I closed the door of the box softly, and came forward. The rolling, Italian eyes of Hamlet glanced up at me. There came a new impulse over the Court of Denmark.

Enrico looked a sad fool in his melancholy black. The doublet sat close, making him stout and vulgar, the knee-breeches seemed to exaggerate the commonness of his thick, rather short, strutting legs. And he carried a long black rag, as a cloak, for histrionic purposes. And he had on his face a portentous grimace of melancholy and philosophic importance. His was the caricature of Hamlet's melancholy self-absorption.

I stooped to arrange my footstool and compose my countenance. I was trying not to grin. For the first time, attired in philosophic melancholy of black silk, Enrico looked a boor and a fool. His close-cropped, rather animal head was common above the effeminate

142

doublet, his sturdy, ordinary figure looked absurd in a melancholic droop.

All the actors alike were out of their element. Their Majesties of Denmark were touching. The Queen, burly little peasant woman, was ill-at-ease in her pink satin. Enrico had had no mercy. He knew she loved to be the scolding servant or housekeeper, with her head tied up in a handkerchief, shrill and vulgar. Yet here she was pranked out in an expanse of satin, la Regina. Regina, indeed!

She obediently did her best to be important. Indeed, she rather fancied herself; she looked sideways at the audience, self-consciously, quite ready to be accepted as an imposing and noble person, if they would esteem her such. Her voice sounded hoarse and common, but whether it was the pink satin in contrast, or a cold, I do not know. She was almost childishly afraid to move. Before she began a speech she looked down and kicked her skirt viciously, so that she was sure it was under control. Then she let go. She was a burly, downright little body of sixty, one rather expected her to box Hamlet on the ears.

Only she liked being a queen when she sat on the throne. There she perched with great satisfaction, her train splendidly displayed down the steps. She was as proud as a child, and she looked like Queen Victoria of the Jubilee period.

The King, her noble consort, also had new honours thrust upon him, as well as new garments. His body was real enough, but it had nothing at all to do with his clothes. They established a separate identity by themselves. But wherever he went, they went with him, to the confusion of everybody.

He was a thin, rather frail-looking peasant, pathetic, and very gentle. There was something pure and fine about him, he was so exceedingly gentle and by natural breeding courteous. But he did not feel kingly, he acted the part with beautiful, simple resignation.

Enrico Persevalli had overshot himself in every direction, but worst of all in his own. He had become a hulking fellow, crawling about with his head ducked between his shoulders, pecking and poking, creeping about after other people, sniffing at them, setting traps for them, absorbed by his own self-important self-consciousness. His legs, in their black knee-breeches, had a crawling, slinking look, he always carried the black rag of a cloak, something for him to twist about as he twisted in his own soul, overwhelmed by a sort of inverted perversity.

I had always felt an aversion from Hamlet: a creeping, unclean thing he seems, on the stage, whether he is Forbes Robertson or anybody else. His nasty poking and sniffing at his mother, his setting traps for the King, his conceited perversion with Ophelia make him always intolerable. The character is repulsive in its conception, based on self-dislike and a spirit of disintegration.

There is, I think, this strain of cold dislike, or self-dislike, through much of the Renaissance art, and through all the later Shakspeare. In Shakspeare it is a kind of corruption in the flesh and a conscious revolt from this. A sense of corruption in the flesh makes Hamlet frenzied, for he will never admit that it is his own flesh. Leonardo da Vinci is the same, but Leonardo loves the corruption, maliciously. Michael Angelo rejects any feeling of corruption, he stands by the flesh, the flesh only. It is the corresponding reaction, but in the opposite direction. But that is all four hundred years ago. Enrico Persevalli has just reached the position. He *is* Hamlet, and evidently he has great satisfaction in the part. He is the modern Italian, suspicious, isolated, self-nauseated, labouring in a sense of physical corruption. But he will not admit it is in himself. He creeps about in self-conceit, transforming his own self-loathing. With what satisfaction did he reveal corruption, corruption in his neighbours he gloated in, letting his mother know he had discovered her incest, her uncleanness, gloated in torturing the incestuous King. Of all the unclean ones, Hamlet was the uncleanest. But he accused only the others.

Except in the "great" speeches, and there Enrico was betrayed, Hamlet suffered the extremity of physical self-loathing, loathing of his own flesh. The play is the statement of the most significant philosophic position of the Renaissance. Hamlet is far more even than Orestes, his prototype, a mental creature, anti-physical, anti-sensual. The whole drama is the tragedy of the convulsed reaction of the mind from the flesh, of the spirit from the self, the reaction from the great aristocratic to the great democratic principle.

An ordinary instinctive man, in Hamlet's position, would either have set about murdering his uncle, by reflex action, or else would have gone right away. There would have been no need for Hamlet to murder his mother. It would have been sufficient blood-vengeance if he had killed his uncle. But that is the statement according to the aristocratic principle.

Orestes was in the same position, but the same position two thousand years earlier, with two thousand years of experience wanting. So that the question was not so intricate in him as in Hamlet, he was not nearly so conscious. The whole Greek life was based on the idea of the supremacy of the self, and the self was always male. Orestes was his father's child, he would be the same whatever mother he had. The mother was but the vehicle, the soil in which the paternal seed was planted. When Clytemnestra murdered Agamemnon, it was as if a common individual murdered God, to the Greek.

But Agamemnon, King and Lord, was not infallible. He was fallible. He had sacrificed Iphigenia for the sake of glory in war, for the fulfilment of the superb idea of self, but on the other hand he had made cruel dissension for the sake of the concubines captured in war. The paternal flesh was fallible, ungodlike. It lusted after meaner pursuits than glory, war, and slaying, it was not faithful to the highest idea of the self. Orestes was driven mad by the furies of his mother, because of the justice that they represented. Nevertheless he was in the end exculpated. The third play of the trilogy is almost foolish, with its prating gods. But it means that, according to the Greek conviction, Orestes was right and Clytemnestra entirely wrong. But for all that, the infallible King, the infallible male Self, is dead in Orestes, killed by the furies of Clytemnestra. He gains his peace of mind after the revulsion from his own physical fallibility, but he will never be an unquestioned lord, as Agamemnon was. Orestes is left at peace, neutralised. He is the beginning of non-aristocratic Christianity.

Hamlet's father, the King, is like Agamemnon a warrior-king. But, unlike Agamemnon, he is blameless with regard to Gertrude. Yet Gertrude, like Clytemnestra, is the potential murderer of her husband, as Lady Macbeth is murderess, as the daughters of Lear. The women murder the supreme male, the ideal Self, the King and Father.

This is the tragic position Shakspeare must dwell upon. The woman rejects, repudiates the ideal Self which the male represents to her. The supreme representative, King and Father, is murdered by the Wife and the Daughters.

What is the reason? Hamlet goes mad in a revulsion of rage and nausea. Yet the women-murderers only represent some ultimate judgment in his own soul. At the bottom of his own soul Hamlet has decided that the Self in its supremacy, Father and King, must die. It is a suicidal decision for his involuntary soul to have arrived at. Yet it is inevitable. The great religious, philosophic tide, which had been swelling all through the Middle Ages, had brought him there.

The question, to be or not to be, which Hamlet puts himself, does not mean, to live or not to live. It is not the simple human being who puts himself the question, it is the supreme I, King and Father. To be or not to be King, Father, in the Self supreme? And the decision is, not to be.

It is the inevitable philosophic conclusion of all the Renaissance. The deepest impulse in man, the religious impulse, is the desire to be immortal, or infinite, consummated. And this impulse is satisfied in fulfilment of an idea, a steady progression. In this progression man is satisfied, he seems to have reached his goal, this infinity, this immortality, this eternal being, with every step nearer which he takes.

And so, according to his idea of fulfilment, man establishes the whole order of life. If my fulfilment is the fulfilment and establishment of the unknown divine Self which I am, then I shall proceed in the realising of the greatest idea of the self, the highest conception of the I, my order of life will be kingly, imperial, aristocratic. The body politic also will culminate in this divinity of the flesh, this body imbued with glory, invested with divine power and might, the King, the Emperor. In the body politic also I shall desire a king, an emperor, a tyrant, glorious, mighty, in whom I see myself consummated and fulfilled. This is inevitable!

But during the Middle Ages, struggling within this pagan, original transport, the transport of the Ego, was a small dissatisfaction, a small contrary desire. Amid the pomp of kings and popes was the Child Jesus and the Madonna. Jesus the King gradually dwindled down. There was Jesus the Child, helpless, at the mercy of all the world. And there was Jesus crucified.

The old transport, the old fulfilment of the Ego, the Davidian ecstasy, the assuming of all power and glory unto the self, the becoming infinite through the absorption of all into the Ego, this gradually became unsatisfactory. This was not the infinite, this was not immortality. This was eternal death, this was damnation.

The monk rose up with his opposite ecstasy, the Christian ecstasy. There was a death to die: the flesh, the self, must die, so that the spirit should rise again immortal, eternal, infinite. I am dead unto myself, but I live in the Infinite. The finite Me is no more, only the Infinite, the Eternal, is.

At the Renaissance this great Half-Truth overcame the other great Half-Truth. The Christian Infinite, reached by a process of abnegation, a process of being absorbed, dissolved, diffused into the great Not-Self, supplanted the old pagan Infinite, wherein the self like a root threw out branches and radicles which embraced the whole universe, became the Whole.

There is only one Infinite, the world now cried, there is the great Christian Infinite of renunciation and consummation in the not-self. The other, that old pride, is damnation. The sin of sins is Pride, it is the way to total damnation. Whereas the pagans based their life on pride.

And according to this new Infinite, reached through renunciation and dissolving into the Others, the Neighbour, man must build up his actual form of life. With Savonarola and Martin Luther the living Church actually transformed itself, for the Roman Church was still pagan. Henry VIII. simply said, "There is no Church, there is only the State." But with Shakspeare the transformation had reached the State also. The King, the Father, the representative of the Consummate Self, the maximum of all life, the symbol of the consummate being, the becoming Supreme, Godlike, Infinite, he must perish and pass away. This Infinite was not infinite, this consummation was not consummate, all this was fallible, false. It was rotten, corrupt. It must go. But Shakspeare was also the thing itself. Hence his horror, his frenzy, his self-loathing.

The King, the Emperor is killed in the soul of man, the old order of life is over, the old tree is dead at the root. So said Shakspeare. It was finally enacted in Cromwell. Charles I. took up the old position of kingship by divine right. Like Hamlet's father, he was blameless otherwise. But as representative of the old form of life, which mankind now hated with frenzy, he must be cut down, removed. It was a symbolic act.

The world, our world of Europe, had now really turned, swung round to a new goal, a new idea, the Infinite reached through the omission of Self. God is all that which is Not-Me. I am consummate when my Self, the resistant solid, is reduced and diffused into all that which is Not-Me: my neighbour, my enemy, the great Otherness. Then I am perfect.

And from this belief the world began gradually to form a new State, a new body politic, in which the Self should be removed. There should be no king, no lords, no aristocrats. The world continued in its religious belief, beyond the French Revolution, beyond the great movement of Shelley and Godwin. There should be no Self. That which was supreme was that which was Not-Me, the other. The governing factor in the State was the idea of the good of others; that is, the Common Good. And the *vital* governing idea in the State has been this idea since Cromwell.

Before Cromwell the idea was "For the King," because every man saw himself consummated in the King. After Cromwell the idea was "For the good of my neighbour," or "For the good of the people," or "For the good of the whole." This has been our ruling idea, by which we have more or less lived.

Now this has failed. Now we say that the Christian Infinite is not infinite. We are tempted, like Nietzsche, to return back to the old pagan Infinite, to say that is supreme. Or we are inclined, like the English and the Pragmatist, to say, "There is no Infinite, there is no Absolute. The only Absolute is expediency, the only reality is sensation and momentariness." But we may say this, even act on it, *à la Sanine*. But we never believe it.

What is really Absolute is the mystic Reason which connects both Infinites, the Holy Ghost that relates both natures of God. If we now wish to make a living State, we must build it up to the idea of the Holy Spirit, the supreme Relationship. We must say, the pagan Infinite is infinite, the Christian Infinite is infinite: these are our two Consummations, in both of these we are consummated. But that which relates them alone is absolute.

This Absolute of the Holy Ghost we may call Truth or Justice or Right. These are partial names, indefinite and unsatisfactory unless there be kept the knowledge of the two Infinites, pagan and Christian, which they go between. When both are there, they are like a superb bridge, on which one can stand and know the whole world, my world, the two halves of the universe.

"Essere, o non essere, è qui il punto."

To be or not to be was the question for Hamlet to settle. It is no longer our question, at least, not in the same sense. When it is a question of death, the fashionable young suicide declares that his self-destruction is the final proof of his own incontrovertible being. And as for not-being in our public life, we have achieved it as much as ever we want to, as much as is necessary. Whilst in private life there is a swing back to paltry selfishness as a creed. And in the war there is the position of neutralisation and nothingness. It is a question of knowing how *to be*, and how *not to be*, for we must fulfil both.

Enrico Persevalli was detestable with his "Essere, o non essere." He whispered it in a hoarse whisper as if it were some melodramatic murder he was about to commit. As a matter of fact, he knows quite well, and has known all his life, that his pagan Infinite, his transport of the flesh and the supremacy of the male in fatherhood, is all unsatis-

148

factory. All his life he has really cringed before the northern Infinite of the Not-Self, although he has continued in the Italian habit of Self. But it is mere habit, sham.

How can he know anything about being and not-being when he is only a maudlin compromise between them, and all he wants is to be a maudlin compromise? He is neither one nor the other. He has neither being nor not-being. He is as equivocal as the monks. He was detestable, mouthing Hamlet's sincere words. He has still to let go, to know what not-being is, before he can *be*. Till he has gone through the Christian negation of himself, and has known the Christian consummation, he is a mere amorphous heap.

For the soliloquies of Hamlet are as deep as the soul of man can go, in one direction, and as sincere as the Holy Spirit itself in their essence. But thank heaven, the bog into which Hamlet struggled is almost surpassed.

It is a strange thing, if a man covers his face, and speaks with his eyes blinded, how significant and poignant he becomes. The ghost of this Hamlet was very simple. He was wrapped down to the knees in a great white cloth, and over his face was an open-work woollen shawl. But the naïve blind helplessness and verity of his voice was strangely convincing. He seemed the most real thing in the play. From the knees downward he was Laertes, because he had on Laertes' white trousers and patent leather slippers. Yet he was strangely real, a voice out of the dark.

The Ghost is really one of the play's failures, it is so trivial and unspiritual and vulgar. And it was spoilt for me from the first. When I was a child I went to the twopenny travelling theatre to see *Hamlet*. The Ghost had on a helmet and a breastplate. I sat in pale transport.

"'Amblet, 'Amblet, I *am* thy father's ghost."

Then came a voice from the dark, silent audience, like a cynical knife to my fond soul:

"Why tha arena, I can tell thy voice."

The peasants loved Ophelia: she was in white with her hair down her back. Poor thing, she was pathetic, demented. And no wonder, after Hamlet's "O, that this too, too solid flesh would melt!" What then of her young breasts and her womb? Hamlet with her was a very disagreeable sight. The peasants loved her. There was a hoarse roar, half of indignation, half of roused passion, at the end of her scene.

The graveyard scene, too, was a great success, but I could not bear Hamlet. And the grave-digger in Italian was a mere buffoon. The whole scene was farcical to me because of the Italian, "Questo cranio, Signore——" And Enrico, dainty fellow, took the skull in a corner of his black cloak. As an Italian, he would not willingly touch it. It was unclean. But he looked a fool, hulking himself in his lugubriousness. He was as self-important as D'Annunzio.

The close fell flat. The peasants had applauded the whole graveyard scene wildly. But at the end of all they got up and crowded to the doors, as if to hurry away: this in spite of Enrico's final feat: he fell backwards, smack down three steps of the throne platform, on to the stage. But planks and braced muscle will bounce, and Signor Amleto bounced quite high again.

It was the end of *Amleto*, and I was glad. But I loved the theatre, I loved to look down on the peasants, who were so absorbed. At the end of the scenes the men pushed back their black hats, and rubbed their hair across their brows with a pleased, excited movement. And the women stirred in their seats.

Just one man was with his wife and child, and he was of the same race as my old woman at San Tommaso. He was fair, thin, and clear, abstract, of the mountains. He seemed to have gathered his wife and child together into another, finer atmosphere, like the air of the mountains, and to guard them in it. This is the real Joseph, father of the child. He has a fierce, abstract look, wild and untamed as a hawk, but like a hawk at its own nest, fierce with love. He goes out and buys a tiny bottle of lemonade for a penny, and the mother and child sip it in tiny sips, whilst he bends over, like a hawk arching its wings.

It is the fierce spirit of the Ego come out of the primal infinite, but detached, isolated, an aristocrat. He is not an Italian, dark-blooded. He is fair, keen as steel, with the blood of the mountaineer in him. He is like my old spinning woman. It is curious how, with his wife and child, he makes a little separate world down there in the theatre, like a hawk's nest, high and arid under the gleaming sky.

The bersaglieri sit close together in groups, so that there is a strange, corporal connection between them. They have close-cropped, dark, slightly bestial heads, and thick shoulders, and thick brown hands on each other's shoulders. When an act is over they pick up their cherished hats and fling on their cloaks and go into the hall. They are rather rich, the bersaglieri.

They are like young, half-wild oxen, such strong, sturdy, dark lads, thickly built and with strange hard heads, like young male caryatides. They keep close together, as if there were some physical instinct connecting them. And they are quite womanless. There is a curious inter-absorption among themselves, a sort of physical trance that holds them all, and puts their minds to sleep. There is a strange, hypnotic unanimity among them as they put on their plumed hats and go out together, always very close, as if their bodies must touch. Then they feel safe and content in this heavy, physical trance. They are in love with one another, the young men love the young men. They shrink from the world beyond, from the outsiders, from all who are not bersaglieri of their barracks.

One man is a sort of leader. He is very straight and solid, solid like a wall, with a dark, unblemished will. His cock-feathers slither in a profuse, heavy stream from his black oil-cloth hat, almost to his shoulder. He swings round. His feathers slip in a cascade. Then he goes out to the hall, his feathers tossing and falling richly. He must be well off. The bersaglieri buy their own black cock's-plumes, and some pay twenty or thirty francs for the bunch, so the maestra said. The poor ones have only poor, scraggy plumes.

There is something very primitive about these men. They remind me really of Agamemnon's soldiers clustered on the seashore, men, all men, a living, vigorous, physical host of men. But there is a pressure on these Italian soldiers, as if they were men caryatides, with a great weight on their heads, making their brain hard, asleep, stunned. They all look as if their real brain were stunned, as if there were another centre of physical consciousness from which they lived.

Separate from them all is Pietro, the young man who lounges on the wharf to carry things from the steamer. He starts up from sleep like a wild-cat as somebody claps him on the shoulder. It is the start of a man who has many enemies. He is almost an outlaw. Will he ever find himself in prison? He is the *gamin* of the village, well detested.

He is twenty-four years old, thin, dark, handsome, with a cat-like lightness and grace, and a certain repulsive, *gamin* evil in his face. Where everybody is so clean and tidy, he is almost ragged. His week's beard shows very black in his slightly hollow cheeks. He hates the man who has waked him by clapping him on the shoulder.

Pietro is already married, yet he behaves as if he were not. He has been carrying-on with a loose woman, the wife of the citron-coloured barber, the Siciliano. Then he seats himself on the women's side of the theatre, behind a young person from Bogliaco, who also has no reputation, and makes her talk to him. He leans forward, resting his arms on the seat before him, stretching his slender, cat-like, flexible loins. The padrona of the hotel hates him—"ein frecher Kerl," she says with contempt, and she looks away. Her eyes hate to see him.

In the village there is the clerical party, which is the majority, there is the anti-clerical party, and there are the ne'er-do-wells. The clerical people are dark and pious and cold; there is a curious stone-cold, ponderous darkness over them, moral and gloomy. Then the anti-clerical party, with the Syndaco at the head, is bourgeois and respectable as far as the middle-aged people are concerned, banal, respectable, shut off as by a wall from the clerical people. The young anti-clericals are the young bloods of the place, the men who gather every night in the more expensive and less-respectable café. These young men are all free-thinkers, great dancers, singers, players of the guitar. They are immoral and slightly cynical. Their leader is the young shopkeeper, who has lived in Vienna, who is a bit of a bounder, with a veneer of sneering irony on an original good nature. He is well-to-do, and gives dances to which only the looser women go, with these reckless young men. He also gets up parties of pleasure, and is chiefly responsible for the coming of the players to the theatre this carnival. These young men are disliked, but they belong to the important class, they are well-to-do, and they have the life of the village in their hands. The clerical peasants are priest-ridden and good, because they are poor and afraid and superstitious. There is, lastly, a sprinkling of loose women, one who keeps the inn where the soldiers drink. These women are a definite set. They know what they are, they pretend nothing else. They are not prostitutes, but just loose women. They keep to their own clique, among men and women, never wanting to compromise anybody else.

And beyond all these there are the Franciscan friars in their brown robes, so shy, so silent, so obliterated, as they stand back in the shop, waiting to buy the bread for the monastery, waiting obscure and neutral, till no one shall be in the shop wanting to be served. The village women speak to them in a curious neutral, official, slightly contemptuous voice. They answer neutral and humble, though distinctly.

At the theatre, now the play is over, the peasants in their black hats and cloaks crowd the hall. Only Pietro, the wharf-lounger, has no cloak, and a bit of a cap on the side of his head instead of a black felt hat. His clothes are thin and loose on his thin, vigorous, cat-like body, and he is cold, but he takes no notice. His hands are always in his pockets, his shoulders slightly raised.

The few women slip away home. In the little theatre-bar the well-to-do young atheists are having another drink. Not that they spend much. A tumbler of wine or a glass of vermouth costs a penny. And the wine is horrible new stuff. Yet the little baker, Agostino, sits on a bench with his pale baby on his knee, putting the wine to its lips. And the baby drinks, like a blind fledgling.

Upstairs, the quality has paid its visits and shaken hands: the Syndaco and the well-to-do, half-Austrian owners of the woodyard, the Bertolini, have ostentatiously shown their mutual friendship; our padrone, the Signor Pietro di Paoli, has visited his relatives the Graziani in the box next the stage, and has spent two intervals with us in our box; meanwhile, his two peasants standing down below, pathetic, thin contadini of the old school, like worn stones, have looked up at us as if we are the angels in heaven, with a reverential, devotional eye, they themselves far away below, standing in the bay at the back, below all.

The chemist and the grocer and the schoolmistress pay calls. They have all sat self-consciously posed in the front of their boxes, like framed photographs of themselves. The second grocer and the baker visit each other. The barber looks in on the carpenter, then drops downstairs among the crowd. Class distinctions are cut very fine. As we pass with the padrona of the hotel, who is a Bavarian, we stop to speak to our own padroni, the di Paoli. They have a warm handshake and effusive polite conversation for us; for Maria Samuelli, a distant bow. We realise our mistake.

The barber—not the Siciliano, but flashy little Luigi with the big tie-ring and the curls—knows all about the theatre. He says that Enrico Persevalli has for his mistress Carina, the servant in *Ghosts*: that the thin, gentle, old-looking king in *Hamlet* is the husband of Adelaida, and Carina is their daughter: that the old, sharp, fat little body of a queen is Adelaida's mother: that they all like Enrico Persevalli, because he is a very clever man: but that the "Comic," Il Brillante, Francesco, is unsatisfied.

In three performances in Epiphany week, the company took two hundred and sixty-five francs, which was phenomenal. The manager, Enrico Persevalli, and Adelaida pay twenty-four francs for every performance, or every evening on which a performance is given, as rent for the theatre, including light. The company is completely satisfied with its reception on the Lago di Garda.

So it is all over. The bersaglieri go running all the way home, because it is already past half-past ten. The night is very dark. About four miles up the lake the searchlights of the Austrian border are swinging, looking for smugglers. Otherwise the darkness is complete.

IV. San Gaudenzio

In the autumn the little rosy cyclamens blossom in the shade of this west side of the lake. They are very cold and fragrant, and their scent seems to belong to Greece, to the Bacchae. They are real flowers of the past. They seem to be blossoming in the landscape of Phaedra and Helen. They bend down, they brood like little chill fires. They are little living myths that I cannot understand.

After the cyclamens the Christmas roses are in bud. It is at this season that the cachi are ripe on the trees in the garden, whole naked trees full of lustrous, orange-yellow, paradisal fruit, gleaming against the wintry blue sky. The monthly roses still blossom frail and pink, there are still crimson and yellow roses. But the vines are bare and the lemon-houses shut. And then, in mid-winter, the lowest buds of the Christmas roses appear under the hedges and rocks and by the streams. They are very lovely, these first, large, cold, pure buds, like violets, like magnolias, but cold, lit up with the light from the snow.

The days go by, through the brief silence of winter, when the sunshine is so still and pure, like iced wine, and the dead leaves gleam brown, and water sounds hoarse in the ravines. It is so still and transcendent, the cypress trees poise like flames of forgotten darkness, that should have been blown out at the end of the summer. For as we have candles to light the darkness of night, so the cypresses are candles to keep the darkness aflame in the full sunshine.

Meanwhile, the Christmas roses become many. They rise from their budded, intact humbleness near the ground, they rise up, they throw up their crystal, they become handsome, they are heaps of confident, mysterious whiteness in the shadow of a rocky stream. It is almost uncanny to see them. They are the flowers of darkness, white and wonderful beyond belief.

Then their radiance becomes soiled and brown, they thaw, break, and scatter and vanish away. Already the primroses are coming out, and the almond is in bud. The winter is passing away. On the mountains the fierce snow gleams apricot gold as evening approaches, golden, apricot, but so bright that it is almost frightening. What can be so fiercely gleaming when all is shadowy? It is something inhuman and unmitigated between heaven and earth.

The heavens are strange and proud all the winter, their progress goes on without reference to the dim earth. The dawns come white and translucent, the lake is a moonstone in the dark hills, then across the lake there stretches a vein of fire, then a whole, orange, flashing track over the whiteness. There is the exquisite silent passage of the day, and then at evening the afterglow, a huge incandescence of rose, hanging above and gleaming, as if it were the presence of a host of angels in rapture. It gleams like a rapturous chorus, then passes away, and the stars appear, large and flashing.

Meanwhile, the primroses are dawning on the ground, their light is growing stronger, spreading over the banks and under the bushes. Between the olive roots the violets are out, large, white, grave violets, and less serious blue ones. And looking down the hill, among the grey smoke of olive leaves, pink puffs of smoke are rising up. It is the almond and the apricot trees, it is the Spring.

Soon the primroses are strong on the ground. There is a bank of small, frail crocuses shooting the lavender into this spring. And then the tussocks and tussocks of primroses are fully out, there is full morning everywhere on the banks and roadsides and stream-sides, and around the olive roots, a morning of primroses underfoot, with an invisible threading of many violets, and then the lovely blue clusters of hepatica, really like pieces of blue sky showing through a clarity of primrose. The few birds are piping thinly and shyly, the streams sing again, there is a strange flowering shrub full of incense, overturned flowers of crimson and gold, like Bohemian glass. Between the olive roots new grass is coming, day is leaping all clear and coloured from the earth, it is full Spring, full first rapture.

Does it pass away, or does it only lose its pristine quality? It deepens and intensifies, like experience. The days seem to be darker and richer, there is a sense of power in the strong air. On the banks by the lake the orchids are out, many, many pale bee-orchids standing clear from the short grass over the lake. And in the hollows are the grape hyacinths, purple as noon, with the heavy, sensual fragrance of noon. They are many-breasted, and full of milk, and ripe, and sun-darkened, like many-breasted Diana.

We could not bear to live down in the village any more, now that the days opened large and spacious and the evenings drew out in sunshine. We could not bear the indoors, when above us the mountains shone in clear air. It was time to go up, to climb with the sun.

So after Easter we went to San Gaudenzio. It was three miles away, up the winding mule-track that climbed higher and higher along the lake. Leaving the last house of the village, the path wound on the steep, cliff-like side of the lake, curving into the hollow where the landslip had tumbled the rocks in chaos, then out again on to the bluff of a headland that hung over the lake.

Thus we came to the tall barred gate of San Gaudenzio, on which was the usual little fire-insurance tablet, and then the advertisements for beer, "Birra, Verona," which is becoming a more and more popular drink.

Through the gate, inside the high wall, is the little Garden of Eden, a property of three or four acres fairly level upon a headland over the lake. The high wall girds it on the land side, and makes it perfectly secluded. On the lake side it is bounded by the sudden drops of the land, in sharp banks and terraces, overgrown with ilex and with laurel bushes, down to the brink of the cliff, so that the thicket of the first declivities seem to safeguard the property.

The pink farmhouse stands almost in the centre of the little territory, among the olive trees. It is a solid, six-roomed place, about fifty years old, having been rebuilt by Paolo's uncle. Here we came to live for a time with the Fiori, Maria and Paolo, and their three children, Giovanni and Marco and Felicina.

Paolo had inherited, or partly inherited, San Gaudenzio, which had been in his family for generations. He was a peasant of fifty-three, very grey and wrinkled and worn-looking, but at the same time robust, with full strong limbs and a powerful chest. His face was old, but his body was solid and powerful. His eyes were blue like upper ice, beautiful. He had been a fair-haired man, now he was almost white.

He was strangely like the pictures of peasants in the northern Italian pictures, with the same curious nobility, the same aristocratic, eternal look of motionlessness, something statuesque. His head was hard and fine, the bone finely constructed, though the skin of his face was loose and furrowed with work. His temples had that fine, hard clarity which is seen in Mantegna, an almost jewel-like quality.

We all loved Paolo, he was so finished in his being, detached, with an almost classic simplicity and gentleness, an eternal kind of sureness. There was also something concluded and unalterable about him, something inaccessible.

Maria Fiori was different. She was from the plain, like Enrico Persevalli and the bersaglieri from the Venetian district. She reminded me again of oxen, broad-boned and massive in physique, dark-skinned, slow in her soul. But, like the oxen of the plain, she knew her work, she knew the other people engaged in the work. Her intelligence was attentive and purposive. She had been a housekeeper, a servant, in

Venice and Verona before her marriage. She had got the hang of this world of commerce and activity, she wanted to master it. But she was weighted down by her heavy animal blood.

Paolo and she were the opposite sides of the universe, the light and the dark. Yet they lived together now without friction, detached, each subordinated in their common relationship. With regard to Maria, Paolo omitted himself, Maria omitted herself with regard to Paolo. Their souls were silent and detached, completely apart, and silent, quite silent. They shared the physical relationship of marriage as if it were something beyond them, a third thing.

They had suffered very much in the earlier stages of their connection. Now the storm had gone by, leaving them, as it were, spent. They were both by nature passionate, vehement. But the lines of their passion were opposite. Hers was the primitive, crude, violent flux of the blood, emotional and undiscriminating, but wanting to mix and mingle. His was the hard, clear, invulnerable passion of the bones, finely-tempered and unchangeable. She was the flint and he the steel. But in continual striking together they only destroyed each other. The fire was a third thing, belonging to neither of them.

She was still heavy and full of desire. She was much younger than he.

"How long did you know your Signora before you were married?" she asked me.

"Six weeks," I said.

"Il Paolo e me, venti giorni, tre settimani," she cried vehemently. Three weeks they had known each other when they married. She still triumphed in the fact. So did Paolo. But it was past, strangely and rather terribly past.

What did they want when they came together, Paolo and she? He was a man over thirty, she was a woman of twenty-three. They were both violent in desire and of strong will. They came together at once, like two wrestlers almost matched in strength. Their meetings must have been splendid. Giovanni, the eldest child, was a tall lad of sixteen, with soft brown hair and grey eyes, and a clarity of brow, and the same calm simplicity of bearing which made Paolo so complete, but the son had at the same time a certain brownness of skin, a heaviness of blood, which he had from his mother. Paolo was so clear and translucent.

In Giovanni the fusion of the parents was perfect, he was a perfect spark from the flint and steel. There was in Paolo a subtle intelligence in feeling, a delicate appreciation of the other person. But the mind was unintelligent, he could not grasp a new order. Maria Fiori was much sharper and more adaptable to the ways of the world. Paolo had an almost glass-like quality, fine and clear and perfectly tempered; but he was also finished and brittle. Maria was much coarser, more vulgar, but also she was more human, more fertile, with crude potentiality. His passion was too fixed in its motion, hers too loose and over-whelming.

But Giovanni was beautiful, gentle, and courtly like Paolo, but warm, like Maria, ready to flush like a girl with anger or confusion. He stood straight and tall, and seemed to look into the far distance with his clear grey eyes. Yet also he could look at one and touch one with his look, he could meet one. Paolo's blue eyes were like the eyes of the old spinning-woman, clear and blue and belonging to the mountains, their vision seemed to end in space, abstract. They reminded me of the eyes of the eagle, which looks into the sun, and which teaches its young to do the same, although they are unwilling.

Marco, the second son, was thirteen years old. He was his mother's favourite. Giovanni loved his father best. But Marco was his mother's son, with the same brown-gold and red complexion, like a pome-granate, and coarse black hair, and brown eyes like pebble, like agate, like an animal's eyes. He had the same broad, bovine figure, though he was only a boy. But there was some discrepancy in him. He was not unified, he had no identity.

He was strong and full of animal life, but always aimless, as though his wits scarcely controlled him. But he loved his mother with a fundamental, generous, undistinguishing love. Only he always forgot what he was going to do. He was much more sensitive than Maria, more shy and reluctant. But his shyness, his sensitiveness only made him more aimless and awkward, a tiresome clown, slack and un-controlled, witless. All day long his mother shouted and shrilled and scolded at him, or hit him angrily. He did not mind, he came up like a cork, warm and roguish and curiously appealing. She loved him with a fierce protective love, grounded on pain. There was such a split, a contrariety in his soul, one part reacting against the other, which landed him always into trouble.

It was when Marco was a baby that Paolo had gone to America. They were poor on San Gaudenzio. There were the few olive trees, the grapes, and the fruit; there was the one cow. But these scarcely made a living. Neither was Maria content with the real peasants' lot any more, polenta at mid-day and vegetable soup in the evening, and no way out, nothing to look forward to, no future, only this eternal present. She had been in service, and had eaten bread and drunk coffee, and known the flux and variable chance of life. She had departed from the old static conception. She knew what one might be, given a certain chance. The fixture was the thing she militated against. So Paolo went to America, to California, into the gold mines.

Maria wanted the future, the endless possibility of life on earth. She wanted her sons to be freer, to achieve a new plane of living. The peasant's life was a slave's life, she said, railing against the poverty and the drudgery. And it was quite true, Paolo and Giovanni worked twelve and fourteen hours a day at heavy laborious work that would have broken an Englishman. And there was nothing at the end of it. Yet Paolo was even happy so. This was the truth to him.

It was the mother who wanted things different. It was she who railed and railed against the miserable life of the peasants. When we were going to throw to the fowls a dry broken penny roll of white bread, Maria said, with anger and shame and resentment in her voice. "Give it to Marco, he will eat it. It isn't too dry for him."

White bread was a treat for them even now, when everybody eats bread. And Maria Fiori hated it, that bread should be a treat to her children, when it was the meanest food of all the rest of the world. She was in opposition to this order. She did not want her sons to be peasants, fixed and static as posts driven in the earth. She wanted them to be in the great flux of life, in the midst of all possibilities. So she at length sent Paolo to America to the gold-mines. Meanwhile, she covered the wall of her parlour with picture postcards, to bring the outer world of cities and industries into her house.

Paolo was entirely remote from Maria's world. He had not yet even grasped the fact of money, not thoroughly. He reckoned in land and olive trees. So he had the old fatalistic attitude to his circumstances, even to his food. The earth was the Lord's and the fulness thereof: also the leanness thereof. Paolo could only do his part and leave the rest. If he ate in plenty, having oil and wine and sausage in the house, and plenty of maize-meal, he was glad with the Lord. If he ate meagrely, of poor polenta, that was fate, it was the skies that ruled these things, and no man ruled the skies. He took his fate as it fell from the skies.

Maria was exorbitant about money. She would charge us all she could for what we had and for what was done for us.

Yet she was not mean in her soul. In her soul she was in a state of anger because of her own closeness. It was a violation to her strong animal nature. Yet her mind had wakened to the value of money. She knew she could alter her position, the position of her children, by virtue of money. She knew it was only money that made the difference between master and servant. And this was all the difference she would acknowledge. So she ruled her life according to money. Her supreme passion was to be mistress rather than servant, her supreme aspiration for her children was that in the end they might be masters and not servants.

Paolo was untouched by all this. For him there was some divinity about a master which even America had not destroyed. If we came in for supper whilst the family was still at table he would have the children at once take their plates to the wall, he would have Maria at once set the table for us, though their own meal were never finished. And this was not servility, it was the dignity of a religious conception. Paolo regarded us as belonging to the Signoria, those who are elect, near to God. And this was part of his religious service. His life was a ritual. It was very beautiful, but it made me unhappy, the purity of his spirit was so sacred and the actual facts seemed such a sacrilege to it. Maria was nearer to the actual truth when she said that money was the only distinction. But Paolo had hold of an eternal truth, where hers was temporal. Only Paolo misapplied this eternal truth. He should not have given Giovanni the inferior status and a fat, mean, Italian tradesman the superior. That was false, a real falsity. Maria knew it and hated it. But Paolo could not distinguish between the accident of riches and the aristocracy of the spirit. So Maria rejected him altogether, and went to the other extreme. We were all human beings like herself; naked, there was no distinction between us, no higher nor lower. But we were possessed of more money than she. And she had to steer her course between these two conceptions. The money alone made the real distinction, the separation; the being, the life made the common level.

Paolo had the curious peasants' avarice also, but it was not meanness. It was a sort of religious conservation of his own power, his own self. Fortunately he could leave all business transactions on our account to Maria, so that his relation with us was purely ritualistic. He would have given me anything, trusting implicitly that I would fulfil my own nature as Signore, one of those more god-like, nearer the light of perfection than himself, a peasant. It was pure bliss to him to bring us the first-fruit of the garden, it was like laying it on an altar.

And his fulfilment was in a fine, subtle, exquisite relationship, not of manners, but subtle interappreciation. He worshipped a finer understanding and a subtler tact. A further fineness and dignity and freedom in bearing was to him an approach towards the divine, so he loved men best of all, they fulfilled his soul. A woman was always a woman, and sex was a low level whereon he did not esteem himself. But a man, a doer, the instrument of God, he was really god-like.

Paolo was a conservative. For him the world was established and divine in its establishment. His vision grasped a small circle. A finer nature, a higher understanding, took in a greater circle, comprehended the whole. So that when Paolo was in relation to a man of further vision, he himself was extended towards the whole. Thus he was fulfilled. And his initial assumption was that every Signore, every gentleman, was a man of further, purer vision than himself. This assumption was false. But Maria's assumption, that no one had a further vision, no one was more elect than herself, that we are all one flesh and blood and being, was even more false. Paolo was mistaken in actual life, but Maria was ultimately mistaken.

Paolo, conservative as he was, believing that a priest must be a priest of God, yet very rarely went to church. And he used the religious oaths that Maria hated, even *Porca-Maria*. He always used oaths, either Bacchus or God or Mary or the Sacrament. Maria was always offended. Yet it was she who, in her soul, jeered at the Church and at religion. She wanted the human society as the absolute, without religious abstractions. So Paolo's oaths enraged her, because of their profanity, she said. But it was really because of their subscribing to another superhuman order. She jeered at the clerical people. She made a loud clamour of derision when the parish priest of the village above went down to the big village on the lake, and across the piazza, the quay, with two pigs in a sack on his shoulder. This was a real picture of the sacred minister to her.

One day, when a storm had blown down an olive tree in front of the house, and Paolo and Giovanni were beginning to cut it up, this same priest of Mugiano came to San Gaudenzio. He was an iron-grey, thin, disreputable-looking priest, very talkative and loud and queer. He seemed like an old ne'er-do-well in priests' black, and he talked loudly, almost to himself, as drunken people do. At once *he* must show the Fiori how to cut up the tree, he must have the axe from Paolo. He shouted to Maria for a glass of wine. She brought it out to him with a sort of insolent deference, insolent contempt of the man and traditional deference to the cloth. The priest drained the tumblerful of wine at one drink, his thin throat with its Adam's apple working. And he did not pay the penny.

Then he stripped off his cassock and put away his hat, and, a ludicrous figure in ill-fitting black knee-breeches and a not very clean shirt, a red handkerchief round his neck, he proceeded to give great extravagant blows at the tree. He was like a caricature. In the doorway Maria was encouraging him rather jeeringly, whilst she winked at me. Marco was stifling his hysterical amusement in his mother's apron, and prancing with glee. Paolo and Giovanni stood by the fallen tree, very grave and unmoved, inscrutable, abstract. Then the youth came away to the doorway, with a flush mounting on his face and a grimace distorting its youngness. Only Paolo, unmoved and detached, stood by the tree with unchanging, abstract face, very strange, his eyes fixed in the ageless stare which is so characteristic.

Meanwhile the priest swung drunken blows at the tree, his thin buttocks bending in the green-black broadcloth, supported on thin shanks, and thin throat growing dull purple in the red-knotted kerchief. Nevertheless he was doing the job. His face was wet with sweat. He wanted another glass of wine.

He took no notice of us. He was strangely a local, even a mountebank figure, but entirely local, an appurtenance of the district.

It was Maria who jeeringly told us the story of the priest, who shrugged her shoulders to imply that he was a contemptible figure. Paolo sat with the abstract look on his face, as of one who hears and does not hear, is not really concerned. He never opposed or contradicted her, but stayed apart. It was she who was violent and brutal in her ways. But sometimes Paolo went into a rage, and then Maria, everybody, was afraid. It was a white, heavy rage, when his blue eyes shone unearthly, and his mouth opened with a curious drawn blindness of the old Furies. There was something of the cruelty of a falling mass of snow, heavy, horrible. Maria drew away, there was a silence. Then the avalanche was finished.

They must have had some cruel fights before they learned to withdraw from each other so completely. They must have begotten Marco in hatred, terrible disintegrated opposition and otherness. And it was after this, after the child of their opposition was born, that Paolo went away to California, leaving his San Gaudenzio, travelling with several companions, like blind beasts, to Havre, and thence to New York, then to California. He stayed five years in the gold-mines, in a wild valley, living with a gang of Italians in a town of corrugated iron.

All the while he had never really left San Gaudenzio. I asked him, "Used you to think of it, the lake, the Monte Baldo, the laurel trees down the slope?" He tried to see what I wanted to know. Yes, he said—but uncertainly. I could see that he had never been really homesick. It had been very wretched on the ship going from Havre to New York. That he told me about. And he told me about the gold-mines, the galleries, the valley, the huts in the valley. But he had never really fretted for San Gaudenzio whilst he was in California.

In real truth he was at San Gaudenzio all the time, his fate was riveted there. His going away was an excursion from reality, a kind of sleep-walking. He left his own reality there in the soil above the lake of Garda. That his body was in California, what did it matter? It was merely for a time, and for the sake of his own earth, his land. He would pay off the mortgage. But the gate at home was his gate all the time, his hand was on the latch.

As for Maria, he had felt his duty towards her. She was part of his little territory, the rooted centre of the world. He sent her home the money. But it did not occur to him, in his soul, to miss her. He wanted her to be safe with the children, that was all. In his flesh perhaps he missed the woman. But his spirit was even more completely isolated since marriage. Instead of having united with each other, they had made each other more terribly distinct and separate. He could live alone eternally. It was his condition. His sex was functional, like eating and drinking. To take a woman, a prostitute at the camp, or not to take her, was no more vitally important than to get drunk or not to get drunk of a Sunday. And fairly often on Sunday Paolo got drunk. His world remained unaltered.

But Maria suffered more bitterly. She was a young, powerful, passionate woman, and she was unsatisfied body and soul. Her soul's unsatisfaction became a bodily unsatisfaction. Her blood was heavy, violent, anarchic, insisting on the equality of the blood in all, and therefore on her own absolute right to satisfaction.

She took a wine licence for San Gaudenzio, and she sold wine. There were many scandals about her. Somehow it did not matter very much, outwardly. The authorities were too divided among themselves to enforce public opinion. Between the clerical party and the radicals and the socialists, what canons were left that were absolute? Besides, these wild villages had always been ungoverned.

Yet Maria suffered. Even she, according to her conviction, belonged to Paolo. And she felt betrayed, betrayed and deserted. The iron had

163

gone deep into her soul. Paolo had deserted her, she had been betrayed to other men for five years. There was something cruel and implacable in life. She sat sullen and heavy, for all her quick activity. Her soul was sullen and heavy.

I could never believe Felicina was Paolo's child. She was an unprepossessing little girl, affected, cold, selfish, foolish. Maria and Paolo, with real Italian greatness, were warm and natural towards the child in her. But they did not love her in their very souls, she was the fruit of ash to them. And this must have been the reason that she was so self-conscious and foolish and affected, small child that she was.

Paolo had come back from America a year before she was born—a year before she was born, Maria insisted. The husband and wife lived together in a relationship of complete negation. In his soul he was sad for her, and in her soul she felt annulled. He sat at evening in the chimney-seat, smoking, always pleasant and cheerful, not for a moment thinking he was unhappy. It had all taken place in his subconsciousness. But his eyebrows and eyelids were lifted in a kind of vacancy, his blue eyes were round and somehow finished, though he was so gentle and vigorous in body. But the very quick of him was killed. He was like a ghost in the house, with his loose throat and powerful limbs, his open, blue, extinct eyes, and his musical, slightly husky voice, that seemed to sound out of the past.

And Maria, stout and strong and handsome like a peasant woman, went about as if there were a weight on her, and her voice was high and strident. She, too, was finished in her life. But she remained unbroken, her will was like a hammer that destroys the old form.

Giovanni was patiently labouring to learn a little English. Paolo knew only four or five words, the chief of which were "a' right," "boss," "bread," and "day." The youth had these by heart, and was studying a little more. He was very graceful and lovable, but he found it difficult to learn. A confused light, like hot tears, would come into his eyes when he had again forgotten the phrase. But he carried the paper about with him, and he made steady progress.

He would go to America, he also. Not for anything would he stay in San Gaudenzio. His dream was to be gone. He would come back. The world was not San Gaudenzio to Giovanni.

The old order, the order of Paolo and of Pietro di Paoli, the aristocratic order of the supreme God, God the Father, the Lord, was passing away from the beautiful little territory. The household no longer receives its food, oil and wine and maize, from out of the earth in the motion of fate. The earth is annulled, and money takes its place. The landowner, who is the lieutenant of God and of Fate, like Abraham, he, too, is annulled. There is now the order of the rich, which supersedes the order of the Signoria.

It is passing away from Italy as it has passed from England. The peasant is passing away, the workman is taking his place. The stability is gone. Paolo is a ghost, Maria is the living body. And the new order means sorrow for the Italian more even than it has meant for us. But he will have the new order.

San Gaudenzio is already becoming a thing of the past. Below the house, where the land drops in sharp slips to the sheer cliff's edge, over which it is Maria's constant fear that Felicina will tumble, there are the deserted lemon gardens of the little territory, snug down below. They are invisible till one descends by tiny paths, sheer down into them. And there they stand, the pillars and walls erect, but a dead emptiness prevailing, lemon trees all dead, gone, a few vines in their place. It is only twenty years since the lemon trees finally perished of a disease and were not renewed. But the deserted terrace, shut between great walls, descending in their openness full to the south, to the lake and the mountain opposite, seem more terrible than Pompeii in their silence and utter seclusion. The grape hyacinths flower in the cracks, the lizards run, this strange place hangs suspended and forgotten, forgotten for ever, its erect pillars utterly meaningless.

I used to sit and write in the great loft of the lemon house, high up, far, far from the ground, the open front giving across the lake and the mountain snow opposite flush with twilight. The old matting and boards, the old disused implements of lemon culture made shadows in the deserted place. Then there would come the call from the back, away above: "Venga, venga mangiare."

We ate in the kitchen, where the olive and laurel wood burned in the open fireplace. It was always soup in the evening. Then we played games or cards, all playing; or there was singing, with the accordion, and sometimes a rough mountain peasant with a guitar.

But it is all passing away. Giovanni is in America, unless he has come back to the war. He will not want to live in San Gaudenzio when he is a man, he says. He and Marco will not spend their lives wringing a little oil and wine out of the rocky soil, even if they are not killed in the fighting which is going on at the end of the lake. In my loft by the lemon houses now I should hear the guns. And Giovanni kissed me with a kind of supplication when I went on to the steamer, as if he were beseeching for a soul. His eyes were bright and clear and lit up with courage. He will make a good fight for the new soul he wants—that is, if they do not kill him in this war.

V. The Dance

Maria had no real licence for San Gaudenzio, yet the peasants always called for wine. It is easy to arrange in Italy. The penny is paid another time.

The wild old road that skirts the lake-side, scrambling always higher as the precipice becomes steeper, climbing and winding to the villages perched high up, passes under the high boundary-wall of San Gaudenzio, between that and the ruined church. But the road went just as much between the vines and past the house as outside, under the wall; for the high gates were always open, and men or women and mules come into the property to call at the door of the homestead. There was a loud shout, "Ah—a—a—ah—Mari—'a. O—O—Oh Pa'o'!" from outside, another wild, inarticulate cry from within, and one of the Fiori appeared in the doorway to hail the new-comer.

It was usually a man, sometimes a peasant from Mugiano, high up, sometimes a peasant from the wilds of the mountain, a wood-cutter, or a charcoal-burner. He came in and sat in the house-place, his glass of wine in his hand between his knees, or on the floor between his feet, and he talked in a few wild phrases, very shy, like a hawk indoors, and unintelligible in his dialect.

Sometimes we had a dance. Then, for the wine to drink, three men came with mandolines and guitars, and sat in a corner playing their rapid tunes, while all danced on the dusty brick floor of the little parlour. No strange women were invited, only men; the young bloods from the big village on the lake, the wild men from above. They danced the slow, trailing, lilting polka-waltz, round and round the small room, the guitars and mandolines twanging rapidly, the dust rising from the soft bricks. There were only the two English women: so men danced with men, as the Italians love to do. They love even better to dance with men, with a dear, blood-friend, than with women.

"It's better like this, two men?" Giovanni says to me, his blue eyes hot, his face curiously tender.

The wood-cutters and peasants take off their coats, their throats are bare. They dance with strange intentness, particularly if they have for partner an English Signora. Their feet in thick boots are curiously swift and significant. And it is strange to see the Englishwomen, as they dance with the peasants, transfigured with a kind of brilliant surprise. All the while the peasants are very courteous, but quiet. They see the women dilate and flash, they think they have found a footing, they are certain. So the male dancers are quiet, but even grand-iloquent, their feet nimble, their bodies wild and confident.

They are at a loss when the two English Signoras move together and laugh, excitedly, at the end of the dance.

"Isn't it fine?"

"Fine! Their arms are like iron, carrying you round."

"Yes! Yes! And the muscles on their shoulders! I never knew there were such muscles! I'm almost frightened."

"But it's fine, isn't it? I'm getting into the dance."

"Yes—yes—you've only to let them take you."

Then the glasses are put down, the guitars give their strange, vibrant, almost painful summons, and the dance begins again.

It is a strange dance, strange and lilting, and changing as the music changed. But it had always a kind of leisurely dignity, a trailing kind of polka-waltz, intimate, passionate, yet never hurried, never violent in its passion, always becoming more intense. The women's faces changed to a kind of transported wonder, they were in the very rhythm of delight. From the soft bricks of the floor the red ochre rose in a thin cloud of dust, making hazy the shadowy dancers; the three musicians, in their black hats and their cloaks, sat obscurely in the corner, making a music that came quicker and quicker, making a dance that grew swifter and more intense, more subtle, the men seeming to fly and to implicate other strange, inter-rhythmic dance into the women, the women drifting and palpitating as if their souls shook and resounded to a breeze that was subtly rushing upon them, through them; the men worked their feet, their thighs swifter, more vividly, the music came to an almost intolerable climax, there was a moment when the dance passed into a possession, the men caught up the women and swung them from the earth, leapt with them for a second, and then the next phase of the dance had begun, slower again, more subtly interwoven, taking perfect, oh, exquisite delight in every inter-related movement, a rhythm within a rhythm, a subtle approaching and drawing nearer to a climax, nearer, till, oh, there was the surpassing lift and swing of the women, when the woman's body seemed like a boat lifted over the powerful, exquisite wave of the man's body, perfect, for a moment, and then once more the slow, intense, nearer movement of the dance began, always nearer, nearer, always to a more perfect climax.

And the women waited as if in transport for the climax, when they would be flung into a movement surpassing all movement. They were flung, borne away, lifted like a boat on a supreme wave, into the zenith and nave of the heavens, consummate.

Then suddenly the dance crashed to an end, and the dancers stood stranded, lost, bewildered, on a strange shore. The air was full of red dust, half-lit by the lamp on the wall; the players in the corner were putting down their instruments to take up their glasses.

And the dancers sat round the wall, crowding in the little room, faint with the transport of repeated ecstasy. There was a subtle smile on the face of the men, subtle, knowing, so finely sensual that the conscious eyes could scarcely look at it. And the women were dazed, like creatures dazzled by too much light. The light was still on their faces, like a blindness, a reeling, like a transfiguration. The men were bringing wine, on a little tin tray, leaning with their proud, vivid loins, their faces flickering with the same subtle smile. Meanwhile, Maria Fiori was splashing water, much water, on the red floor. There was the smell of water among the glowing, transfigured men and women who sat gleaming in another world, round the walls.

The peasants have chosen their women. For the dark, handsome Englishwoman, who looks like a slightly malignant Madonna, comes Il Duro; for the "bella bionda," the wood-cutter. But the peasants have always to take their turn after the young well-to-do men from the village below.

Nevertheless, they are confident. They cannot understand the middle-class diffidence of the young men who wear collars and ties and finger-rings.

The wood-cutter from the mountain is of medium height, dark, thin, and hard as a hatchet, with eyes that are black like the very flaming thrust of night. He is quite a savage. There is something strange about his dancing, the violent way he works one shoulder. He has a wooden leg, from the knee-joint. Yet he dances well, and is inordinately proud. He is fierce as a bird, and hard with energy as a thunderbolt. He will dance with the blonde Signora. But he never speaks. He is like some violent natural phenomenon rather than a person. The woman begins to wilt a little in his possession.

"È bello—il ballo?" he asks at length, one direct, flashing question.

"Si—molto bello," cries the woman, glad to have speech again.

The eyes of the wood-cutter flash like actual possession. He seems now to have come into his own. With all his senses, he is dominant, sure.

He is inconceivably vigorous in body, and his dancing is almost perfect, with a little catch in it, owing to his lameness, which brings almost a pure intoxication. Every muscle in his body is supple as steel, supple, as strong as thunder, and yet so quick, so delicately swift, it is almost unbearable. As he draws near to the swing, the climax, the ecstasy, he seems to lie in wait, there is a sense of a great strength crouching ready. Then it rushes forth, liquid, perfect, transcendent, the woman swoons over in the dance, and it goes on, enjoyment, infinite, incalculable enjoyment. He is like a god, a strange natural phenomenon, most intimate and compelling, wonderful.

But he is not a human being. The woman, somewhere shocked in her independent soul, begins to fall away from him. She has another being, which he has not touched, and which she will fall back upon. The dance is over, she will fall back on herself. It is perfect, too perfect.

During the next dance, while she is in the power of the educated Ettore, a perfect and calculated voluptuary, who knows how much he can get out of this Northern woman, and only how much, the wood-cutter stands on the edge of the darkness, in the open doorway, and watches. He is fixed upon her, established, perfect. And all the while she is aware of the insistent hawk-like poising of the face of the wood-cutter, poised on the edge of the darkness, in the doorway, in possession, unrelinquishing.

And she is angry. There is something stupid, absurd, in the hard, talon-like eyes watching so fiercely and so confidently in the doorway, sure, unmitigated. Has the creature no sense?

The woman reacts from him. For some time she will take no notice of him. But he waits, fixed. Then she comes near to him, and his will seems to take hold of her. He looks at her with a strange, proud, inhuman confidence, as if his influence with her was already accomplished.

"Venga—venga un po'," he says, jerking his head strangely to the darkness.

"What?" she replies, and passes shaken and dilated and brilliant, consciously ignoring him, passes away among the others, among those who are safe.

There is food in the kitchen, great hunks of bread, sliced sausage that Maria has made, wine, and a little coffee. But only the quality come to eat. The peasants may not come in. There is eating and drinking in the little house, the guitars are silent. It is eleven o'clock.

Then there is singing, the strange bestial singing of these hills. Sometimes the guitars can play an accompaniment, but usually not. Then the men lift up their heads and send out the high, half-howling music, astounding. The words are in dialect. They argue among themselves for a moment: will the Signoria understand? They sing. The Signoria does not understand in the least. So with a strange, slightly malignant triumph, the men sing all the verses of their song, sitting round the walls of the little parlour. Their throats move, their faces have a slight, mocking smile. The boy capers in the doorway like a faun, with glee, his straight black hair falling over his forehead. The elder brother sits straight and flushed, but even his eyes glitter with a kind of yellow light of laughter. Paolo also sits quiet, with the invisible smile on his face. Only Maria, large and active, prospering now, keeps collected, ready to order a shrill silence in the same way as she orders the peasants, violently, to keep their places.

The boy comes to me and says:

"Do you know, Signore, what they are singing?"

"No," I say.

So he capers with furious glee. The men with the watchful eyes, all roused, sit round the wall and sing more distinctly:

> Si verrà la primavera
> Fiorann' le mandoline,
> Vienn' di basso le Trentine
> Coi 'taliani far' l'amor.

But the next verses are so improper that I pretend not to understand. The women, with wakened, dilated faces, are listening, listening hard, their two faces beautiful in their attention, as if listening to something magical, a long way off. And the men sitting round the wall sing more plainly, coming nearer to the correct Italian. The song comes loud and vibrating and maliciously from their reedy throats, it penetrates everybody. The foreign women can understand the sound, they can feel the malicious, suggestive mockery. But they cannot catch the words. The smile becomes more dangerous on the faces of the men.

Then Maria Fiori sees that I have understood, and she cries, in her loud, overriding voice:

"Basta—basta."

The men get up, straighten their bodies with a curious, offering movement. The guitars and mandolines strike the vibrating strings. But the vague Northern reserve has come over the Englishwomen. They dance again, but without the fusion in the dance. They have had enough.

The musicians are thanked, they rise and go into the night. The men pass off in pairs. But the wood-cutter, whose name and whose nickname I could never hear, still hovered on the edge of the darkness.

Then Maria sent him also away, complaining that he was too wild, *proprio selvatico*, and only the "quality" remained, the well-to-do youths from below. There was a little more coffee, and a talking, a story of a man who had fallen over a declivity in a lonely part going home drunk in the evening, and had lain unfound for eighteen hours. Then a story of a donkey who had kicked a youth in the chest and killed him.

But the women were tired, they would go to bed. Still the two young men would not go away. We all went out to look at the night.

The stars were very bright overhead, the mountain opposite and the mountains behind us faintly outlined themselves on the sky. Below, the lake was a black gulf. A little wind blew cold from the Adige.

In the morning the visitors had gone. They had insisted on staying the night. They had eaten eight eggs each and much bread at one o'clock in the morning. Then they had gone to sleep, lying on the floor in the sitting-room.

In the early sunshine they had drunk coffee and gone down to the village on the lake. Maria was very pleased. She would have made a good deal of money. The young men were rich. Her cupidity seemed like her very blossom.

VI. Il Duro

The first time I saw Il Duro was on a sunny day when there came up a party of pleasure-makers to San Gaudenzio. They were three women and three men. The women were in cotton frocks, one a large, dark, florid woman in pink, the other two rather insignificant. The men I scarcely noticed at first, except that two were young and one elderly.

They were a queer party, even on a feast day, coming up purely for pleasure, in the morning, strange, and slightly uncertain, advancing between the vines. They greeted Maria and Paolo in loud, coarse voices. There was something blowsy and uncertain and hesitating about the women in particular, which made one at once notice them.

Then a picnic was arranged for them out of doors, on the grass. They sat just in front of the house, under the olive tree, beyond the well. It should have been pretty, the women in their cotton frocks and their friends, sitting with wine and food in the spring sunshine. But somehow it was not: it was hard and slightly ugly.

But since they were picnicking out of doors, we must do so too. We were at once envious. But Maria was a little unwilling, and then she set a table for us.

The strange party did not speak to us, they seemed slightly uneasy and angry at our presence. I asked Maria who they were. She lifted her shoulders, and, after a second's cold pause, said they were people from down below, and then, in her rather strident, shrill, slightly bitter, slightly derogatory voice, she added:

"They are not people for you, Signore. You don't know them."

She spoke slightly angrily and contemptuously of them, rather protectively of me. So that vaguely I gathered that they were not quite "respectable."

Only one man came into the house. He was very handsome, beautiful rather, a man of thirty-two or -three, with a clear golden skin, and perfectly turned face, something godlike. But the expression was strange. His hair was jet black and fine and smooth, glossy as a bird's wing, his brows were beautifully drawn, calm above his grey eyes, that had long, dark lashes.

His eyes, however, had a sinister light in them, a pale, slightly repelling gleam, very much like a god's pale-gleaming eyes, with the same vivid pallor. And all his face had the slightly malignant, suffering look of a satyr. Yet he was very beautiful.

He walked quickly and surely, with his head rather down, passing from his desire to his object, absorbed, yet curiously indifferent, as if the transit were in a strange world, as if none of what he was doing were worth the while. Yet he did it for his own pleasure, and the light on his face, a pale, strange gleam through his clear skin, remained like a translucent smile, unchanging as time.

He seemed familiar with the household, he came and fetched wine at his will. Maria was angry with him. She railed loudly and violently. He was unchanged. He went out with the wine to the party on the grass. Maria regarded them all with some hostility.

They drank a good deal out there in the sunshine. The women and the older man talked floridly. Il Duro crouched at the feast in his curious fashion—he had strangely flexible loins, upon which he seemed to crouch forward. But he was separate, like an animal that remains quite single, no matter where it is.

The party remained until about two o'clock. Then, slightly flushed, it moved on in a ragged group up to the village beyond. I do not know if they went to one of the inns of the stony village, or to the large strange house which belonged to the rich young grocer of the village below, a house kept only for feasts and riots, uninhabited for the most part. Maria would tell me nothing about them. Only the young well-to-do grocer, who had lived in Vienna, the Bertolotti, came later in the afternoon enquiring for the party.

And towards sunset I saw the elderly man of the group stumbling home very drunk down the path, after the two women, who had gone on in front. Then Paolo sent Giovanni to see the drunken one safely past the landslip, which was dangerous. Altogether it was an unsatisfactory business, very much like any other such party in any other country.

Then in the evening Il Duro came in. His name is Faustino, but everybody in the village has a nickname, which is almost invariably used. He came in and asked for supper. We had all eaten. So he ate a little food alone at the table, whilst we sat round the fire.

Afterwards we played "Up, Jenkins." That was the one game we played with the peasants, except that exciting one of theirs, which consists in shouting in rapid succession your guesses at the number of fingers rapidly spread out and shut into the hands again upon the table.

Il Duro joined in the game. And that was because he had been in America, and now was rich. He felt he could come near to the strange Signori. But he was always inscrutable.

It was queer to look at the hands spread on the table: the Englishwomen, having rings on their soft fingers; the large fresh hands of the elder boy, the brown paws of the younger; Paolo's distorted great hard hands of a peasant; and the big, dark brown, animal, shapely hands of Faustino.

He had been in America first for two years and then for five years—seven years altogether—but he only spoke a very little English. He was always with Italians. He had served chiefly in a flag factory, and had had very little to do save to push a trolley with flags from the dyeing-room to the drying-room—I believe it was this.

Then he had come home from America with a fair amount of money, he had taken his uncle's garden, had inherited his uncle's little house, and he lived quite alone.

He was rich, Maria said, shouting in her strident voice. He at once disclaimed it, peasant-wise. But before the Signori he was glad also to appear rich. He was mean, that was more, Maria cried, half-teasing, half getting at him.

He attended to his garden, grew vegetables all the year round, lived in his little house, and in spring made good money as a vine-grafter: he was an expert vine-grafter.

After the boys had gone to bed he sat and talked to me. He was curiously attractive and curiously beautiful, but somehow like stone in his clear colouring and his clear-cut face. His temples, with the black hair, were distinct and fine as a work of art.

But always his eyes had this strange, half-diabolic, half-tortured pale gleam, like a goat's, and his mouth was shut almost uglily, his cheeks stern. His moustache was brown, his teeth strong and spaced. The women said it was a pity his moustache was brown.

"Peccato!—sa, per bellezza, i baffi neri—ah-h!"

Then a long-drawn exclamation of voluptuous appreciation.

"You live quite alone?" I said to him.

He did. And even when he had been ill he was alone. He had been ill two years before. His cheeks seemed to harden like marble, and to become pale at the thought. He was afraid, like marble with fear.

"But why?" I said, "why do you live alone? You are sad—è triste."

He looked at me with his queer, pale eyes.

I felt a great static misery in him, something very strange.

"Triste!" he repeated, stiffening up, hostile. I could not understand.

"Vuol' dire che hai l'aria dolorosa," cried Maria, like a chorus interpreting. And there was always a sort of loud ring of challenge somewhere in her voice.

"Sad," I said, in English.

"Sad!" he repeated, also in English. And he did not smile or change, only his face seemed to become more stone-like. And he only looked at me, into my eyes, with the long, pale, steady, inscrutable look of a goat, I can only repeat, something stone-like.

"Why," I said, "don't you marry? Man doesn't live alone."

"I don't marry," he said to me, in his emphatic, deliberate, cold fashion, "because I've seen too much. Ho visto troppo."

"I don't understand," I said.

Yet I could feel that Paolo, sitting silent, like a monolith also, in the chimney opening, he understood: Maria also understood.

Il Duro looked again steadily into my eyes.

"Ho visto troppo," he repeated, and the words seemed engraved on stone. "I've seen too much."

"But you can marry," I said, "however much you have seen, if you have seen all the world."

He watched me steadily, like a strange creature looking at me.

"What woman?" he said to me.

"You can find a woman—there are plenty of women," I said.

"Not for me," he said. "I have known too many. I've known too much, I can marry nobody."

"Do you dislike women?" I said.

"No—quite otherwise. I don't think ill of them."

"Then why can't you marry? Why must you live alone?"

"Why live with a woman?" he said to me, and he looked mockingly. "Which woman is it to be?"

"You can find her," I said. "There are many women."

Again he shook his head in the stony, final fashion.

"Not for me. I have known too much."

"But does that prevent you from marrying?"

He looked at me steadily, finally. And I could see it was impossible for us to understand each other, or for me to understand him. I could not understand the strange white gleam of his eyes, where it came from.

Also I knew he liked me very much, almost loved me, which again was strange and puzzling. It was as if he were a fairy, a faun, and had no soul. But he gave me a feeling of vivid sadness, a sadness that gleamed like phosphorescence. He himself was not sad. There was a completeness about him, about the pallid otherworld he inhabited, which excluded sadness. It was too complete, too final, too defined. There was no yearning, no vague merging off into mistiness. . . . He was as clear and fine as semi-transparent rock, as a substance in moonlight. He seemed like a crystal that has achieved its final shape and has nothing more to achieve.

That night he slept on the floor of the sitting-room. In the morning he was gone. But a week after he came again, to graft the vines.

All the morning and the afternoon he was among the vines, crouching before them, cutting them back with his sharp, bright knife, amazingly swift and sure, like a god. It filled me with a sort of panic to see him crouched flexibly, like some strange animal god, doubled on his haunches, before the young vines, and swiftly, vividly, without thought, cut, cut, cut at the young budding shoots, which fell unheeded on to the earth. Then again he strode with his curious, half goat-like movement across the garden, to prepare the lime.

He mixed the messy stuff, cow-dung and lime and water and earth, carefully with his hands, as if he understood that too. He was not a worker. He was a creature in intimate communion with the sensible world, knowing purely by touch the limey mess he mixed amongst, knowing as if by relation between that soft matter and the matter of himself.

Then again he strode over the earth, a gleaming piece of earth himself, moving to the young vines. Quickly, with a few clean cuts of the knife, he prepared the new shoot, which he had picked out of a handful which lay beside him on the ground, he went finely to the quick of the plant, inserted the graft, then bound it up, fast, hard.

It was like God grafting the life of man upon the body of the earth, intimately, conjuring with his own flesh.

All the while Paolo stood by, somehow excluded from the mystery, talking to me, to Faustino. And Il Duro answered easily, as if his mind were disengaged. It was his senses that were absorbed in the sensible life of the plant and the lime and the cow-dung he handled.

Watching him, watching his absorbed, bestial, and yet god-like crouching before the plant, as if he were the god of lower life, I somehow understood his isolation, why he did not marry. Pan and the ministers of Pan do not marry, the sylvan gods. They are single and isolated in their being.

It is in the spirit that marriage takes place. In the flesh there is connection, but only in the spirit is there a new thing created out of two different antithetic things. In the body I am conjoined with the woman. But in the spirit my conjunction with her creates a third thing, an absolute, a Word, which is neither me nor her, nor of me nor of her, but which is absolute.

And Faustino had none of this spirit. In him sensation itself was absolute—not spiritual consummation, but physical sensation. So he could not marry, it was not for him. He belonged to the god Pan, to the absolute of the senses.

All the while his beauty, so perfect and so defined, fascinated me, a strange static perfection about him. But his movements, whilst they fascinated, also repelled. I can always see him crouched before the vines on his haunches, his haunches doubled together in a complete animal unconsciousness, his face seeming in its strange golden pallor and its hardness of line, with the gleaming black of the fine hair on the brow and temples, like something reflective, like the reflecting surface of a stone that gleams out of the depths of night. It was like darkness revealed in its steady, unchanging pallor.

Again he stayed through the evening, having quarrelled once more with the Maria about money. He quarrelled violently, yet coldly. There was something terrifying in it. And as soon as the matter of dispute was settled, all trace of interest or feeling vanished from him.

Yet he liked, above all things, to be near the English Signori. They seemed to exercise a sort of magnetic attraction over him. It was something of the purely physical world, as a magnetised needle swings towards soft iron. He was quite helpless in the relation. Only by mechanical attraction he gravitated into line with us.

But there was nothing between us except our complete difference. It was like night and day flowing together.

VII. John

Besides Il Duro, we found another Italian who could speak English, this time quite well. We had walked about four or five miles up the lake, getting higher and higher. Then quite suddenly, on the shoulder of a bluff far up, we came on a village, icy cold, and as if forgotten.

We went into the inn to drink something hot. The fire of olive sticks was burning in the open chimney, one or two men were talking at a table, a young woman with a baby stood by the fire watching something boil in a large pot. Another woman was seen in the house-place beyond.

In the chimney-seats sat a young mule-driver, who had left his two mules at the door of the inn, and opposite him an elderly stout man. They got down and offered us the seats of honour, which we accepted with due courtesy.

The chimneys are like the wide open chimney-places of old English cottages, but the hearth is raised about a foot and a half or two feet from the floor, so that the fire is almost level with the hands, and those who sit in the chimney-seats are raised above the audience in the room, something like two gods flanking the fire, looking out of the cave of ruddy darkness into the open, lower world of the room.

We asked for coffee with milk and rum. The stout landlord took a seat near us below. The comely young woman with the baby took the tin coffee-pot that stood among the grey ashes, put in fresh coffee among the old bottoms, filled it with water, then pushed it more into the fire.

The landlord turned to us with the usual naïve, curious deference, and the usual question:

"You are Germans?"

"English."

"Ah—Inglesi."

Then there is a new note of cordiality—or so I always imagine—and the rather rough, cattle-like men who are sitting with their wine round the table look up more amicably. They do not like being intruded upon. Only the landlord is always affable.

"I have a son who speaks English," he says: he is a handsome, courtly old man, of the Falstaff sort.

"Oh!"

"He has been in America."

"And where is he now?"

"He is at home. O—— Nicoletta, where is the Giovann'?"

The comely young woman with the baby came in.

"He is with the band," she said.

The old landlord looked at her with pride.

"This is my daughter-in-law," he said.

She smiled readily to the Signora.

"And the baby?" we asked.

"Mio figlio," cried the young woman, in the strong, penetrating voice of these women. And she came forward to show the child to the Signora.

It was a bonny baby: the whole company was united in adoration and service of the bambino. There was a moment of suspension, when religious submission seemed to come over the inn-room.

Then the Signora began to talk, and it broke upon the Italian child-reverence.

"What is he called?"

"Oscare," came the ringing note of pride. And the mother talked to the baby in dialect. All, men and women alike, felt themselves glorified by the presence of the child.

At last the coffee in the tin coffee-pot was boiling and frothing out of spout and lid. The milk in the little copper pan was also hot, among the ashes. So we had our drink at last.

The landlord was anxious for us to see Giovanni, his son. There was a village band performing up the street, in front of the house of a colonel who had come home wounded from Tripoli. Everybody in the village was wildly proud about the colonel and about the brass band, the music of which was execrable.

We just looked into the street. The band of uncouth fellows was playing the same tune over and over again before a desolate, newish house. A crowd of desolate, forgotten villagers stood round, in the cold upper air. It seemed altogether that the place was forgotten by God and man.

But the landlord, burly, courteous, handsome, pointed out with a flourish the Giovanni, standing in the band playing a cornet. The band itself consisted only of five men, rather like beggars in the street. But Giovanni was the strangest! He was tall and thin and somewhat German-looking, wearing shabby American clothes and a very high double collar and a small American crush hat. He looked entirely like a ne'er-do-well who plays a violin in the street, dressed in the most down-at-heel, sordid respectability.

"That is he—you see, Signore—the young one under the balcony."

The father spoke with love and pride, and the father was a gentleman, like Falstaff, a pure gentleman. The daughter-in-law also peered out to look at Il Giovann', who was evidently a figure of repute, in his sordid, degenerate American respectability. Meanwhile, this figure of repute blew himself red in the face, producing staccato strains on his cornet. And the crowd stood desolate and forsaken in the cold, upper afternoon.

Then there was a sudden rugged "Evviva, Evviva!" from the people, the band stopped playing, somebody valiantly broke into a line of the song:

> Tripoli, sarà italiana,
> Sarà italiana al rombo del cannon'.

The colonel had appeared on the balcony, a smallish man, very yellow in the face, with grizzled black hair and very shabby legs. They all seemed so sordidly, hopelessly shabby.

He suddenly began to speak, leaning forward, hot and feverish and yellow, upon the iron rail of the balcony. There was something hot and marshy and sick about him, slightly repulsive, less than human. He told his fellow-villagers how he loved them, how, when he lay uncovered on the sands of Tripoli, week after week, he had known they were watching him from the Alpine height of the village, he could feel that where he was they were all looking. When the Arabs came rushing like things gone mad, and he had received his wound, he had known that in his own village, among his own dear ones, there was recovery. Love would heal the wounds, the home country was a lover who would heal all her sons' wounds with love.

Among the grey, desolate crowd were sharp, rending "Bravos!"— the people were in tears—the landlord at my side was repeating softly, abstractedly: "Caro—caro—Ettore, caro colonello———" and when it was finished, and the little colonel with shabby, humiliated legs was gone in, he turned to me, and said, with challenge that almost frightened me:

"Un brav' uomo."

"Bravissimo," I said.

Then we, too, went indoors.

It was all, somehow, grey and hopeless and acrid, unendurable.

The colonel, poor devil—we knew him afterwards—is now dead. It is strange that he is dead. There is something repulsive to me in the thought of his lying dead: such a humiliating, somehow degraded corpse. Death has no beauty in Italy, unless it be violent. The death of man or woman through sickness is an occasion of horror, repulsive. They belong entirely to life, they are so limited to life, these people.

Soon the Giovanni came home, and took his cornet upstairs. Then he came to see us. He was an ingenuous youth, sordidly shabby and dirty. His fair hair was long and uneven, his very high starched collar made one aware that his neck and his ears were not clean, his American crimson tie was ugly, his clothes looked as if they had been kicking about on the floor for a year.

Yet his blue eyes were warm and his manner and speech very gentle.

"You will speak English with us," I said.

"Oh," he said, smiling and shaking his head, "I could speak English very well. But it is two years that I don't speak it now, over two years now, so I don't speak it."

"But you speak it very well."

"No. It is two years that I have not spoke, not a word—so, you see, I have——"

"You have forgotten it? No, you haven't. It will quickly come back."

"If I hear it—when I go to America—then I shall—I shall——"

"You will soon pick it up."

"Yes—I shall pick it up."

The landlord, who had been watching with pride, now went away. The wife also went away, and we were left with the shy, gentle, dirty, and frowsily-dressed Giovanni.

He laughed in his sensitive, quick fashion.

"The women in America, when they came into the store, they said, 'Where is John, where is John?' Yes, they liked me."

And he laughed again, glancing with vague, warm, blue eyes, very shy, very coiled upon himself with sensitiveness.

He had managed a store in America, in a smallish town. I glanced at his reddish, smooth, rather knuckly hands, and thin wrists in the frayed cuff. They were real shopman's hands.

The landlord brought some special feast-day cake, so overjoyed he was to have his Giovanni speaking English with the Signoria.

When we went away, we asked "John" to come down to our villa to see us. We scarcely expected him to turn up.

Yet one morning he appeared, at about half-past nine, just as we were finishing breakfast. It was sunny and warm and beautiful, so we asked him please to come with us picnicking.

He was a queer shoot, again, in his unkempt longish hair and slovenly clothes, a sort of very vulgar down-at-heel American in appearance. And he was transported with shyness. Yet ours was the world he had chosen as his own, so he took his place bravely and simply, a hanger-on.

We climbed up the water-course in the mountain-side, up to a smooth little lawn under the olive trees, where daisies were flowering and gladioli were in bud. It was a tiny little lawn of grass in a level crevice, and sitting there we had the world below us, the lake, the distant island, the far-off, low Verona shore.

Then "John" began to talk, and he talked continuously, like a foreigner, not saying the things he would have said in Italian, but following the suggestion and scope of his limited English.

In the first place, he loved his father—it was "my father, my father" always. His father had a little shop as well as the inn in the village above. So John had had some education. He had been sent to Brescia and then to Verona to school, and there had taken his examinations to become a civil engineer. He was clever, and could pass his examinations. But he never finished his course. His mother died, and his father, disconsolate, had wanted him at home. Then he had gone back, when he was sixteen or seventeen, to the village beyond the lake, to be with his father and to look after the shop.

"But didn't you mind giving up all your work?" I said.

He did not quite understand.

"My father wanted me to come back," he said.

It was evident that Giovanni had had no definite conception of what he was doing or what he wanted to do. His father, wishing to make a gentleman of him, had sent him to school in Verona. By accident he had been moved on into the engineering course. When it all fizzled to an end, and he returned half-baked to the remote, desolate village of the mountain-side, he was not disappointed or chagrined. He had never conceived of a coherent purposive life. Either one stayed in the village, like a lodged stone, or one made random excursions into the world, across the world. It was all aimless and purposeless.

So he had stayed a while with his father, then he had gone, just as aimlessly, with a party of men who were emigrating to America. He had taken some money, had drifted about, living in the most comfortless, wretched fashion, then he had found a place somewhere in Pennsylvania, in a dry goods store. This was when he was seventeen or eighteen years old.

All this seemed to have happened to him without his being very much affected, at least consciously. His nature was simple and self-complete. Yet not so self-complete as that of Il Duro or Paolo. They had passed through the foreign world and been quite untouched. Their souls were static, it was the world that had flowed unstable by.

But John was more sensitive, he had come more into contact with his new surroundings. He had attended night classes almost every evening, and had been taught English like a child. He had loved the American free school, the teachers, the work.

But he had suffered very much in America. With his curious, over-sensitive, wincing laugh, he told us how the boys had followed him and jeered at him, calling after him, "You damn Dago, you damn Dago." They had stopped him and his friend in the street and taken away their hats, and spat into them, and made water into them. So that at last he had gone mad. They were youths and men who always tortured him, using bad language which startled us very much as he repeated it, there on the little lawn under the olive trees, above the perfect lake: English obscenities and abuse so coarse and startling that we bit our lips, shocked almost into laughter, whilst John, simple and natural, and somehow, for all his long hair and dirty appearance, flower-like in soul, repeated to us these things which may never be repeated in decent company.

"Oh," he said, "at last, I get mad. When they come one day, shouting, 'You damn Dago, dirty dog,' and will take my hat again, oh, I get mad, and I would kill them. I would kill them, I am so mad. I run to them, and throw one to the floor, and I tread on him while I go upon another, the biggest. Though they hit me and kick me all over, I feel nothing, I am mad. I throw the biggest to the floor, a man, he is older than I am, and I hit him, so hard I would kill him. When the others see it they are afraid, they throw stones and hit me on the face. But I don't feel it—I don't know nothing. I hit the man on the floor, I almost kill him. I forget everything except I will kill him——"

"But you didn't?"

"No—I don't know——" and he laughed his queer, shaken laugh. "The other man, what was with me, my friend, he came to me and we went away. Oh, I was mad, I completely mad. I would have killed them."

He was trembling slightly, and his eyes were dilated with a strange, greyish-blue fire that was very painful and elemental. He looked beside himself. But he was by no means mad.

We were shaken by the vivid, lambent excitement of the youth, we wished him to forget. We were shocked, too, in our souls to see the pure elemental flame shaken out of his gentle, sensitive nature. By his slight, crinkled laugh we could see how much he had suffered. He had gone out and faced the world, and he had kept his place, stranger and Dago though he was.

"They never came after me no more, not all the while I was there."

Then he said he became the foreman in the store—at first he was only assistant. It was the best store in the town, and many English ladies came, and some Germans. He liked the English ladies very much: they always wanted him to be in the store. He wore white clothes there, and they would say:

"You look very nice in the white coat, John," or else:

"Let John come, he can find it," or else they said:

"John speaks like a born American."

This pleased him very much.

In the end, he said, he earned a hundred dollars a month. He lived with the extraordinary frugality of the Italians, and had quite a lot of money.

He was not like Il Duro. Faustino had lived in a state of miserliness almost in America, but then he had had his debauches of shows and wine and carousals. John went chiefly to the schools, in one of which he was even asked to teach Italian. His knowledge of his own language was remarkable and most unusual!

"But what," I asked, "brought you back?"

"It was my father. You see, if I did not come to have my military service, I must stay till I am forty. So I think perhaps my father will be dead, I shall never see him. So I came."

He had come home when he was twenty to fulfil his military duties. At home he had married. He was very fond of his wife, but he had no conception of love in the old sense. His wife was like the past, to which he was wedded. Out of her he begot his child, as out of the past. But the future was all beyond her, apart from her. He was going away again, now, to America. He had been some nine months at home after his military service was over. He had no more to do. Now he was leaving his wife and child and his father to go to America.

"But why," I said, "Why? You are not poor, you can manage the shop in your village."

"Yes," he said. "But I will go to America. Perhaps I shall go into the store again, the same."

"But is it not just the same as managing the shop at home?"

"No—no—it is quite different."

Then he told us how he bought goods in Brescia and in Salò for the shop at home, how he had rigged up a funicular with the assistance of the village, an overhead wire by which you could haul the goods up the face of the cliffs right high up, to within a mile of the village. He was very proud of this. And sometimes he himself went down the funicular to the water's edge, to the boat, when he was in a hurry. This also pleased him.

But he was going to Brescia this day to see about going again to America. Perhaps in another month he would be gone.

It was a great puzzle to me why he would go. He could not say himself. He would stay four or five years, then he would come home again to see his father—and his wife and child.

There was a strange, almost frightening destiny upon him, which seemed to take him away, always away from home, from the past, to that great, raw America. He seemed scarcely like a person with individual choice, more like a creature under the influence of fate which was disintegrating the old life and precipitating him, a fragment inconclusive, into the new chaos.

He submitted to it all with a perfect unquestioning simplicity, never even knowing that he suffered, that he must suffer disintegration from the old life. He was moved entirely from within, he never questioned his inevitable impulse.

"They say to me, 'Don't go—don't go'—" he shook his head. "But I say I will go."

And at that it was finished.

So we saw him off at the little quay, going down the lake. He would return at evening, and be pulled up in his funicular basket. And in a month's time he would be standing on the same lake steamer going to America.

Nothing was more painful than to see him standing there in his degraded, sordid American clothes, on the deck of the steamer, waving us good-bye, belonging in his final desire to our world, the world of consciousness and deliberate action. With his candid, open, unquestioning face, he seemed like a prisoner being conveyed from one form of life to another, or like a soul in trajectory, that has not yet found a resting-place.

What were wife and child to him: they were the last steps of the past. His father was the continent behind him; his wife and child the foreshore of the past; but his face was set outwards, away from it all—whither, neither he nor anybody knew, but he called it America.

Italians in Exile

Italians in Exile

When I was in Constance the weather was misty and enervating and depressing, it was no pleasure to travel on the big, flat, desolate lake.

When I went from Constance, it was on a small steamer down the Rhine to Schaffhausen. That was beautiful. Still, the mist hung over the waters, over the wide shallows of the river, and the sun, coming through the morning, made lovely yellow lights beneath the bluish haze, so that it seemed like the beginning of the world. And there was a hawk in the upper air fighting with two crows, or two rooks. Ever they rose higher and higher, the crow flickering above the attacking hawk, the fight going on like some strange symbol in the sky, the Germans on deck watching with pleasure.

Then we passed out of sight, between wooded banks and under bridges where quaint villages of old romance piled their red and coloured pointed roofs beside the water, very still, remote, lost in the vagueness of the past. It could not be that they were real. Even when the boat put in to shore, and the customs officials came to look, the village remained remote in the romantic past of High Germany, the Germany of fairy tales and minstrels and craftsmen. The poignancy of the past was almost unbearable, floating there in colour upon the haze of the river.

We went by some swimmers, whose white, shadowy bodies trembled near the side of the steamer, under water. One man with a round, fair head, lifted his face and one arm from the water and shouted a greeting to us, as if he were a Niebelung, saluting with bright arm lifted from the water, his face laughing, the fair moustache hanging over his mouth. Then his white body swirled in the water, and he was gone, swimming with the side stroke.

Schaffhausen the town, half old and bygone, half modern, with breweries and industries, that is not very real. Schaffhausen Falls, with their factory in the midst and their hotel at the bottom, and the general cinematograph effect, they are ugly.

It was afternoon when I set out to walk from the Falls to Italy, across Switzerland. I remember the big, fat, rather gloomy fields of this part of Baden, damp and unliving. I remember I found some apples under a tree in a field near a railway embankment, then some mushrooms, and I ate both. Then I came on to a long, desolate high road, with dreary, withered trees on either side, and flanked by great fields where groups of men and women were working. They looked at me as I went by down the long, long road, alone and exposed and out of the world.

I remember nobody came at the border village to examine my pack, I passed through unchallenged. All was quiet and lifeless and hopeless, with big stretches of heavy land.

Till sunset came, very red and purple, and suddenly, from the heavy spacious open land I dropped sharply into the Rhine valley again, suddenly, as if into another glamorous world.

There was the river rushing along between its high, mysterious, romantic banks, which were high as hills, and covered with vine. And there was the village of tall, quaint houses flickering its lights on to the deep-flowing river, and quite silent, save for the rushing of water.

There was a fine covered bridge, very dark. I went to the middle, and looked through the opening at the dark water below, at the façade of square lights, the tall village-front towering remote and silent above the river. The hill rose on either side the flood, down here was a small, forgotten, wonderful world, that belonged to the date of isolated village communities and wandering minstrels.

So I went back to the inn of "The Golden Stag," and, climbing some steps, I made a loud noise. A woman came, and I asked for food. She led me through a room where were enormous barrels, ten feet in diameter, lying fatly on their sides; then through a large stone-clean kitchen, with bright pans, ancient as the Meistersinger; then up some steps and into the long guest-room, where a few tables were laid for supper.

A few people were eating. I asked for Abendessen, and sat by the window looking at the darkness of the river below, the covered bridge, the dark hill opposite, crested with its few lights.

Then I ate a very large quantity of knoedel soup, and bread, and drank beer, and was very sleepy. Only one or two village men came in, and these soon went again, the place was dead still. Only at a long table on the opposite side of the room were seated seven or eight men, ragged, disreputable, some impudent—another came in late—the landlady gave them all thick soup with dumplings and bread and meat, serving them in a sort of brief disapprobation. They sat at the long table, eight or nine tramps and beggars and wanderers out of work, and they ate with a sort of cheerful callousness and brutality for the most part, and as if ravenously, looking round and grinning sometimes, subdued, cowed, like prisoners, and yet impudent. At the end one shouted to know where he was to sleep. The landlady called to the young serving-woman, and in a classic German severity of disapprobation, they were led up the stone stairs to their room. They tramped off in threes and twos, making a bad, mean, humiliated exit. It was not yet eight o'clock. The landlady sat talking to one bearded man, staid and severe, whilst, with her work on the table, she sewed steadily.

As the beggars and wanderers went slinking out of the room, some called impudently, cheerfully:

"Nacht, Frau Wirtin—G'Nacht, Wirtin—'te Nacht, Frau," to all of which the hostess answered a stereotyped "Gute Nacht," never turning her head from her sewing or indicating by the faintest movement that she was addressing the men who were filing raggedly to the doorway.

So the room was empty, save for the landlady and her sewing, the staid, elderly villager to whom she was talking in the unbeautiful dialect, and the young serving-woman who was clearing away the plates and basins of the tramps and beggars.

Then the villager also went.

"Gute Nacht, Frau Seidl," to the landlady; "Gute Nacht," at random, to me.

So I looked at the newspaper. Then I asked the landlady for a cigarette, not knowing how else to begin. So she came to my table, and we talked.

It pleased me to take upon myself a sort of romantic, wandering character; she said my German was "schön"; a little goes a long way.

So I asked her who were the men who had sat at the long table. She became rather stiff and curt.

"They are the men looking for work," she said, as if the subject were disagreeable.

"But why do they come here, so many?" I asked.

Then she told me that they were going out of the country: this was almost the last village of the border: that the relieving officer in each village was empowered to give to every vagrant a ticket entitling the holder to an evening meal, bed, and bread in the morning, at a certain inn. This was the inn for the vagrants coming to this village. The landlady received fourpence per head, I believe it was, for each of these wanderers.

"Little enough," I said.

"Nothing," she replied.

She did not like the subject at all. Only her respect for me made her answer.

"Bettler, Lumpen, und Taugenichtse!" I said, cheerfully.

"And men who are out of work, and are going back to their own parish," she said stiffly.

So we talked a little, and I too went to bed.

"Gute Nacht, Frau Wirtin."

"Gute Nacht, mein Herr."

So I went up more and more stone stairs, attended by the young woman. It was a great, lofty, old, deserted house, with many drab doors.

At last, in the distant topmost floor, I had my bedroom with two beds and bare floor and scant furniture. I looked down at the river far below, at the covered bridge, at the far lights on the hill above, opposite. Strange to be here in this lost, forgotten place, sleeping under the roof with tramps and beggars. I debated whether they would steal my boots if I put them out. But I risked it. The door-latch made a loud noise on the deserted landing, everywhere felt abandoned, forgotten. I wondered where the eight tramps and beggars were asleep. There was no way of securing the door. But somehow I felt that, if I were destined to be robbed or murdered, it would not be by tramps and beggars. So I blew out the candle and lay under the big feather bed, listening to the running and whispering of the mediaeval Rhine.

And when I waked up again it was sunny, it was morning on the hill opposite, though the river deep below ran in shadow.

The tramps and beggars were all gone: they must be cleared out by seven o'clock in the morning. So I had the inn to myself, I, and the landlady, and the serving-woman. Everywhere was very clean, full of the German morning energy and brightness, which is so different from the Latin morning. The Italians are dead and torpid first thing, the Germans are energetic and cheerful.

It was cheerful in the sunny morning, looking down on the swift river, the covered, picturesque bridge, the bank and the hill opposite. Then down the curving road of the facing hill the Swiss cavalry came riding, men in blue uniforms. I went out to watch them. They came thundering romantically through the dark cavern of the roofed-in bridge, and they dismounted at the entrance to the village. There was a fresh morning-cheerful newness everywhere, in the arrival of the troops, in the welcome of the villagers.

The Swiss do not look very military, neither in accoutrement nor in bearing. This little squad of cavalry seemed more like a party of common men riding out on some business of their own than like an army. They were very republican and very free. The officer who commanded them was one of themselves, his authority was by consent.

It was all very pleasant and genuine, there was a sense of ease and peacefulness, quite different from the mechanical, slightly sullen manœuvring of the Germans.

The village baker and his assistant came hot and floury from the bakehouse, bearing between them a great basket of fresh bread. The cavalry were all dismounted by the bridge-head, eating and drinking like business men. Villagers came to greet their friends: one soldier kissed his father, who came wearing a leathern apron. The school bell tang-tang-tanged from above, school-children merged timidly through the grouped horses, up the narrow street, passing unwillingly with their books. The river ran swiftly, the soldiers, very haphazard and slack in uniform, real shack-bags, chewed their bread in large mouthfuls, the young lieutenant, who seemed to be an officer only by consent of the men, stood apart by the bridge-head, gravely. They were all serious and self-contented, very unglamorous. It was like a business excursion on horseback, harmless and uninspiring. The uniforms were almost ludicrous, so ill-fitting and casual.

So I shouldered my own pack and set off, through the bridge over the Rhine, and up the hill opposite.

There is something very dead about this country. I remember I picked apples from the grass by the roadside, and some were very sweet. But for the rest, there was mile after mile of dead, uninspired country, uninspired, so neutral and ordinary that it was almost destructive.

One gets this feeling always in Switzerland, except high up: this feeling of average, of utter, soulless ordinariness, something intolerable. Mile after mile, to Zurich, it was just the same. It was just the same in the tram-car going into Zurich; it was just the same in the town, in the shops, in the restaurant. All was the utmost level of ordinariness and well-being, but so ordinary that it was like a blight. All the picturesqueness of the town is as nothing, it is like a most ordinary, average, usual person in an old costume. The place was soul-killing.

So after two hours' rest, eating in a restaurant, wandering by the quay, and through the market, and sitting on a seat by the lake, I found a steamer that would take me away. That is how I always feel in Switzerland, the only possible living sensation is the sensation of relief in going away, always going away. The horrible average ordinariness of it all, something utterly without flower or soul or transcendence, the horrible vigorous ordinariness, is too much.

So I went on a steamer down the long lake, surrounded by low grey hills. It was Saturday afternoon. A thin rain came on. I thought I would rather be in fiery Hell than in this dead level of average life.

I landed somewhere on the right bank, about three-quarters of the way down the lake. It was almost dark. Yet I must walk away. I climbed a long hill from the lake, came to the crest, looked down the darkness of the valley, and descended into the deep gloom, down into a soulless village.

But it was eight o'clock, and I had had enough. One might as well sleep. I found the "Gasthaus zur Post."

It was a small, very rough inn, having only one common room, with bare tables, and a short, stout, grim, rather surly landlady, and a landlord whose hair stood up on end, and who was trembling on the edge of delirium tremens.

They could only give me boiled ham: so I ate boiled ham and drank beer, and tried to digest the utter cold materialism of Switzerland.

As I sat with my back to the wall, staring blankly at the trembling landlord, who was ready at any moment to foam at the mouth, and at the dour landlady, who was quite capable of keeping him in order, there came in one of those dark, showy Italian girls, with a man. She wore a blouse and skirt, and no hat. Her hair was perfectly dressed. It was really Italy. The man was soft, dark, he would get stout later, *trapu*, he would have somewhat the figure of Caruso. But as yet he was soft, sensuous, young, handsome.

They sat at the long side-table, with their beer, and created another country at once within the room. Another Italian came, fair and fat and slow, one from the Venetian province: then another, a little, thin young man, who might have been a Swiss, save for his vivid movement.

This last was the first to speak to the Germans. The others had just said "Bier." But the little new-comer entered into a conversation with the landlady.

At last there were six Italians sitting talking loudly and warmly at the side-table. The slow, cold German-Swiss at the other tables looked at them occasionally. The landlord, with his crazed, stretched eyes, glared at them with hatred. But they fetched their beer from the bar with easy familiarity, and sat at their table, creating a bonfire of life in the callousness of the inn.

At last they finished their beer, and trooped off down the passage. The room was painfully empty. I did not know what to do.

Then I heard the landlord yelling and screeching and snarling from the kitchen at the back, for all the world like a mad dog. But the Swiss Saturday evening customers at the other tables smoked on and talked in their ugly dialect, without trouble. Then the landlady came in, and soon after the landlord, he collarless, with his waistcoat unbuttoned, showing his loose throat, and accentuating his round, pot belly. His limbs were thin and feverish, the skin of his face hung loose, his eyes were glaring, his hands trembled. Then he sat down to talk to a crony. His terrible appearance was a fiasco; nobody heeded him at all, only the landlady was surly.

From the back came loud noises of pleasure and excitement, and banging about. When the room door was opened I could see down the dark passage opposite another lighted door. Then the fat, fair Italian came in for more beer.

"What is all the noise?" I asked the landlady at last.

"It is the Italians," she said.

"What are they doing?"

"They are doing a play."

"Where?"

She jerked her head: "In the room at the back."

"Can I go and look at them?"

"I should think so."

The landlord glaringly watched me go out. I went down the stone passage, and found a great, half-lighted room, that might be used to hold meetings, with forms piled at the side. At one end was a raised platform or stage. And on this stage was a table and a lamp, and the Italians grouped round the light, gesticulating and laughing. Their beer mugs were on the table and on the floor of the stage: the little sharp youth was intently looking over some papers, the others were bending over the table with him.

They looked up as I entered from the distance, looked at me in the distant twilight of the dusky room, as if I were an intruder, as if I should go away when I had seen them. But I said, in German:

"May I look?"

They were still unwilling to see or to hear me.

"What do you say?" the small one asked in reply.

The others stood and watched, slightly at bay, like suspicious animals.

"If I might come and look," I said in German, then, feeling very uncomfortable, in Italian: "You are doing a drama, the landlady told me."

The big, empty room was behind me, dark; the little company of Italians stood above me, in the light of the lamp which was on the table. They all watched with unseeing, unwilling looks: I was merely an intrusion.

"We are only learning it," said the small youth.

They wanted me to go away. But I wanted to stay.

"May I listen," I said. "I don't want to stay in there." And I indicated, with a movement of the head, the inn-room beyond.

"Yes," said the young intelligent man. "But we are only reading our parts."

They had all become more friendly to me, they accepted me.

"You are a German?" asked one youth.

"No—English."

"English? But do you live in Switzerland?"

"No—I am walking to Italy."

"On foot?"

They looked with wakened eyes.

"Yes."

So I told them about my journey. They were puzzled. They did not quite understand why I wanted to walk. But they were delighted with the idea of going to Lugano and Como and then to Milan.

"Where do you come from?" I asked them.

They were all from the villages between Verona and Venice. They had seen the Garda. I told them of my living there.

"Those peasants of the mountains," they said at once, "they are people of little education. Rather wild folk."

And they spoke with good-humoured contempt.

I thought of Paolo, and Il Duro, and the Signor Pietro, our padrone, and I resented these factory-hands for criticising them.

So I sat on the edge of the stage whilst they rehearsed their parts. The little, thin, intelligent fellow, Giuseppino, was the leader. The others read their parts in the laborious, disjointed fashion of the peasant, who can only see one word at a time, and has then to put the words together, afterwards, to make sense. The play was an amateur melodrama, printed in little penny booklets, for carnival production. This was only the second reading they had given it, and the handsome, dark fellow, who was roused and displaying himself before the girl, a hard, erect piece of callousness, laughed and flushed and stumbled, and understood nothing till it was transferred into him direct through Giuseppino. The fat, fair, slow man was more conscientious. He laboured through his part. The other two men were in the background, more or less.

The most confidential was the fat, fair, slow man, who was called Alberto. His part was not very important, so he could sit by me and talk to me.

He said they were all workers in the factory—silk, I think it was—in the village. They were a whole colony of Italians, thirty or more families. They had all come at different times.

Giuseppino had been longest in the village. He had come when he was eleven, with his parents, and had attended the Swiss school. So he spoke perfect German. He was a clever man, was married, and had two children.

He himself, Alberto, had been seven years in the valley; the girl, la Maddelena, had been here ten years; the dark man, Alfredo, who was flushed with excitement of her, had been in the village about nine years; he alone of all the men was not married.

The others had all married Italian wives, and they lived in the great dwelling whose windows shone yellow by the rattling factory. They lived entirely among themselves, none of them could speak German, more than a few words, except the Giuseppino, who was like a native here.

It was very strange being among these Italians exiled in Switzerland. Alfredo, the dark one, the unmarried, was in the old tradition. Yet even he was curiously subject to a new purpose, as if there were some greater new will that included him, sensuous, mindless as he was. He seemed to give his consent to something beyond himself. In this he was different from Il Duro, in that he had put himself under the control of the outside conception.

It was strange to watch them on the stage, the Italians all lambent, soft, warm, sensuous, yet moving subject round Giuseppino, who was always quiet, always ready, always impersonal. There was a look of purpose, almost of devotion on his face, that singled him out and made him seem the one stable, eternal being among them. They quarrelled, and he let them quarrel up to a certain point; then he called them back. He let them do as they liked, so long as they adhered more or less to the central purpose, so long as they got on in some measure with the play.

All the while they were drinking beer and smoking cigarettes. The Alberto was barman: he went out continually with the glasses. The Maddelena had a small glass. In the lamplight of the stage, the little party read and smoked and practised, exposed to the empty darkness of the big room. Queer and isolated it seemed, a tiny, pathetic magic-land far away from the barrenness of Switzerland. I could believe in the old fairy tales, where, when the rock was opened, a magic underworld was revealed.

The Alfredo, flushed, roused, handsome, but very soft and enveloping in his heat, laughed and threw himself into his pose, laughed foolishly, and then gave himself up to his part. The Alberto, slow and laborious, yet with a spark of vividness and natural intensity flashing through, replied and gesticulated, the Maddelena laid her head on the bosom of Alfredo, the other men started into action, and the play proceeded intently for half an hour.

Quick, vivid, and sharp, the little Giuseppino was always central. But he seemed almost invisible. When I think back, I can scarcely see him, I can only see the others, the lamplight on their faces and on their full, gesticulating limbs. I can see the Maddelena, rather coarse and hard and repellent, declaiming her words in a loud, half-cynical voice, falling on the breast of the Alfredo, who was soft and sensuous, more like a female, flushing, with his mouth getting wet, his eyes moist, as he was roused. I can see the Alberto, slow, laboured, yet with a kind of pristine simplicity in all his movements, that touched his fat commonplaceness with beauty. Then there were the other two men, shy, inflammable, unintelligent, with their sudden Italian rushes of hot feeling. All their faces are distinct in the lamplight, all their bodies are palpable and dramatic.

But the face of the Giuseppino is like a pale luminousness, a sort of gleam among all the ruddy glow, his body is evanescent, like a shadow. And his being seemed to cast its influence over all the others, except perhaps the woman, who was hard and resistant. The other men seemed all overcast, mitigated, in part transfigured by the will of the little leader. But they were very soft stuff, if inflammable.

The young woman of the inn, niece of the landlady, came down and called out across the room.

"We will go away from here now," said the Giuseppino to me. "They close at eleven. But we have another inn in the next parish that is open all night. Come with us and drink some wine."

"But," I said, "you would rather be alone."

No, they pressed me to go, they wanted me to go with them, they were eager, they wanted to entertain me. Alfredo, flushed, wet-mouthed, warm, protested I must drink wine, the real Italian red wine, from their own village at home. They would have no nay.

So I told the landlady. She said I must be back by twelve o'clock.

The night was very dark. Below the road the stream was rushing, there was a great factory on the other side of the water, making faint quivering lights of reflection, and one could see the working of machinery shadowy through the lighted windows. Near by was the tall tenement where the Italians lived.

We went on through the straggling, raw village, deep beside the stream, then over the small bridge, and up the steep hill down which I had come earlier in the evening.

So we arrived at the café. It was so different inside from the German inn, yet it was not like an Italian café either. It was brilliantly lighted, clean, new, and there were red-and-white cloths on the tables. The host was in the room, and his daughter, a beautiful red-haired girl.

Greetings were exchanged with the quick, intimate directness of Italy. But there was another note also, a faint echo of reserve, as though they reserved themselves from the outer world, making a special inner community.

Alfredo was hot: he took off his coat. We all sat freely at a long table, whilst the red-haired girl brought a quart of red wine. At other tables men were playing cards, with the odd Neapolitan cards. They too were talking Italian. It was a warm, ruddy bit of Italy within the cold darkness of Switzerland.

"When you come to Italy," they said to me, "salute it from us, salute the sun, and the earth, l'Italia."

So we drank in salute of Italy. They sent their greeting by me.

"You know in Italy there is the sun, the sun," said Alfredo to me, profoundly moved, wet-mouthed, tipsy.

I was reminded of Enrico Persevalli and his terrifying cry at the end of *Ghosts*:

"Il sole, il sole!"

So we talked for a while of Italy. They had a pained tenderness for it, sad, reserved.

"Don't you want to go back?" I said, pressing them to tell me definitely. "Won't you go back some time?"

"Yes," they said, "we will go back."

But they spoke reservedly, without freedom. We talked about Italy, about songs, and Carnival; about the food, polenta, and salt. They laughed at my pretending to cut the slabs of polenta with a string: that rejoiced them all: it took them back to the Italian mezzo-giorno, the bells jangling in the campanile, the eating after the heavy work on the land.

But they laughed with the slight pain and contempt and fondness which every man feels towards his past, when he has struggled away from that past, from the conditions which made it.

They loved Italy passionately; but they would not go back. All their blood, all their senses were Italian, needed the Italian sky, the speech, the sensuous life. They could hardly live except through the senses. Their minds were not developed, mentally they were children, lovable, naïve, almost fragile children. But sensually they were men: sensually they were accomplished.

Yet a new tiny flower was struggling to open in them, the flower of a new spirit. The substratum of Italy has always been pagan, sensuous, the most potent symbol the sexual symbol. The child is really a non-Christian symbol: it is the symbol of man's triumph of eternal life in procreation. The worship of the Cross never really held good in Italy. The Christianity of Northern Europe has never had any place there.

And now, when Northern Europe is turning back on its own Christianity, denying it all, the Italians are struggling with might and main against the sensuous spirit which still dominates them. When Northern Europe, whether it hates Nietzsche or not, is crying out for the Dionysic ecstasy, practising on itself the Dionysic ecstasy, Southern Europe is breaking free from Dionysos, from the triumphal affirmation of life over death, immortality through procreation.

I could see these sons of Italy would never go back. Men like Paolo and Il Duro broke away only to return. The dominance of the old form was too strong for them. Call it love of country or love of the village, campanilismo, or what not, it was the dominance of the old pagan form, the old affirmation of immortality through procreation, as opposed to the Christian affirmation of immortality through self-death and social love.

But "John," and these Italians in Switzerland were a generation younger, and they would not go back, at least, not to the old Italy. Suffer as they might, and they did suffer, wincing in every nerve and fibre from the cold material insentience of the northern countries and of America, still they would endure this for the sake of something else they wanted. They would suffer a death in the flesh, as "John" had suffered in fighting the street crowd, as these men suffered year after year cramped in their black, gloomy, cold Swiss valley, working in the factory. But there would come a new spirit out of it.

Even Alfredo was submitted to the new process; though he belonged entirely by nature to the sort of Il Duro, he was purely sensuous and mindless. But under the influence of Giuseppino he was thrown down, as fallow to the new spirit that would come.

And then, when the others were all partially tipsy, the Giuseppino began to talk to me. In him was a steady flame burning, burning, burning, a flame of the mind, of the spirit, something new and clear, something that held even the soft, sensuous Alfredo in submission, besides all the others, who had some little development of mind.

"Sa Signore," said the Giuseppino to me, quiet, almost invisible or inaudible, as it seemed, like a spirit addressing me, "l'uomo non ha patria—a man has no country. What has the Italian government to do with us? What does a government mean? It makes us work, it takes part of our wages away from us, it makes us soldiers—and what for? What is government for?"

"Have you been a soldier?" I interrupted him.

He had not, none of them had: that was why they could not really go back to Italy. Now this was out; this explained partly their curious reservation in speaking about their beloved country. They had forfeited parents as well as homeland.

"What does the government do? It takes taxes, it has an army, and police, and it makes roads. But we could do without an army, and we could be our own police, and we could make our own roads. What is this government? Who wants it? Only those who are unjust, and want to have advantage over somebody else. It is an instrument of injustice and of wrong.

"Why should we have a government? Here, in this village, there are thirty families of Italians. There is no government for them, no Italian government. And we live together better than in Italy. We are richer and freer, we have no policemen, no poor laws. We help each other, and there are no poor.

"Why are these governments always doing what we don't want them to do? We should not be fighting in the Cirenaica if we were all Italians. It is the government that does it. They talk and talk and do things with us: but we don't want them."

The others, tipsy, sat round the table with the terrified gravity of children who are somehow responsible for things they do not understand. They stirred in their seats, turning aside, with gestures almost of pain, of imprisonment. Only Alfredo, laying his hand on mine, was laughing, loosely, floridly. He would upset all the government with a jerk of his well-built shoulder, and then he would have a spree—such a spree. He laughed wetly to me.

The Giuseppino waited patiently during this tipsy confidence, but his pale clarity and beauty was something constant and star-like, in comparison with the flushed, soft handsomeness of the other. He waited patiently, looking at me.

But I did not want him to go on: I did not want to answer. I could feel a new spirit in him, something strange and pure and slightly frightening. He wanted something which was beyond me. And my soul was somewhere in tears, crying helplessly like an infant in the night. I could not respond: I could not answer. He seemed to look at me, me, an Englishman, an educated man, for corroboration. But I could not corroborate him. I knew the purity and new struggling towards birth of a true, star-like spirit. But I could not confirm him in his utterance: my soul could not respond. I did not believe in the perfectibility of man. I did not believe in infinite harmony among men. And this was his star, this belief.

It was nearly mid-night. A Swiss came in and asked for beer. The Italians gathered round them a curious darkness of reserve. And then I must go.

They shook hands with me warmly, truthfully, putting a sort of implicit belief in me, as representative of some further knowledge. But there was a fixed, calm resolve over the face of the Giuseppino, a sort of steady faith, even in disappointment. He gave me a copy of a little Anarchist paper published in Geneva. *L'Anarchista*, I believe it was called. I glanced at it. It was in Italian, naïve, simple, rather rhetorical. So they were all Anarchists, these Italians.

I ran down the hill in the thick Swiss darkness to the little bridge, and along the uneven, cobbled street. I did not want to think, I did not want to know. I wanted to arrest my activity, to keep it confined to the moment, to the adventure.

When I came to the flight of stone steps which led up to the door of the inn, at the side, I saw in the darkness two figures. They said a low good-night and parted, the girl began to knock at the door, the man disappeared. It was the niece of the landlady parting from her lover.

We waited outside the locked door, at the top of the stone steps, in the darkness of midnight. The stream rustled below. Then came a shouting and an insane snarling within the passage; the bolts were not withdrawn.

"It is the gentleman, it is the strange gentleman," called the girl.

Then came again the furious shouting snarls, and the landlord's mad voice:

"Stop out, stop out there. The door won't be opened again."

"The strange gentleman is here," repeated the girl.

Then more movement was heard, and the door was suddenly open, and the landlord rushing out upon us, wielding a broom. It was a strange sight, in the half-lighted passage. I stared blankly in the doorway. The landlord dropped the broom he was waving and collapsed as if by magic, looking at me, though he continued to mutter madly, unintelligibly. The girl slipped past me, and the landlord snarled. Then he picked up the brush, at the same time crying:

"You are late, the door was shut, it will not be opened. We shall have the police in the house. We said twelve o'clock, at twelve o'clock the door must be shut, and must not be opened again. If you are late you stay out——"

So he went snarling, his voice rising higher and higher, away into the kitchen.

"You are coming to your room?" the landlady said to me coldly. And she led me upstairs.

The room was over the road, clean, but rather ugly, with a large tin, that had once contained lard or Swiss-milk, to wash in. But the bed was good enough, which was all that mattered.

I heard the landlord yelling, and there was a long and systematic thumping somewhere, thump, thump, thump, and banging. I wondered where it was. I could not locate it at all, because my room lay beyond another large room: I had to go through a large room, by the foot of two beds, to get to my door: so I could not quite tell where anything was.

But I went to sleep whilst I was wondering.

I woke in the morning and washed in the tin. I could see a few people in the street, walking in the Sunday morning leisure. It felt like Sunday in England, and I shrank from it. I could see none of the Italians. The factory stood there, raw and large and sombre, by the stream, and the drab-coloured stone tenements were close by. Otherwise the village was a straggling Swiss street, almost untouched.

The landlord was quiet and reasonable, even friendly, in the morning. He wanted to talk to me: where had I bought my boots, was his first question. I told him in Munich. And how much had they cost? I told him twenty-eight marks. He was much impressed by them: such good boots, of such soft, strong, beautiful leather, he had not seen such boots for a long time.

Then I knew it was he who had cleaned my boots. I could see him fingering them and wondering over them. I rather liked him. I could see he had had imagination, once, and a certain fineness of nature. Now he was corrupted with drink, too far gone to be even a human being. I hated the village.

They set bread and butter and a piece of cheese weighing about five pounds, and large, fresh, sweet cakes for breakfast. I ate and was thankful: the food was good.

A couple of village youths came in, in their Sunday clothes. They had the Sunday stiffness. It reminded me of the stiffness and curious self-consciousness that comes over life in England on a Sunday. But the landlord sat with his waistcoat hanging open over his shirt, pot-bellied, his ruined face leaning forward, talking, always talking, wanting to know.

So in a few minutes I was out on the road again, thanking God for the blessing of a road that belongs to no man, and travels away from all men.

I did not want to see the Italians. Something had got tied up in me, and I could not bear to see them again. I liked them so much; but, for some reason or other, my mind stopped like clockwork if I wanted to think of them and of what their lives would be, their future. It was as if some curious negative magnetism arrested my mind, prevented it from working, the moment I turned it towards these Italians.

I do not know why it was. But I could never write to them, or think of them, or even read the paper they gave me, though it lay in my drawer for months, in Italy, and I often glanced over six lines of it. And often, often my mind went back to the group, the play they were rehearsing, the wine in the pleasant café, and the night. But the moment my memory touched them, my whole soul stopped and was null; I could not go on. Even now I cannot really consider them in thought. I shrink involuntarily away. I do not know why this is.

The Return Journey

When one walks, one must travel west or south. If one turn northward or eastward it is like walking down a *cul-de-sac*, to the blind end.

So it has been since the Crusaders came home satiated, and the Renaissance saw the western sky as an archway into the future. So it is still. We must go westwards and southwards.

It is a sad and gloomy thing to travel even from Italy into France. But it is a joyful thing to walk south to Italy, south and west. It is so. And there is a certain exaltation in the thought of going west, even to Cornwall, to Ireland. It is as if the magnetic poles were south-west and north-east, for our spirits, with the south-west, under the sunset, as the positive pole. So whilst I walk through Switzerland, though it is a valley of gloom and depression, a light seems to flash out under every footstep, with the joy of progression.

It was Sunday morning when I left the valley where the Italians lived. I went quickly over the stream, heading for Lucerne. It was a good thing to be out of doors, with one's pack on one's back, climbing uphill. But the trees were thick by the roadside; I was not yet free. It was Sunday morning, very still.

In two hours I was at the top of the hill, looking out over the intervening valley at the long lake of Zurich, spread there beyond with its girdle of low hills, like a relief-map. I could not bear to look at it, it was so small and unreal. I had a feeling as if it were false, a large relief-map that I was looking down upon, and which I wanted to smash. It seemed to intervene between me and some reality. I could not believe that that was the real world. It was a figment, a fabrication, like a dull landscape painted on a wall, to hide the real landscape.

So I went on, over to the other side of the hill, and I looked out again. Again there were the smoky-looking hills and the lake like a piece of looking-glass. But the hills were higher: that big one was the Rigi. I set off down the hill.

There was fat agricultural land and several villages. And church was over. The church-goers were all coming home: men in black broadcloth and old, chimney-pot silk hats, carrying their umbrellas; women in ugly dresses, carrying books and umbrellas. The streets were dotted with these black-clothed men and stiff women, all reduced to a Sunday nullity. I hated it. It reminded me of that which I knew in my boyhood, that stiff, null "propriety" which used to come over us, like a sort of deliberate and self-inflicted cramp, on Sundays. I hated these elders in black broadcloth, with their neutral faces, going home piously to their Sunday dinners. I hated the feeling of these villages, comfortable, well-to-do, clean, and proper.

And my boot was chafing two of my toes. That always happens. I had come down to a wide, shallow valley-bed, marshy. So about a mile out of the village I sat down by a stone bridge, by a stream, and tore up my handkerchief, and bound up the toes. And as I sat binding my toes, two of the elders in black, with umbrellas under their arms, approached from the direction of the village.

They made me so furious, I had to hasten to fasten my boot, to hurry on again, before they should come near me. I could not bear the way they walked and talked, so crambling and material and mealy-mouthed.

Then it did actually begin to rain. I was just going down a short hill. So I sat under a bush and watched the trees drip. I was so glad to be there, homeless, without place or belonging, crouching under the leaves in the copse by the road, that I felt I had, like the meek, inherited the earth. Some men went by, with their coat-collars turned up, and the rain making still blacker their black broadcloth shoulders. They did not see me. I was as safe and separate as a ghost. So I ate the remains of my food, that I had bought in Zurich, and waited for the rain.

Later, in the wet Sunday afternoon, I went on to the little lake, past many inert, neutral, material people, down an ugly road where trams ran. The blight of Sunday was almost intolerable near the town.

So on I went, by the side of the steamy, reedy lake, walking the length of it. Then suddenly I went in to a little villa by the water for tea. In Switzerland every house is a villa.

But this villa was kept by two old ladies and a delicate dog, who must not get his feet wet. I was very happy there. I had good jam and strange honey-cakes for tea, that I liked, and the little old ladies pattered round in a great stir, always whirling like two dry leaves after the restless dog.

"Why must he not go out?" I said.

"Because it is wet," they answered, "and he coughs and sneezes."

"Without a handkerchief, that is not *angenehm*," I said.

So we became bosom friends.

"You are Austrian?" they said to me.

I said I was, from Graz; that my father was a doctor in Graz, and that I was walking for my pleasure through the countries of Europe.

I said this because I knew a doctor from Graz who was always wandering about, and because I did not want to be myself, an Englishman, to these two old ladies. I wanted to be something else. So we exchanged confidences.

They told me, in their queer, old, toothless fashion, about their visitors, a man who used to fish all day, every day for three weeks, fish every hour of the day, though many a day he caught nothing—nothing at all—still he fished from the boat: and so on, such trivialities. Then they told me of a third sister who had died, a third little old lady. One could feel the gap in the house. They cried; and I, being an Austrian from Graz, to my astonishment felt my tears slip over on to the table. I also *was* sorry, and I would have kissed the little old ladies to comfort them.

"Only in heaven it is warm, and it doesn't rain, and no one dies," I said, looking at the wet leaves.

Then I went away. I would have stayed the night at this house: I wanted to. But I had developed my Austrian character too far.

So I went on to a detestable brutal inn in the town. And the next day I climbed over the back of the detestable Rigi, with its vile hotel, to come to Lucerne. There, on the Rigi, I met a lost young Frenchman who could speak no German, and who said he could not find people to speak French. So we sat on a stone and became close friends, and I promised faithfully to go and visit him in his barracks in Algiers: I was to sail from Naples to Algiers. He wrote me the address on his card, and told me he had friends in the regiment, to whom I should be introduced, and we could have a good time, if I would stay a week or two, down there in Algiers.

How much more real Algiers was than the rock on the Rigi where we sat, or the lake beneath, or the mountains beyond. Algiers is very real, though I have never seen it, and my friend is my friend for ever, though I have lost his card and forgotten his name. He was a Government clerk from Lyons, making this his first foreign tour before he began his military service. He showed me his "circular excursion ticket." Then at last we parted, for he must get to the top of the Rigi, and I must get to the bottom.

Lucerne and its lake were as irritating as ever: like the wrapper round milk chocolate. I could not sleep even one night there: I took the steamer down the lake, to the very last station. There I found a good German inn, and was happy.

There was a tall thin young man, whose face was red and inflamed from the sun. I thought he was a German tourist. He had just come in. And he was eating bread and milk. He and I were alone in the eating-room. He was looking at an illustrated paper.

"Does the steamer stop here all night?" I asked him in German, hearing the boat bustling and blowing her steam on the water outside, and glancing round at her lights, red and white, in the pitch darkness.

He only shook his head over his bread and milk, and did not lift his face.

"Are you English, then?" I said.

No one but an Englishman would have hidden his face in a bowl of milk, and have shaken his red ears in such painful confusion.

"Yes," he said, "I am."

And I started almost out of my skin at the unexpected London accent. It was as if one suddenly found oneself in the Tube.

"So am I," I said. "Where have you come from?"

Then he began, like a general explaining his plans, to tell me. He had walked round over the Furka Pass, had been on foot four or five days. He had walked tremendously. Knowing no German, and nothing of the mountains, he had set off alone on this tour: he had a fortnight's holiday. So he had come over the Rhone Glacier across the Furka and down from Andermatt to the Lake. On this last day he had walked about thirty mountain miles.

"But weren't you tired?" I said, aghast.

He was. Under the inflamed redness of his sun- and wind- and snow-burned face he was sick with fatigue. He had done over a hundred miles in the last four days.

"Did you enjoy it?" I asked.

"Oh yes. I wanted to do it all." He wanted to do it, and he *had* done it. But God knows what he wanted to do it for. He had now one day at Lucerne, one day at Interlaken and Berne, then London.

I was sorry for him in my soul, he was so cruelly tired, so perishingly victorious.

"Why did you do so much?" I said. "Why did you come on foot all down the valley when you could have taken the train? Was it worth it?"

"I think so," he said.

Yet he was sick with fatigue and over-exhaustion. His eyes were quite dark, sightless: he seemed to have lost the power of seeing, to be virtually blind. He hung his head forward when he had to write a post card, as if he felt his way. But he turned his post card so that I should not see to whom it was addressed; not that I was interested; only I noticed his little, cautious, English movement of privacy.

"What time will you be going on?" I asked.

"When is the first steamer?" he said, and he turned out a guide-book with a timetable. He would leave at about seven.

"But why so early?" I said to him.

He must be in Lucerne at a certain hour, and at Interlaken in the evening.

"I suppose you will rest when you get to London?" I said.

He looked at me quickly, reservedly.

I was drinking beer: I asked him wouldn't he have something. He thought a moment, then said he would have another glass of hot milk. The landlord came—"And bread?" he asked.

The Englishman refused. He could not eat, really. Also he was poor; he had to husband his money. The landlord brought the milk and asked me, when would the gentleman want to go away. So I made arrangements between the landlord and the stranger. But the Englishman was slightly uncomfortable at my intervention. He did not like me to know what he would have for breakfast.

I could feel so well the machine that had him in its grip. He slaved for a year, mechanically, in London, riding in the Tube, working in the office. Then for a fortnight he was let free. So he rushed to Switzerland, with a tour planned out, and with just enough money to see him through, and to buy presents at Interlaken: bits of the edelweiss pottery: I could see him going home with them.

So he arrived, and with amazing, pathetic courage set forth on foot in a strange land, to face strange landlords, with no language but English at his command, and his purse definitely limited. Yet he wanted to go among the mountains, to cross a glacier. So he had walked on and on, like one possessed, ever forward. His name might have been Excelsior, indeed.

But then, when he reached his Furka, only to walk along the ridge and to descend on the same side! My God, it, was killing to the soul. And here he was, down again from the mountains, beginning his journey home again: steamer and train and steamer and train and Tube, till he was back in the machine.

It hadn't let him go, and he knew it. Hence his cruel self-torture of fatigue, his cruel exercise of courage. He who hung his head in his milk in torment when I asked him a question in German, what courage had he not needed to take this his very first trip out of England, alone, on foot!

His eyes were dark and deep with unfathomable courage. Yet he was going back in the morning. He was going back. All he had courage for was to go back. He would go back, though he died by inches. Why not? It was killing him, it was like living loaded with irons. But he had the courage to submit, to die that way, since it was the way allotted to him.

The way he sank on the table in exhaustion, drinking his milk, his will, nevertheless, so perfect and unblemished, triumphant, though his body was broken and in anguish, was almost too much to bear. My heart was wrung for my countryman, wrung till it bled.

I could not bear to understand my countryman, a man who worked for his living, as I had worked, as nearly all my countrymen work. He would not give in. On his holiday he would walk, to fulfil his purpose, walk on; no matter how cruel the effort were, he would not rest, he would not relinquish his purpose nor abate his will, not by one jot or tittle. His body must pay whatever his will demanded, though it were torture.

It all seemed to me so foolish. I was almost in tears. He went to bed. I walked by the dark lake, and talked to the girl in the inn. She was a pleasant girl: it was a pleasant inn, a homely place. One could be happy there.

In the morning it was sunny, the lake was blue. By night I should be nearly at the crest of my journey. I was glad.

The Englishman had gone. I looked for his name in the book. It was written in a fair, clerkly hand. He lived at Streatham. Suddenly I hated him. The dogged fool, to keep his nose on the grindstone like that. What was all his courage but the very tip-top of cowardice? What a vile nature—almost Sadish, proud, like the infamous Red Indians, of being able to stand torture.

The landlord came to talk to me. He was fat and comfortable and too respectful. But I had to tell him all the Englishman had done, in the way of a holiday, just to shame his own fat, ponderous, inn-keeper's luxuriousness that was too gross. Then all I got out of his enormous comfortableness was:

"Yes, that's a *very* long step to take."

So I set off myself, up the valley between the close, snow-topped mountains, whose white gleamed above me as I crawled, small as an insect, along the dark, cold valley below.

There had been a cattle fair earlier in the morning, so troops of cattle were roving down the road, some with bells tang-tanging, all with soft faces and startled eyes and a sudden swerving of horns. The grass was very green by the roads and by the streams; the shadows of the mountain slopes were very dark on either hand, overhead, and the sky with snowy flanks and tips was high up.

Here, away from the world, the villages were quiet and obscure— left behind. They had the same fascinating atmosphere of being forgotten, left out of the world, that old English villages have. And buying apples and cheese and bread in a little shop that sold everything and smelled of everything, I felt at home again.

But climbing gradually higher, mile after mile, always between the shadows of the high mountains, I was glad I did not live in the Alps. The villages on the slopes, the people there, seemed as if they *must* gradually, bit by bit, slide down and tumble to the water-course, and be rolled on away, away to the sea. Straggling, haphazard little villages ledged on the slope, high up, beside their wet, green, hanging meadows, with pine trees behind and the valley bottom far below, and rocks right above, on both sides, seemed like little temporary squat-tings of outcast people. It seemed impossible that they should persist there, with great shadows wielded over them, like a menace, and gleams of brief sunshine, like a window. There was a sense of momen-tariness and expectation. It seemed as though some dramatic upheaval must take place, the mountains fall down into their own shadows. The valley beds were like deep graves, the sides of the mountains like the collapsing walls of a grave. The very mountain-tops above, bright with transcendent snow, seemed like death, eternal death.

There, it seemed, in the glamorous snow, was the source of death, which fell down in great waves of shadow and rock, rushing to the level earth. And all the people of the mountains, on the slopes, in the valleys, seemed to live upon this great, rushing wave of death, of breaking-down, of destruction.

The very pure source of breaking-down, decomposition, the very quick of cold death, is the snowy mountain-peak above. There, eternally, goes on the white foregathering of the crystals, out of the deathly cold of the heavens; this is the static nucleus where death meets life in its elementality. And thence, from their white, radiant nucleus of death in life, flows the great flux downwards, towards life and warmth. And we below, we cannot think of the flux upwards, that flows from the needle-point of snow to the unutterable cold and death.

The people under the mountains, they seem to live in the flux of death, the last, strange, overshadowed units of life. Big shadows wave over them, there is the eternal noise of water falling icily downwards from the source of death overhead.

And the people under the shadows, dwelling in the tang of snow and the noise of icy water, seem dark, almost sordid, brutal. There is no flowering or coming to flower, only this persistence, in the ice-touched air, of reproductive life.

But it is difficult to get a sense of a native population. Everywhere are the hotels and the foreigners, the parasitism. Yet there is, unseen, this overshadowed, overhung, sordid mountain population, ledged on the slopes and in the crevices. In the wider valleys there is still a sense of cowering among the people. But they catch a new tone from their contact with the foreigners. And in the towns are nothing but tradespeople.

So I climbed slowly up, for a whole day, first along the high-road, sometimes above and sometimes below the twisting, serpentine railway, then afterwards along a path on the side of the hill—a path that went through the crew-yards of isolated farms and even through the garden of a village priest. The priest was decorating an archway. He stood on a chair in the sunshine, reaching up with a garland, whilst the serving-woman stood below, talking loudly.

The valley here seemed wider, the great flanks of the mountains gave place, the peaks above were further back. So one was happier. I was pleased as I sat by the thin track of single flat stones that dropped swiftly downhill.

At the bottom was a little town with a factory or quarry, or a foundry, some place with long, smoking chimneys. Which made me feel quite at home among the mountains.

It is the hideous rawness of the world of men, the horrible, desolating harshness of the advance of the industrial world upon the world of nature that is so painful. It looks as though the industrial spread of mankind were a sort of dry disintegration advancing and advancing, a process of dry disintegration. If only we could learn to take thought for the whole world instead of for merely tiny bits of it.

I went through the little, hideous, crude factory-settlement in the high valley, where the eternal snows gleamed, past the enormous advertisements for chocolate and hotels, up the last steep slope of the pass to where the tunnel begins. Göschenen, the village at the mouth of the tunnel, is all railway sidings and haphazard villas for tourists, post cards, and touts and weedy carriages; disorder and sterile chaos, high up. How should any one stay there!

I went on up the pass itself. There were various parties of visitors on the roads and tracks, people from towns incongruously walking and driving. It was drawing on to evening. I climbed slowly, between the great cleft in the rock where are the big iron gates, through which the road winds, winds half-way down the narrow gulley of solid, living rock, the very throat of the path, where hangs a tablet in memory of many Russians killed.

Emerging through the dark rocky throat of the pass I came to the upper world, the level upper world. It was evening, livid, cold. On either side spread the sort of moorland of the wide pass-head. I drew near along the high road, to Andermatt.

Everywhere were soldiers moving about the livid, desolate waste of this upper world. I passed the barracks and the first villas for visitors. Darkness was coming on, the straggling, inconclusive street of Andermatt looked as if it were some accident: houses, hotels, barracks, lodging-places tumbled at random as the caravan of civilisation crossed this high, cold, arid bridge of the European world.

I bought two post cards and wrote them out of doors in the cold livid twilight. Then I asked a soldier where was the post-office. He directed me. It was something like sending post cards from Skegness or Bognor, there in the post-office.

I was trying to make myself agree to stay in Andermatt for the night. But I could not. The whole place was so terribly raw and flat and accidental, as if great pieces of furniture had tumbled out of a pantechnicon and lay discarded by the road. I hovered in the street, in the twilight, trying to make myself stay. I looked at the announcements of lodgings and boarding for visitors. It was no good. I could not go into one of these houses.

So I passed on, through the old, low, broad-eaved houses that cringe down to the very street, out into the open again. The air was fierce and savage. On one side was a moorland, level, on the other a sweep of naked hill, curved concave, and sprinkled with snow. I could see how wonderful it would all be, under five or six feet of winter snow, ski-ing and tobogganing at Christmas. But it needed the snow. In the summer there is to be seen nothing but the winter's broken detritus.

The twilight deepened, though there was still the strange, glassy translucency of the snow-lit air. A fragment of moon was in the sky. A carriage-load of French tourists passed me. There was the loud noise of water, as ever, something eternal and maddening in its sound, like the sound of Time itself, rustling and rushing and wavering, but never for a second ceasing. The rushing of Time that continues throughout eternity, this is the sound of the icy streams of Switzerland, something that mocks and destroys our warm being.

So I came, in the early darkness, to the little village with the broken castle that stands for ever frozen at the point where the track parts, one way continuing along the ridge to the Furka Pass, the other swerving over the hill to the left, over the Gotthard.

In this village I must stay. I saw a woman looking hastily, furtively from a doorway. I knew she was looking for visitors. I went on up the hilly street. There were only a few wooden houses and a gaily lighted wooden inn, where men were laughing, and strangers, men, standing talking loudly in the doorway.

It was very difficult to go to a house this night. I did not want to approach any of them. I turned back to the house of the peering woman. She had looked hen-like and anxious. She would be glad of a visitor to help her pay her rent.

It was a clean, pleasant wooden house, made to keep out the cold. That seemed its one function: to defend the inmates from the cold. It was furnished like a hut, just tables and chairs and bare, wooden walls. One felt very close and secure in the room, as in a hut, shut away from the outer world.

The hen-like woman came.

"Can I have a bed," I said, "for the night?"

"Abendessen, ja!" she replied. "Will you have soup and boiled beef and vegetables?"

I said I would, so I sat down to wait, in the utter silence. I could scarcely hear the ice-stream, the silence seemed frozen, the house empty. The woman seemed to be flitting aimlessly, scurriedly, in reflex against the silence. One could almost touch the stillness as one could touch the walls, or the stove, or the table with white American oil-cloth.

Suddenly she appeared again.

"What will you drink?"

She watched my face anxiously, and her voice was pathetic, slightly pleading in its quickness.

"Wine or beer?" she said.

I would not trust the coldness of beer.

"A half of red wine," I said.

I knew she was going to keep me an indefinite time.

She appeared with the wine and bread.

"Would you like omelette after the beef?" she asked. "Omelette with cognac; I can make it *very* good."

I knew I should be spending too much, but I said yes. After all, why should I not eat, after the long walk?

So she left me again, whilst I sat in the utter isolation and stillness, eating bread and drinking the wine, which was good. And I listened for any sound: only the faint noise of the stream. And I wondered, Why am I here, on this ridge of the Alps, in the lamp-lit, wooden, close-shut room, alone? Why am I here?

Yet somehow I was glad, I was happy even: such splendid silence and coldness and clean isolation. It was something eternal, unbroachable: I was free, in this heavy, ice-cold air, this upper world, alone. London, far away below, beyond, England, Germany, France—they were all so unreal in the night. It was a sort of grief that this continent all beneath was so unreal, false, non-existent in its activity. Out of the silence one looked down on it, and it seemed to have lost all importance, all significance. It was so big, yet it had no significance. The kingdoms of the world had no significance: what could one do but wander about?

The woman came with my soup. I asked her, did not many people come in the summer. But she was scared away, she did not answer, she went like a leaf in the wind. However, the soup was good and plentiful.

She was a long time before she came with the next course. Then she put the tray on the table, and looking at me, then looking away, shrinking, she said:

"You must excuse me if I don't answer you—I don't hear well—I am rather deaf."

I looked at her, and I winced also. She shrank in such simple pain from the fact of her defect. I wondered if she were bullied because of it, or only afraid lest visitors would dislike it.

She put the dishes in order, set me my plate, quickly, nervously, and was gone again, like a scared chicken. Being tired, I wanted to weep over her, the nervous, timid hen, so frightened by her own deafness. The house was silent of her, empty. It was perhaps her deafness which created this empty soundlessness.

When she came with the omelette, I said to her loudly:

"That was very good, the soup and meat." So she quivered nervously, and said, "Thank you," and I managed to talk to her. She was like most deaf people, in that her terror of not hearing made her six times worse than she actually was.

She spoke with a soft, strange accent, so I thought she was perhaps a foreigner. But when I asked her she misunderstood, and I had not the heart to correct her. I can only remember she said her house was always full in the winter, about Christmas-time. People came for the winter sport. There were two young English ladies who always came to her.

She spoke of them warmly. Then, suddenly afraid, she drifted off again. I ate the omelette with cognac, which was very good, then I looked in the street. It was very dark, with bright stars, and smelled of snow. Two village men went by. I was tired, I did not want to go to the inn.

So I went to bed, in the silent, wooden house. I had a small bedroom, clean and wooden and very cold. Outside, the stream was rushing. I covered myself with a great depth of feather-bed, and looked at the stars, and the shadowy upper world, and went to sleep.

In the morning I washed in the ice-cold water, and was glad to set out. An icy mist was over the noisy stream, there were a few meagre, shredded pine trees. I had breakfast and paid my bill: it was seven francs, more than I could afford. But that did not matter, once I was out in the air.

The sky was blue and perfect, it was a ringing morning, the village was very still. I went up the hill till I came to the sign-post. I looked down the direction of the Furka, and thought of my tired Englishman from Streatham, who would be on his way home. Thank God I need not go home: never, perhaps. I turned up the track to the left, to the Gothard.

Standing looking round at the mountain-tops, at the village and the broken castle below me, at the scattered débris of Andermatt on the moor in the distance, I was jumping in my soul with delight. Should one ever go down to the lower world?

Then I saw another figure striding along, a youth with knee-breeches and Alpine hat and braces over his shirt, walking manfully, his coat slung in his Rucksack behind. I laughed, and waited. He came my way.

"Are you going over the Gothard?" I said.

"Yes," he replied. "Are you also?"

"Yes," I said. "We will go together."

So we set off, climbing a track up the heathy rocks.

He was a pale, freckled town youth from Basel, seventeen years old. He was a clerk in a baggage-transport firm—Gondrand Frères, I believe. He had a week's holiday, in which time he was going to make a big circular walk, something like the Englishman's. But he was accustomed to this mountain walking: he belonged to a Sportverein.

Manfully he marched in his thick, hob-nailed boots, earnestly he scrambled up the rocks.

We were in the crest of the pass. Broad, snow-patched slopes came down from the pure sky, the defile was full of stones, all bare stones, enormous ones as big as a house, and small ones, pebbles. Through these the road wound in silence, through this upper, transcendent desolation, wherein was only the sound of the stream. Sky and snow-patched slopes, then the stony, rocky bed of the defile, full of morning sunshine: this was all. We were crossing in silence from the northern world to the southern.

But he, Emil, was going to take the train back, through the tunnel, in the evening, to resume his circular walk at Göschenen.

I, however, was going on, over the ridge of the world, from the north into the south. So I was glad.

We climbed up the gradual incline for a long time. The slopes above became lower, they began to recede. The sky was very near, we were walking under the sky.

Then the defile widened out, there was an open place before us, the very top of the pass. Also there were low barracks, and soldiers. We heard firing. Standing still, we saw on the slopes of snow, under the radiant blue heaven, tiny puffs of smoke, then some small black figures crossing the snow patch, then another rattle of rifle-fire, rattling dry and unnatural in the upper, skyey air, between the rocks.

"Das ist schön," said my companion, in his simple admiration.

"Hübsch," I said.

"But that would be splendid, to be firing up there, manœuvring up in the snow."

And he began to tell me how hard a soldier's life was, how hard the soldier was drilled.

"You don't look forward to it?" I said.

"Oh yes, I do. I want to be a soldier, I want to serve my time."

"Why?" I said.

"For the exercise, the life, the drilling. One becomes strong."

"Do all the Swiss want to serve their time in the army?" I asked.

"Yes—they all want to. It is good for every man, and it keeps us all together. Besides, it is only for a year. For a year it is very good. The Germans have three years—that is too long, that is bad."

I told him how the soldiers in Bavaria hated the military service.

"Yes," he said, "that is true of Germans. The system is different. Ours is much better, in Switzerland a man enjoys his time as a soldier. I want to go."

So we watched the black dots of soldiers crawling over the high snow, listened to the unnatural dry rattle of guns, up there.

Then we were aware of somebody whistling, of soldiers yelling down the road. We were to come on, along the level, over the bridge. So we marched quickly forward, away from the slopes, towards the hotel, once a monastery, that stood in the distance. The light was blue and clear on the reedy lakes of this upper place; it was a strange desolation of water and bog and rocks and road, hedged by the snowy slopes round the rim, under the very sky.

The soldier was yelling again. I could not tell what he said.

"He says if we don't run we can't come at all," said Emil.

"I won't run," I said.

So we hurried forwards, over the bridge, where the soldier on guard was standing.

"Do you want to be shot?" he said, angrily, as we came up.

"No, thanks," I said.

Emil was very serious.

"How long should we have had to wait if we hadn't got through now?" he asked the soldier, when we were safely out of danger.

"Till one o'clock," was the reply.

"Two hours!" said Emil, strangely elated. "We should have had to wait two hours before we could come on. He was riled that we didn't run," and he laughed with glee.

So we marched over the level to the hotel. We called in for a glass of hot milk. I asked in German. But the maid, a pert hussy, elegant and superior, was French. She served us with great contempt, as two worthless creatures, poverty-stricken. It abashed poor Emil, but we managed to laugh at her. This made her very angry. In the smoking-room she raised up her voice in French:

"Du lait chaud pour les chameaux."

"Some hot milk for the camels, she says," I translated for Emil. He was covered with confusion and youthful anger.

But I called to her, tapped the table and called:

"Mademoiselle!"

She appeared flouncingly in the doorway.

"Encore du lait pour les chameaux," I said.

And she whisked our glasses off the table, and flounced out without a word.

But she would not come in again with the milk. A German girl brought it. We laughed, and she smiled primly.

When we set forth again, Emil rolled up his sleeves and turned back his shirt from his neck and breast, to do the thing thoroughly. Besides, it was mid-day, and the sun was hot; and, with his bulky pack on his back, he suggested the camel of the French maid more than ever.

We were on the downward slope. Only a short way from the hotel, and there was the drop, the great cleft in the mountains running down from this shallow pot among the peaks.

The descent on the south side is much more precipitous and wonderful than the ascent from the north. On the south, the rocks are craggy and stupendous, the little river falls headlong down, it is not a stream, it is one broken, panting cascade far away in the gulley below, in the darkness.

But on the slopes the sun pours in, the road winds down with its tail in its mouth, always in endless loops returning on itself. The mules that travel upward seem to be treading in a mill.

Emil took the narrow tracks, and, like the water, we cascaded down, leaping from level to level, leaping, running, leaping, descending headlong, only resting now and again when we came down on to another level of the high-road.

Having begun, we could not help ourselves, we were like two stones bouncing down. Emil was highly elated. He waved his thin, bare, white arms as he leapt, his chest grew pink with the exercise. Now he felt he was doing something that became a member of his Sportverein. Down we went, jumping, running, britching.

It was wonderful on this south side, so sunny, with feathery trees and deep black shadows. It reminded me of Goethe, of the romantic period:

"Kennst du das Land, wo die Citronen blühen?"

So we went tumbling down into the south, very swiftly, along with the tumbling stream. But it was very tiring. We went at a great pace down the gulley, between the sheer rocks. Trees grew in the ledges high over our heads, trees grew down below. And ever we descended.

Till gradually the gulley opened, then opened into a wide valley-head, and we saw Airolo away below us, the railway emerging from its hole, the whole valley like a cornucopia full of sunshine.

Poor Emil was tired, more tired than I was. And his big boots had hurt his feet in the descent. So, having come to the open valley-head, we went more gently. He had become rather quiet.

The head of the valley had that half-tamed, ancient aspect that reminded me of the Romans. I could only expect the Roman legions to be encamped down there: and the white goats feeding on the bushes belonged to a Roman camp.

But no, we saw again the barracks of the Swiss soldiery, and again we were in the midst of rifle-fire and manœuvres. But we went evenly, tired now, and hungry. We had nothing to eat.

It is strange how different the sun-dried, ancient, southern slopes of the world are, from the northern slopes. It is as if the god Pan really had his home among these sun-bleached stones and tough, sun-dark trees. And one knows it all in one's blood, it is pure, sun-dried memory. So I was content, coming down into Airolo.

We found the streets were Italian, the houses sunny outside and dark within, like Italy, there were laurels in the road. Poor Emil was a foreigner all at once. He rolled down his shirt sleeves and fastened his shirt-neck, put on his coat and collar, and became a foreigner in his soul, pale and strange.

I saw a shop with vegetables and grapes, a real Italian shop, a dark cave.

"Quanto costa l'uva?" were my first words in the south.

"Sessanta al chilo," said the girl.

And it was as pleasant as a drink of wine, the Italian.

So Emil and I ate the sweet black grapes, as we went to the station.

He was very poor. We went into the third-class restaurant at the station. He ordered beer and bread and sausage: I ordered soup and boiled beef and vegetables.

They brought me a great quantity, so, whilst the girl was serving coffee-with-rum to the men at the bar, I took another spoon and knife and fork and plates for Emil, and we had two dinners from my one. When the girl—she was a woman of thirty-five—came back, she looked at us sharply. I smiled at her coaxingly; so she gave a small, kindly smile in reply.

"Ja, dies ist reizend," said Emil, *sotto voce*, exulting. He was very shy. But we were curiously happy, in that railway restaurant.

Then we sat very still, on the platform, and waited for the train. It was like Italy, pleasant and social to wait in the railway station, all the world easy and warm in its activity, with the sun shining.

I decided to take a franc's worth of train-journey. So I chose my station. It was one franc-twenty, third class. Then my train came, and Emil and I parted, he waving to me till I was out of sight. I was sorry he had to go back, he did so want to venture forth.

So I slid for a dozen miles or more, sleepily, down the Ticino valley, sitting opposite two fat priests in their feminine black.

When I got out at my station I felt for the first time ill at ease. Why was I getting out at this wayside place, on to the great, raw high-road? I did not know. But I set off walking. It was nearly tea-time.

Nothing in the world is more ghastly than these Italian roads, new, mechanical, belonging to a machine life. The old roads are wonderful, skilfully aiming their way. But these new great roads are desolating, more desolating than all the ruins in the world.

I walked on and on, down the Ticino valley, towards Bellinzona. The valley was perhaps beautiful: I don't know. I can only remember the road. It was broad and new, and it ran very often beside the railway. It ran also by quarries and by occasional factories, also through villages. And the quality of its sordidness is something that does not bear thinking of, a quality that has entered Italian life now, if it was not there before.

Here and there, where there were quarries or industries, great lodging-houses stood naked by the road, great, grey, desolate places. And squalid children were playing round the steps, and dirty men slouched in. Everything seemed under a weight.

Down the road of the Ticino valley I felt again my terror of this new world which is coming into being on top of us. One always feels it in a suburb, on the edge of a town, where the land is being broken under the advance of houses. But this is nothing, in England, to the terror one feels on the new Italian roads, where these great blind cubes of dwellings rise stark from the destroyed earth, swarming with a sort of verminous life, really verminous, purely destructive.

It seems to happen when the peasant suddenly leaves his home and becomes a workman. Then an entire change comes over everywhere. Life is now a matter of selling oneself to slave-work, building roads or labouring in quarries or mines or on the railways, purposeless, meaningless, really slave-work, each integer doing his mere labour, and all for no purpose, except to have money, and to get away from the old system.

These Italian navvies work all day long, their whole life is engaged in the mere brute labour. And they are the navvies of the world. And whilst they are navvying, they are almost shockingly indifferent to their circumstances, merely callous to the dirt and foulness.

It is as if the whole social form were breaking down, and the human element swarmed within the disintegration, like maggots in cheese.

The roads, the railways are built, the mines and quarries are excavated, but the whole organism of life, the social organism, is slowly crumbling and caving in, in a kind of process of dry rot, most terrifying to see. So that it seems as though we should be left, at last, with a great system of roads and railways and industries, and a world of utter chaos seething upon these fabrications: as if we had created a steel framework, and the whole body of society were crumbling and rotting in between. It is most terrifying to realise: and I have always felt this terror upon a new Italian high-road: more there than anywhere.

The remembrance of the Ticino valley is a sort of nightmare to me. But it was better when at last, in the darkness of night, I got into Bellinzona. In the midst of the town one felt the old organism still living. It is only at its extremities that it is falling to pieces, as in dry rot.

In the morning, leaving Bellinzona, again I went in terror of the new, evil high-road, with its skirting of huge, cubical houses, and its seething navvy population. Only the peasants driving in with fruit were consoling. But I was afraid of them: the same spirit had set in in them.

I was no longer happy in Switzerland, not even when I was eating great blackberries and looking down at the Lago Maggiore, at Locarno, lying by the lake: the terror of the callous, disintegrating process was too strong in me.

At a little inn a man was very good to me. He went into his garden and fetched me the first grapes and apples and peaches, bringing them in amongst leaves, and heaping them before me. He was Italian-Swiss: he had been in a bank in Bern, now he had retired, had bought his paternal home, and was a free man. He was about fifty years old: he spent all his time in his garden: his daughter attended to the inn.

He talked to me, as long as I stayed, about Italy and Switzerland and work and life. He was retired, he was free. But he was only nominally free. He had only achieved freedom from labour. He knew that the system he had escaped at last, persisted, and would consume his sons and his grandchildren. He himself had more or less escaped back to the old form; but as he came with me on to the hill-side, looking down the high-road at Lugano in the distance, he knew that his old order was collapsing by a slow process of disintegration.

Why did he talk to me as if I had any hope, as if I represented any positive truth as against this great negative truth that was advancing up the hill-side. Again I was afraid. I hastened down the high-road, past the houses, the grey, raw crystals of corruption.

I saw a girl with handsome bare legs, legs shining like brass in the sun. She was working in a field, on the edge of a vineyard. I stopped to look at her, suddenly fascinated by her handsome naked flesh that shone like brass.

Then she called out to me, in a jargon I could not understand, something mocking and challenging. And her voice was raucous and challenging, I went on, afraid.

In Lugano I stayed at a German hotel. I remember sitting on a seat in the darkness by the lake, watching the stream of promenaders patrolling the edge of the water, under the trees and the lamps. I can still see many of their faces: English, German, Italian, French. And it seemed here, here in this holiday-place, was the quick of the disintegration, the dry-rot, in this dry, friable flux of people backwards and forwards on the edge of the lake, men and women from the big hotels, in evening dress, curiously sinister, and ordinary visitors, and tourists, and workmen, youths, men of the town, laughing, jeering. It was curiously and painfully sinister, almost obscene.

I sat a long time among them, thinking of the girl with her limbs of glowing brass. Then at last I went up to the hotel, and sat in the lounge looking at the papers. It was the same here as down below, though not so intense, the feeling of horror.

So I went to bed. The hotel was on the edge of a steep declivity. I wondered why the whole hills did not slide down, in some great natural catastrophe.

In the morning I walked along the side of the Lake of Lugano, to where I could take a steamer to ferry me down to the end. The lake is not beautiful, only picturesque. I liked most to think of the Romans coming to it.

So I steamed down to the lower end of the water. When I landed and went along by a sort of railway I saw a group of men. Suddenly they began to whoop and shout. They were hanging on to an immense pale bullock, which was slung up to be shoed. And it was lunging and kicking with terrible energy. It was strange to see that mass of pale, soft-looking flesh working with such violent frenzy, convulsed with violent, active frenzy, whilst men and women hung on to it with ropes, hung on and weighed it down. But again it scattered some of them in its terrible convulsion. Human beings scattered into the road, the whole place was covered with hot dung. And when the bullock began to lunge again, the men set up a howl, half of triumph, half of derision.

I went on, not wanting to see. I went along a very dusty road. But it was not so terrifying, this road. Perhaps it was older.

In dreary little Chiasso I drank coffee, and watched the come and go through the Customs. The Swiss and the Italian Customs officials had their offices within a few yards of each other, and everybody must stop. I went in and showed my Rucksack to the Italian, then I mounted a tram, and went to the Lake of Como.

In the tram were dressed-up women, fashionable, but business-like. They had come by train to Chiasso, or else had been shopping in the town.

When we came to the terminus a young miss, dismounting before me, left behind her parasol. I had been conscious of my dusty, grimy appearance as I sat in the tram, I knew they thought me a workman on the roads. However, I forgot that when it was time to dismount.

"Pardon, Mademoiselle," I said to the young miss. She turned and withered me with a rather overdone contempt, "bourgeoise," I said to myself, as I looked at her—"Vous avez laissé votre parasol."

She turned, and with a rapacious movement darted upon her parasol. How her soul was in her possessions! I stood and watched her. Then she went into the road and under the trees, haughty, a demoiselle. She had on white kid boots.

I thought of the Lake of Como what I had thought of Lugano: it must have been wonderful when the Romans came there. Now it is all villas. I think only the sunrise is still wonderful, sometimes.

I took the steamer down to Como, and slept in a vast old stone cavern of an inn, a remarkable place, with rather nice people. In the morning I went out. The peace and the bygone beauty of the cathedral created the glow of the great past. And in the market-place they were selling chestnuts wholesale, great heaps of bright, brown chestnuts, and sacks of chestnuts, and peasants very eager selling and buying. I thought of Como, it must have been wonderful even a hundred years ago. Now it is cosmopolitan, the cathedral is like a relic, a museum object, everywhere stinks of mechanical money-pleasure.

I dared not risk walking to Milan: I took a train. And there, in Milan, sitting in the Cathedral Square, on Saturday afternoon, drinking Bitter Campari and watching the swarm of Italian city-men drink and talk vivaciously, I saw that here the life was still vivid, here the process of disintegration was vigorous, and centred in a multiplicity of mechanical activities that engage the human mind as well as the body. But always there was the same purpose stinking in it all, the mechanising, the perfect mechanising of human life.

Appendix I

Christs in the Tirol (first version)

Note on the Text

The base-text for the superseded first version of 'Christs in the Tirol' is the autograph manuscript at the Harry Ransom Humanities Research Center, University of Texas at Austin. As 'painted shrines on the Lake Garda' (229:7) are mentioned, this essay was probably written soon after the arrival of DHL and Frieda at Riva del Garda in September 1912. It was published for the first time in the *Fortnightly Review* (July 1933) and in the first American edition of *Love Among the Haystacks & Other Pieces* (Viking Press, October 1933).

Christs in the Tirol

The real Tirol seems to come not far south of the Brenner, and to extend right north to the Starnberger See. Even at Sterzing the rather gloomy atmosphere of the Tyrolese Alps is dispersing, the approach of the South is felt. And strangely enough, the roadside Crucifixes become less and less interesting, after Sterzing. Walking from Munich down to Italy, I have looked at hundreds of Martertafeln, and now I miss them; these painted shrines on the Lake Garda are not the same.

I, who see a tragedy in every cow, began by seeing one in the Secession pictures in Munich. All these new paintings seemed so shrill and restless. Those that were meant for joy shrieked joy, and sorrow was dished as a sensation, curiously, subtly spiced. I thought of some of our English artists, that seem to suck their sadness like a mournful lollipop. That is at any rate a more comfortable way. And then, for miles and endless miles, one must walk past Crucifixes.

I got rather scared of them in the end. At first they were mostly factory made, so that I did not notice them, any more than I noticed the boards with warnings, except just to observe they were there. And then, coming among the others carved in wood by the peasant artists, I began to notice. They create almost an atmosphere, an atmosphere of their own on the country side.

The first I really *saw*, and the one that startled me into awareness was in a marshy place at the foot of the mountains. A dead Christ hung in an old shrine. He was broad and handsome, he was a Bavarian peasant. I looked at his body and at his limbs, and recognised him, almost as one of the men I had seen in the Gasthaus the evening before, a peasant farmer working himself to the bone, but not giving in. His plain, rudimentary face stared straight in front, and the neck was stiffened. He might have said: 'Yes, I am suffering. I look at you, and you can see me. *Perhaps* something will happen, will help. If not, I'll stick it'. I loved him. He seemed stubborn and struggling from the root of his soul, his human soul. No Godship had been thrust upon him. He was human clay, a peasant Prometheus Christ, his poor soul bound in him, blind, but stubborn, struggling against the fact of the nails.

And after him, when I see so many Christs posing on the Cross, à la Guido Reni, I recognise them as the mere conventional symbol, as devoid of personal meaning as is our St George and the Dragon, and I go by.

But then there are so many Christs that are men, carved by men. In the Zemm valley, right in the middle of the Tyrol, there are half a dozen crucifixes, evidently by the same worker. They have all got the same body and the same face, though one has a fair beard. The largest of them is more than life size. He has a strangely brutal face, that aches with weariness of pain, and he looks as if he were just dead. He has fallen forward on the cross, the weight of his full-grown, mature body, tearing his hands on the nails. And on his rather ugly, passionate mouth, is despair and bitterness and death. The peasants, as they drive their pack-horses along the dark valley, take off their hats in passing, half afraid. It is sombre and damp, and there hangs the falling body of the man, who has died in bitterness of spirit. There is something dreadful about the bitter despair of the crucifix. I think of the man that carved it. He was afraid. They were nearly all afraid, when they carved and erected these monuments to physical pain, just as the sturdy peasants are afraid, as they take off their hats in the mountain gloom.

They are afraid of physical pain. It terrifies them. They raise, in their startled helplessness of suffering, these Christs, these human attempts at deciphering the riddle of pain. In the same way, more or less, they paint the little pictures of some calamity – a man drowned in a stream, or killed by a falling tree – and nail it up near the spot where the accident occurred. There are thousands of these pictures, painted just as a child would do them. A man is seen immersed in water up to the waist, his hands in the air. The water flows wildly, a bridge stands serenely, the man must either have his feet on the bottom or must be performing some rare swimming miracle. But it says the bridge broke beneath him and he was drowned. Yet he is seen hallooing wildly, the water not up to his breast. His neighbour painted the picture, partly out of a curious love of sensational mishap, partly out of genuine dread lest a bridge should fall under himself also. His family nailed the picture to the tree at the end of the broken bridge, partly to get prayers for his soul, partly to insist on the fact that 'in the midst of life we are in death.' And we, as we look at it – when we are not amused – wonder if we have as great a horror and terror of death and pain, as these people have; or if our horror and terror are only a little more complex; and if all art is not a kind of accustoming ourselves to the idea of suffering and death, so that we can more and more comprehend them, even if we do not really understand.

I can do with all the Christs that have a bit of fight in them, or some stillness of soul. But I hate the Christs who just suffer, or who just whine. Some of them look up to heaven, turn their eyes skyward and pull down the corners of their mouths. Then I say '*You* have n't got it bad enough, my dear fellow. Your cross is n't much more than an ailment for you to whine about.' Some of them look pale and done-for, and I think 'Poor devil, he had n't got much spunk.' And then, some are just nothings. Indeed, I used to think I never should see a Christus who was anything but neutral. In their attempts at drawing Jesus, the artists have made so many bloodless creatures, neither man nor woman, and a good deal less interesting than either. They have extracted so many mundane qualities, that they have left nothing but a fishy neutrality, usually with curled hair, and offered it to us as pictures of Jesus.

I return to my peasant Christs, that I love. I have mentioned the stubborn, Prometheus Christ, and the bitter, despairing Christ, and the Christ like a pale, dead young man who has suffered too much, and the rather sentimental Christ: all of them men, and rather real.

Then, in a tiny glass case beside a high-road in the mountains, sits another Christ that half makes me laugh and half makes me want to sit down and weep. His little head rests on his hand, his elbow on his knee, and he meditates, half wearily. I am strongly reminded of Walther von der Vogelweide, and the German mediaeval spirit. Detached, he sits and dreams and broods, in his little golden crown of thorns and his little red flannel cloak, that some peasant woman has stitched. 'Couvre-toi de gloire – couvre-toi de flannelle,' I think to myself. But he sits and dreams and broods. I think he is the forefather of the warmhearted German Philosopher and Professor.

Beyond the Brenner, there seems again a kind of falsity in the Christs. The wayside Chapels become fearfully ornate and florid, the Christus neutral, or sensational. There is in a chapel near St. Jakob the most ghastly Christus it is possible to imagine. He is seated, after the crucifixion, and in the most dreadful bloody mess. His eyes, which are turned slightly to look at you, are blood-shot till they are scarlet and glistening, and the very iris seems crimsoned. Where the skin is torn away at the wounds, the living red muscles are bare, and one can almost see the intestines, red with blood, bulging from the hole in the side. And the misery, and the almost low hate, the almost criminal look on the bloody disfigured face, is shocking. That is a Christ of the new, sensational sort.

I have not seen anyone salute the Christus, south of the Brenner, in the

Austrian Tyrol. There is a queer feeling about Austria, as if it were waiting to take its impression from some other nation. On the Franco–German frontier, one feels two distinct and antagonistic nationalities, mixing but not mingling. But Austria merges into Germany on one side, and merges into Italy on the other, till one looks for Austria, and wonders where it is. And Austria seems to be looking for itself. Its soldiers have no more nationality than the 'Chocolate Soldiers,' and the Austrian official uniform is worthy of an essay to itself. It creates a dandy and a decent fellow, but no impression of office. At the back of the German official is Germany, at the back of an Austrian official – a gentle deprecation.

So, in Austria, I have seen a fallen Christus. It was on the Jaufen, not so very far from Meran. I was looking at the snow, and descending through the cold morning air, when I noticed a little Christus shed, very old. It was all of aged, silvery grey wood, covered on the top with a thicket of grey-green lichen. And on the rocks at the foot of the cross was the armless Christus who had tumbled down, and lay on his back, in a weird attitude. It was one of the old peasant Christs, carved out of wood, with the curious long, wedge shaped shins that are characteristic. The arms had broken off at the shoulders, and hung on their nails, as the ex voto limbs are hung in the shrines. But these dangled from their palms, upside down, the muscles carved in wood looking startling. And the icy cold wind blew them backwards and forwards. I dared not touch the fallen image, nor the arms. I wish a priest would go and make it right. And I wish he would wash off the nasty and sensational streams of blood that flow from the brow and breast and knees and feet, hundreds of red stripes, down the body of so many Austrian Christs. They hide the man, and make a messy horror.

And I suppose most of the carvers of these wayside crucifixes were right. There was a Christ who rebelled against his suffering, and one who was bitter with a sense of futility, and one who gave in to his misery, and one who hated his persecutors, and one who dreamed wistfully, all on the same cross. And perhaps there was one who was peaceful in his sense of right, and one who was ashamed for having let the crowd make beasts of themselves, batten on his suffering, and one who thought 'I am of you, I might be among you, yelling at myself in the same cruel way. But I am not, and that is something—.'

All those Christs, like a populace, hang in the mountains under their little sheds. And perhaps they are falling, one by one. And I suppose our Christs in England are such as Hamlet and Tom Jones and Jude the Obscure.

Appendix II

The Travel Routes

The Alpine Region in 1912

0   10   20   30   40   50 miles
0 10 20 30 40 50 60 70 80 km

FRANCE

GE

Überling

Schaffhausen
Neuhausen
Rhine Falls

Basel
R. Rhine (Rhein)

Constance

Lake Constac

Eglisau

Zürich
Mönchhof   Zürichsee
Adliswil
Langnau-Gattikon   Thalwil
Albispass

Zuger See   Zug
Lucerne   Walchwil
(Luzern)   Küssnacht
Rigi   Arth
Rigi Pass

LIECHTENS

SWITZERLAND

Lake of Lucerne

Flüelen
Altdorf
Erstfeld
Silenen
Santis 8,209 ft   Amsteg
Gurtnellen

Göschenen

Hospental   Andermatt
Lago di Lucendro
Furka Pass   St Gotthard
St Gotthard Pass   Tunnel
6,916 ft   Airolo   Lukmanier Pass
6,286 ft

Lake Geneva

Val Tremola   Ticino Valley
(Valle Leventina)

Lavorgo
R. Ticino
Osogna

Locarno   Bellinzona

Lago Maggiore   Lake of Lugano
Lugano

Capolago   Cernobbio
Chiasso   Como

I   T

Milan

AUSTRIA   Riva
Limone
Campione
Gardola di Tignale
Muslone
Gargnano   San Gaudenzio
Villa di Gargnano
Bogliaco
Toscolano
Gardone
Riviera
Salò
Isola
di Garda
Desenzano   Sirmione

R. Adige

Montecastello

ITALY

0   5 miles
0   5   10 km

The Travel Routes

The following account, together with the maps, gives the routes, dates and other details of Lawrence's walking tours from Bavaria to Lake Garda in 1912 (the subject of 'A Chapel Among the Mountains', 'A Hay-Hut Among the Mountains', the two versions of 'Christs in the Tyrol' and 'The Crucifix Across the Mountains') and from Bavaria to Milan in 1913 ('Italians in Exile' and 'The Return Journey').

METZ AND WALDBRÖL IN MAY 1912

'The English and the Germans' and 'How a Spy is Arrested' are set in Metz which DHL visited 4–8 May 1912. Probably on 6 May he made the excursion recounted in 'French Sons of Germany'. As he left Metz, he passed the **ridiculous imitation-mediæval church** (17:21), Le Temple Protestant, built 1901–4 in a romanesque style and with a bulky spire out of proportion to the size of the church. It stands on an island in the Mosel River, L'Ile d'Amour (Island of Love – which DHL calls **The Place of Love**, 17:23). Walking south-west among **this Mosel valley** (17:37), he climbed a hill, perhaps passing a Madonna shrine (unlocated, but DHL may have transferred to this sketch the one he saw outside Trier on 9 May), walked through **vineyards** (17:34) and came upon a **cemetery** below a church (18:10) before emerging at the church with a **terrace** (18:18): the church of St Rémi at Scy (20:6) which is on a hill above a cemetery and beside a small park studded with horse-chestnuts and overlooking Montigny and Metz. The boys' school (18:23) is on one side of the adjoining village square.

On 15 May, during his stay in Waldbröl (11–24 May), DHL walked through the countryside with 'Johanna' **to Nümbrecht**, seven miles away (cf. 21:27), before being caught in the hailstorm described in 'Hail in the Rhine-Land'.

BAVARIA TO LAKE GARDA IN AUGUST–SEPTEMBER 1912

From June to early August 1912, DHL and Frieda lived in Icking, south of Munich. On 5 August they set out for Italy. They walked through Wolfratshausen along the Isartal, shortly afterwards taking a train along the Loisachtal for twelve miles, probably to Bichl. They then walked back to the Isartal at Bad Tölz. Along the way they ate at the inn described in 'A Chapel Among the Mountains' (27:17) and 'Christs in the Tirol' (first version). DHL may then have seen the **Bavarian peasant** crucifix ('The Crucifix Across the Mountains', 91:38–92:16 unlocated), although the next day is also a possibility (229:25–6), or on another unrelated occasion. They stayed overnight at Bad Tölz, walking on the next day to Winkel.

Hearing about a shortcut to Glashütte from Winkel (or from the hamlet of Hohenwiesen just beyond), they took the path, passing a waterfall on the Klaffenbach east of Winkel; they became lost, and after a steep climb found the (old) Röhrlmoos **chapel** (of 'A Chapel Among the Mountains'), looked at the ex-voto paintings and slept the night in the nearby **hay-hut** ('A Hay-Hut Among the Mountains'). The next morning they passed the Röhrlmoos **farm-house** (41:13; about half a mile east and below the hay-hut) and walked down to near Glashütte, resting in **the home of a forester** (described in the deleted ending of 'A Hay-Hut': see Note on the Texts).

In the afternoon they took a bus to the north end of the Achensee, and stayed overnight in a farmhouse. The next day (8 August) they walked along the (old) elevated lake road to Jenbach, then travelled by train east to Kufstein to collect their luggage, which they had sent ahead, and sent it on again, staying the night there. On 9 August, they returned by train to Jenbach and travelled up the Zillertal to Mayrhofen – probably taking a train at least some of the way, for they arrived that evening. They stayed over a fortnight, making excursions into the nearby valleys, including the Tuxer Tal where they saw what may be the original of the **dead Hyacinth** crucifix (98:15). They were joined by David Garnett (1892–1981) on *c.* 18 August and, a few days later, by his close friend Harold Hobson (1891–1974).

The four set out on 26 August, walking up the Zemmtal through the Dornauberg-Klamm which Baedeker describes as 'a picturesque valley enclosed by lofty pine-clad hills, skirting the left bank of the Zemmbach, which is precipitated in numerous cascades through a rocky ravine' (Baedeker's *Austria-Hungary*, Leipzig, 1900, 137) – cf. 96:14–19. Here they saw, on the first day, the crucifix **deep in the Klamm** (96:14). This **large, pale Christ** (96:21–2) remains, in the position described. In 1987, Josef Kröll (b. 1899), a farmer of Ginzling in the Zemmtal, confirmed the existence of the crucifix prior to 1912. But the Christ's attitude differs from DHL's account: the body has sunk down rather than forward on the cross, and it hangs from nails in the wrists rather than the hands. Shortly after, they saw the fair-bearded Christ **at the end of a bridge** (97:15).

Passing Ginzling, they slept in a hay-hut and, on the next day (27 August), walked on to stay overnight at the old Dominicushütte (rebuilt in 1918 after a fire, and again in 1971 in a different position because of the construction of a dam). On 28 August, they crossed the Pfitscher Joch – the probable location of **the last crucifix** (100:9) – and stayed the night at an inn in the Pfitscher Tal, probably the Gasthof Elefant (no longer an inn) north of Afens.

They had passed the **seated sensational Christus** (99:4–5) in a small, baroque roadside chapel at Wieden (of stone, 1828, replacing a wooden one: an ex-voto painting shows what appears to be the same Christ and is dated 1771). The Christ has a crown of thorns and a reed sceptre, but no stigmata: this is the traditional *Christus im Elend* (Christ in Distress) pose, before the crucifixion but after the flagellation.

The original of the **D'Annunzio's son** crucifix is probably one just below (west of) Afens which they would have seen the next morning (97:39). It is probably Austrian – but Tyrolean rather than **Viennese** (98:4). The region belonged to Austria until 1919: crucifixes were made at nearby Sterzing, and there was a flourishing manufacturing centre of hand-carved religious statuary at St Ulrich (Ortisei) in the Grödnertal (Val Gardena, north-east of Bozen and also Austrian).

DHL and Frieda reached Sterzing (Vipiteno) the next day, Hobson and Garnett having left the inn very early that morning to catch a train for Munich at Sterzing. On 1 September, DHL and Frieda began the walk to Meran (Merano) via the Jaufenpass and St Leonard; leaving the high-road, they took a bridle-path up the Jaufental to the inn near the top of the Jaufenpass and stayed overnight. Next morning, they picked up the high-road again but went the wrong way and returned to Sterzing; it was probably on this downhill walk that they saw **the fallen Christ** (100:29). From Sterzing they took the train to Bozen (Bolzano), and next day (3 September) went on to Trient (Trento) and the following day to Riva on Lake Garda.

LAKE GARDA IN SEPTEMBER 1912–APRIL 1913

On 18 September 1912 DHL and Frieda moved to Villa di Gargnano, on the west side of the lake where the 1913 essays, 'By the Lago di Garda', and their counterparts 'On the Lago di Garda' in *Twilight in Italy* are set. DHL and Frieda made an excursion on 16 February 1913 up the lake to Campione, and then went on foot to Gardola di Tignale in the mountains above. 'John' is based on this visit. 'San Gaudenzio', 'The Dance' and 'Il Duro' stem from the week DHL and Frieda spent at a farmhouse, San Gaudenzio, in the mountains near Muslone a few miles north of Villa (*c.* 3–11 April 1913), just prior to leaving Lake Garda for Germany and England.

BAVARIA TO MILAN IN 1913

DHL and Frieda returned to Germany in August 1913, staying at Irschenhausen, near Munich; here he witnessed the artillery practice described in 'With the Guns'. On 17 or 18 September 1913 he left for Italy; Frieda went to Baden-Baden to visit her mother, planning to meet DHL in Basel. DHL travelled to Überlingen, probably by train; and took the steamer across Lake Constance to the town of **Constance** (189:1), thus entering Switzerland. He had taken the **steamer . . . to Schaffhausen** (189:3–4), passing **quaint villages of old romance** (189:13): a former nunnery, monastery and mansions, all converted to other purposes by 1913; and churches and several chateaux would have been visible among the smaller dwellings (Baedeker's *Switzerland*, Leipzig, 1913, 35–6, hereafter referred to as *Switzerland*). The **bridges** (189:13) included 'a covered wooden bridge, below which the steamer lowers its funnel' (*Switzerland*, 35) – at Diessenhofen (the bridge still exists). Parts of the right bank are in Germany (hence the **customs officials** at 189:16).

Then, because 'the great Water Works' at Schaffhausen prevents further river traffic (*Switzerland* 34), DHL walked or took a tram two miles to Neuhausen near the **ugly** Rhine Falls (189:31). On the right bank he walked 10½ miles with the road, leaving and finally returning to the Rhine, to **the village of tall, quaint houses**, Eglisau (190:11), going across the border into the Duchy of **Baden** (part of Germany, 189:34) during his walk, and back again. He stayed overnight in **The Golden Stag** – the *Goldene Hirsch* inn situated next to the position of the former **covered bridge** (190:13; built in 1811, replaced in 1919).

On 20 September, he set off on foot towards Zürich along a flat river valley, hence the **feeling of average** he complains of (193:28). He finished the trip by **tram-car** (193:30), and that afternoon took **a steamer down the long lake** (the Zürichsee, 194:3). DHL believed he had landed **about three-quarters of the way down the lake** (194:6–7) – which is 25 miles long. But the lake turns south-east towards the lower end, creating the impression that it ends at about two-thirds of its actual length.

He got off either at Mönchhof or Thalwil and walked to a village where he came upon the Italians: his route is unclear at this point. Because the next day it took him over a pass where he sees the Zürichsee from one side and the Zuger See and the mountain, Rigi, from the other (the Albispass, given his onward route), and because the previous evening he had climbed one **long hill** (194:8) from the lake and descended immediately into a dark valley (Sihl) to **a soulless village** with a silk factory (194:9–10), the village must be Adliswil or Langnau–Gattikon.

'The Return Journey' starts with DHL's walking the next day (21 September) up to the Albispass (207:19–21). Descending in the afternoon, he passed **fat agricultural land and several villages** on the way to Zug (207:31). He saw **church-goers . . . all coming home** (207:32). Proceeding through Zug, he walked down the east side of the Zuger See, having tea in the **little villa by the water** (208:27) probably at Walchwil or at the end of the lake at Arth where he stayed overnight in a **detestable brutal inn** (209:18). In the morning (22 September) he climbed the Rigi Pass – **the detestable Rigi** (209:19) – and then descended (209:34–5), probably walking through Küssnacht (since he does not say he took a steamer) and on to Lucerne (209:36). Taking the steamer down to **the very last station** on the Lake of Lucerne (209:38), he stayed overnight at Flüelen where he met the Englishman (209:40–212:18).

The following day he walked through the Reusstal past Altdorf, Erstfeld, Silenen, Amsteg and **a little town with a factory or quarry, or a foundry, some place with long, smoking chimneys** (214:26–7) – Gurtnellen, with its 'large granite-quarries, a carbide factory, and steel-works' (*Switzerland* 144). Continuing (the account telescopes the intervening distance), he reached Göschenen **where the tunnel begins** (214:38) – the St Gotthard Tunnel (1872–82) to Airolo. A train took 14–20 minutes, but DHL decided to continue walking. Climbing, he passed the **tablet in memory of many Russians killed** (215:6–7) and the Swiss Army training camp on the outskirts of Andermatt (215:11–13). He walked on to **the little village with the broken castle**, Hospental, where he stayed the night (216:3–4). On 24 September, he climbed to the St Gotthard Pass, meeting Emil (218:29–35). The **bridge** at 220:4 which the soldiers instruct them to cross quickly was probably the Rodont Bridge over the Reuss near the Lago di Lucendro, one mile north of the pass (again telescoping the distance), and itself one and a half miles south of the 'First Cantoniera . . . now used for Military purposes' (*Switzerland* 149) – the **low barracks** which DHL would have passed on his ascent (219:19). DHL and Emil stopped at the Hotel Monte Prosa just south of the pass (220:6), and then set out on the **precipitous and wonderful** descent (221:8–9) for Airolo: the 'road crosses . . . the Ticino . . . and enters the dismal Val Tremola; it then descends . . . in numerous windings, avoided by the old bridle-path' (*Switzerland* 151). Near the Swiss army barracks (222:4), a view of the Ticino Valley (Valle Leventina) opens up (221:33–4); closer to Airolo are other barracks. From Airolo, Emil returned to Göschenen by train through the tunnel (219:11–12). DHL proceeded by train **a dozen miles or more** (223:1) down the Ticino Valley, probably to Lavorgo where he resumed walking, passing **quarries and . . . factories** (223:13) probably near Osogna, the present site of quarries, and the 'large electric power-works' Baedeker notes at Bodio (*Switzerland* 533). He arrived in Bellinzona **in the darkness of night** (224:11).

On 25 September he walked towards Lugano: from near Monte Ceneri he would have looked down on Locarno on **Lago Maggiore** (224:21), and, soon after, have seen the girl with **legs shining like brass** (225:1). He stayed in **Lugano** that night (225:8). The next day, to get to Como, he took a steamer down the Lake of Lugano **to the lower end of the water** (i.e. Capolago, 225:29); from there he walked to **dreary little Chiasso** (226:1), the last Swiss town, stopping to go through customs into Italy. Although there was a direct tram to Como, DHL took another to its **terminus** at Cernobbio (226:9), on the west shore of the Lake of Como, and then went by **steamer down to Como** (226:23). There he saw the **cathedral** (226:26) and stayed the night. The next day (27 September) he took a train to Milan – where, with changed plans, he was now to meet Frieda. He sat **in the Cathedral Square . . . drinking Bitter Campari** (226:33–4).

Explanatory Notes

7 The English and the Germans The title is editorial.

7:5 Germans to the front ... from the Chinese War [7:7] A popular allusion to German military dominance, referring to the arrival of German reinforcements at Peking during the Boxer Uprising of 1900.

7:10 Metz A town in the north of the Alsace-Lorraine region, on the border between Germany and France. In 1871, following the Franco-Prussian War, the town was ceded to Germany along with the rest of Alsace-Lorraine. It was returned to France after the First World War in accordance with the Treaty of Versailles (1919).

8:7 the Germans are not as old a nation Compared with England and France, Germany is very young: unification only took place in 1871.

9:2–3 safe from any German attack ... mania for self-starvation Germany's increasing naval expansion was felt by England as a threat to essential lines of supply.

11 How a Spy is Arrested In the manuscript the title was originally 'How One is Arrested as a Spy' and then 'A Spy is Arrested'.

11:8 Anita Fictionalization of Frieda Weekley (1879–1956). Her sister (11:37) was Else Jaffe (1874–1973) and her father (13:20) Freiherr Friedrich von Richthofen (1845–1915). Anita/Frieda also appears in 'A Chapel Among the Mountains' and in 'A Hay-Hut Among the Mountains'.

13:30 Montigny South-western district of Metz, corresponding to the French name of the town.

14:14 Lübeck A port in the north-west of Germany.

15:11 the Kaiser Emperor Wilhelm II (1859–1941) was King of Prussia 1888–1918.

16:3–4 the Cathedral ... lofty nave The Gothic cathedral of Saint-Etienne (1280–1380); the length of the choir is only a fraction of that of the nave.

16:15–17 The barber ... speaks no German The local (French-speaking) people's resentment against Germany has always been strongly felt; even today people of the older generation scornfully refuse to speak German.

17:2–3 great-grandfather ... revolution DHL's family believed that they had French ancestors: in *Sons and Lovers* Walter Morel has a grandfather who 'was a French refugee and had married an English barmaid' (*Sons and Lovers*, eds. Helen Baron and Carl Baron, Penguin Books, 1994, 17:38–9). This is just one version of the story. See John Worthen, *D. H. Lawrence: The Early Years 1885–1912*, Cambridge University Press, 1991, pp. 7–8.

19:15–16 The boys used French . . . the soldiers in German DHL is well aware that language is an instrument for strengthening or defending one's identity – as in the case of the French barber (16:22–3) – but it also discloses existing power relationships.

20:9 the vines The whole of Alsace-Lorraine is famous for its wine.

21:15 as Kaiserly as did his own The Kaiser (see note on 15:11) had a luxuriant moustache with turned-up ends.

21:23 Johanna In this sketch Johanna is not based on Frieda, but on DHL's Waldbröl cousin Hannah Krenkow.

23:34 Stollwerck's chocolate machine Stollwerck is a famous Cologne manufacturer of chocolate.

25:8 dished Caught out.

25:11 Entry to Jerusalem Christ's entry into Jerusalem was 'strewn' with 'branches from the trees' (Matthew xxi. 8). All quotations from the Bible are from the King James version.

26:3 tiles, so many smashed As reported in the local paper the *Waldbröler Zeitung* (17 May 1912), many roofs and windows in the surrounding villages were smashed by the hail storm.

26:5 the Asylum A mental hospital, founded in the 1890s in Waldbröl.

27:23 armoured like Ivanhoe The hero of the novel of the same name (1819) by Walter Scott (1771–1832), he became a prototype for stories of love and chivalry till the beginning of the present century. He fits perfectly into the Romantic atmosphere created at the beginning of the essay, and then immediately debunked.

27:27 Glashütte The name of a very old Gasthaus (once a changing post), just over the border between Austria and Germany, after which the cluster of houses is named. DHL and Frieda rested there after the night they spent in the hay-hut. The Gasthaus is now a well-known restaurant.

30:22–3 the tiny chapel Little chapels, often of wood, are disseminated all over the mountains.

30:23 ex-voto pictures I.e., presented in recognition of answered prayers; quite common in small mountain communities, where life is every day exposed to danger and to the violence of uncontrollable elements. They often represent a man or a woman who has been saved from an impending tragedy in front of a landscape with cattle or horses. For a full account of the pictures surviving in the early 1970s, see Frederick Owen, 'A Chapel Among the Mountains', *The Human World*, n. 15–16, 1974, pp. 75–83. Cf. ex-voto limbs at 99:34.

31:9–10 in the open doorway . . . eternal angel Cf. Abraham's welcome of the 'three men' as he 'sat in the tent door in the heat of the day' (Genesis xviii. 1–2).

32:22–3 In the midst of life . . . death Cf. the *Book of Common Prayer*, the service for the Burial of the Dead.

32:31–3 Catherine of Russia . . . Vicar of Wakefield attire Catherine II, the Great, of Russia (1729–96) and the hero of Oliver Goldsmith's (1728–74) novel *The Vicar of Wakefield* (1766).

33:12 **history of the Tyrol . . . 1783 period** DHL is trying to explain the painting, the mother begging for the freedom of her son, in terms of a particularly repressive historical situation; as a matter of fact, Karl Theodor (1724–99), Prince Elector of Bavaria from 1777, was known for his repressive measures.

33:29 **little cow-girl Kate** As Owen discovered (see note on 30:23), DHL's error: he misread 'Kalb' (a little calf) for 'Kate' which is why the little girl is not mentioned when the animal is found again.

36:12 **Anita called it a kettle** DHL is here rendering the German word 'Kessel' which means 'kettle' as well as a circular valley. Cf. the kettle association in *Mr Noon* (ed. Lindeth Vasey and Peter Preston, Penguin Books, 1996, 245:22–3): 'They were at the top of a pass, in a sort of kettle among the mountains.'

36:32 **squilched** Squelched; the same form appears at 41:12. See Note on the Texts.

37:24 **Egyptian darkness** The penultimate of God's plagues on the Egyptian Pharaoh was three days of complete darkness (Exodus x. 21–3).

40:5 **towzled** Extremely untidy; dialect version of 'tousled'.

41:6 **toilet** I.e., washing and dressing.

43:5 **Sterzing** Situated a few miles south of the Brenner Pass, Sterzing/ Vipiteno is the last Italian town before the Austrian border. At the time of DHL's stay in the town, the whole region was still part of the Austro-Hungarian Empire and therefore German-speaking. Nowadays the region from the border almost as far as Trento is officially bilingual.

43:10–11 **Secession pictures in Munich . . . shrill and restless** The reference is to avant-garde movements which arose in Europe at the end of the last century out of dissatisfaction with traditional bourgeois art. The 'Munich Secession', founded in 1882, was immediately followed by similar groups in Vienna (1897) and in Berlin (1899). The pictures DHL saw (three exhibitions were held while he was in Munich) belonged to the avant-garde movement in general and not exclusively to the Secessionists.

44:2 **a peasant Prometheus-Christ** Lawrence connects the suffering of the peasant to two of the main suffering figures in the Christian and pagan traditions. In Greek mythology, Prometheus stole fire from the gods and gave it to man. As a punishment, Zeus chained him to a rock and sent an eagle daily to eat out his liver, which was restored every night.

44:10–11 **à la Guido Reni** The Italian painter Guido Reni (1575–1642) tried to avoid the extreme contrasts of light and shadow by means of intermediate tonalities which better suited his ideal of moderation.

45:32–4 **strange neutrals . . . the Jesus of the New Testament** Portraits in stained-glass and illustrations for children.

45:39 **Walther von der Vogelweide** German medieval epic and lyric poet (*c.* 1170–*c.* 1230), one of the main exponents of the court Minnesinger; commonly regarded as the first national German poet. See note on 189:17–18.

46:7–8 **German philosopher and professor** DHL refers perhaps to Alfred Weber (1868–1958), Professor of Sociology and Political Science at Heidelberg University, and the lover of Frieda's elder sister, Else Jaffe.

46:23 **after the crucifixion** In fact, after the flagellation. Christ is seated, and covered with blood.

51:1 **The church of San Tommaso . . . Franciscan monastery just behind** [56:22–3] The local parish church of Villa di Gargnano has an impressive life-size picture of the saint touching Jesus's wounds over the altar. It was given to the Franciscan monks at the beginning of the century, when they were allowed to come back after being expelled by Napoleon. The monastery and the church of San Francesco, situated on the shores of the lake, where the monks had originally been, had already become the office of the Società Lago di Garda in 1840.

51:12–13 **the Valley of the Shadow of Death** Psalm xxiii. 4. Many towns on the western shore of Lake Garda have little, winding, stony passages between the houses; as a result most passages are always in shadow.

51:25 **Purgatory of a passage** Cf. Dante, *The Divine Comedy, Purgatory*, Cantos III and IV. The way up to the church of San Tommaso is compared to the cliff, steep and sheer, which Dante and Virgil have to climb to gain access to Purgatory.

52:35 **But she was spinning . . . shuttle, her bobbin** [53:1] An old spinning technique whose roots go back to the Roman period; it was possible to spin outside, while watching cattle for instance.

53:39–40 **understand a syllable** In the Lake Garda area, dialect is still very strong, and varies from place to place. An Italian speaker from another region may still have problems understanding it.

54:12 **chuntered** Murmured/blathered (dialect).

55:34 **bird-devouring Italian** Hunting was very popular in Italy (as it still is today, in spite of strict laws); shooting at birds or setting traps for them was common practice. The postman's surprise, 'eight little birds tied together by the necks' (55:38–9), is a special present for a special guest in Italian culture.

56:9 **olive oil in preparation** The production of olive oil was a mainstay of Gargnano's economy, of increasing importance with the decline of the citrus cultivation; an oil factory (now ruined), part of the Società Lago di Garda, existed in the Franciscan monastery next to the church of San Francesco.

56:10–11 ***Strada Vecchia* . . . *Strada Nuova*** Old road . . . new road (Italian). A section of the new road connecting Gargnano to Brescia via Salò was completed at the beginning of the nineteenth century. The Gardesana Occidentale connecting Gargnano to Riva through the mountains was opened in 1930–31; a steamship (see 56:17–18) ran between various points on the lake when DHL and Frieda were there. Baedeker's guide, *Northern Italy*, which DHL used, gave the time-table.

58:3 **pine for what is not** From Shelley's 'To a Skylark' (1820), ll. 86–7 (see note on 121:1). The Spinner is not living for what is not and can never be achieved, but simply in the present, in contrast with the monks who are 'never here' (57:24).

59:14 **speak French** Till a few decades ago, French was the most widely spoken foreign language among the Italian upper classes. It was a sign of prestige which distinguished education as well as social class.

60:7 **Conte B. . . . Palazzo B.** Count Bettoni, one of the few truly aristocratic landowning families originating from Brescia in the sixteenth century, with a splendid neo-classical palace built in the mid-1700s at Bogliaco, one mile south of Gargnano. Its gardens run along the shore of the lake and its land extends far on to the mountain side.

60:28–9 **Poor Hamlet . . . he approaches** The role of Hamlet is opposed to that of Christ, who gives 'light to them that sit in darkness' (Luke i. 79).

66:8 **heavy bouquet** A bunch of green lemon leaves and yellow lemons can be seen in many shops and houses around Gargnano; it is a decoration, and also a kind of perfume.

66:31–2 **leaves and fruit . . . San Francesco** The cultivation of citrus fruits was introduced by the Franciscan monks who arrived at Gargnano in the middle of the thirteenth century; the first Franciscan monastery on Lake Garda was built in Gargnano in 1266 by Fra Bonaventura. In the cloister, the decoration of lemons and oranges can be seen on the capitals of the columns. See 66:26–31.

66:34 **Bacchus** The Roman god of wine and fertility, known to the Greeks as Dionysus; see notes on 118:37 and 154:3.

66:40–67:1 **one of our lemons is as good as *two* from elsewhere** Local people still insist that the lemons of Lake Garda, a thin-skinned variety, are very sweet and juicy and can be eaten just as they are. This is partly true and partly the expression of local pride.

67:8 **'Cedro.'** A lemon liqueur, made from the rind when the fruit is very green and unripe. The distillery, founded in 1869, produced liqueurs, syrups and other herbs and citrus delicacies famous throughout the area. It closed in 1977. The liqueur was actually called 'Doppio Cedro', 35 per cent proof with a sparkling green colour. It had a lighter counterpart in the transparent 'Acqua di Cedro', which at 27 per cent proof was considered a liqueur for women, given, for instance, as a present during pregnancy.

69:8 **'I Spettri.'** 'Gli Spettri' (DHL's error); *Ghosts* (1881) by the Norwegian dramatist, Henrik Ibsen (1828–1906). He was very popular in Europe at the turn of the century and had an enormous influence on modern dramatists. In *Ghosts* he presents the tragic effects of heredity on a young man who inherits what he fears are the depraved instincts of his father.

69:9 **theatre is an old church** In the centre of Gargnano, in the church once devoted to Maria Maddalena, built in 1551 and deconsecrated at the end of the eighteenth century by Napoleon. It was turned into a theatre (Teatro Sociale di Gargnano) in 1806, was very popular in the area and attracted companies from the surrounding regions. It then became a cinema run privately and was bought by the municipality in 1977. Now it is only open to the public on special occasions (shows, talks or exhibitions). The inside has been completely changed from the original structure, whereas the external part of the building and the façade still maintain their original appearance.

69:31 **bersaglieri** A select military corps of sharpshooters founded in the Piedmont army in 1836. A wide-brimmed hat crowned with cock feathers is still a distinguishing part of their uniform. A regiment of bersaglieri was located at the beginning of the century between Bogliaco and Villa in the ex-monastery of San Carlo, which had been turned into a barracks in the middle of the nineteenth century; see also 79:8–24.

72:19 **Feast of the Epiphany** 6 January, celebrating the Magi's visit to Christ.

72:20–21 **D'Annunzio . . . 'La Fiaccola sotto il moggio'** See Introduction, note 37. *La fiaccola sotto il moggio (The Light under the Bushel)* (1905) is a revenge tragedy set in the Abruzzi.

72:39 **church bells** I.e., Italian 'campanilismo' (see 200:28), deriving from 'campanile' (bell-tower), and meaning an almost fanatic attachment to one's native village.

73:8–9 **'La Moglie del Dottore,'** *The Wife of the Doctor,* comedy by the Italian playwright Silvio Zambaldi (1870–1932).

73:17–18 **Gretchen, Dame aux Camélias, Desdemona . . . Lucia, Margherita** [73:35] **. . . Ophelia, Iphigenia, Antigone** [73:36] Tragic literary heroines who suffer or die for love. See also examples at 140:1, 7–8, 26–7.

73:25 **Salò** A few miles south of Gargnano, Salò was a centre of major activities at the beginning of the century. Towards the end of the Second World War the Republic founded by Mussolini on Lake Garda in opposition to the legitimate government was called 'The Social Republic of Salò'.

73:25–6 **daughter of Rigoletto** Gilda in *Rigoletto* (1851), opera by Giuseppe Verdi (1813–1901).

74:12–17 **'Oh wert thou . . my bosom,'** Ballad by the Scottish poet Robert Burns (1759–96) ('plaidie', woollen plaid; 'airt', direction; 'bield', shelter).

74:23–7 **Even Bunty . . carpenter** An allusion to the heroine Bunty in the comedy *Bunty Pulls the Strings* by the Scottish playwright Graham Moffat (1866–1951); she wants to marry an 'uncouth joiner'.

74:37 **Enrico Persevalli** Based on Enrico Marconi, the director of the company owned by Adelia di Giacomo Tadini, the Adelaida of 139:27. DHL was probably unwilling to use the surname Marconi due to the associations with the famous still-living Guglielmo Marconi (1874–1937), the inventor of wireless telegraphy in 1895. As a surname, Persevalli occurs in the area around

Gargnano, although possible associations with Wagner's hero Parsival and an attempt to Italianize the name of the hero should not be excluded.

76:4 **Kind hearts . . . coronets** Popular saying derived from a poem by Alfred, Lord Tennyson (1809–92), 'Lady Clara Vere de Vere' (1842), 1. 55.

76:10–11 **'Uneasy lies . . . a crown.'** Said by Shakespeare's Henry IV in *2 Henry IV*, III. i. 31, not by Richard II.

76:35 **'Father Time' . . . 'Jude the Obscure,'** In Thomas Hardy's (1840–1928) novel *Jude the Obscure* (1895), little Jude, or Old Father Time, hangs himself and the two babies when Jude and Sue separate.

76:38 **phosphorescence** The light emanated by plants, insects and bacteria of putrefaction: the word occurs with negative connotations at 116:27–30 in the description of Aphrodite as 'the phosphorescence of the sea [who] consumes and does not create', and at 176:36–7, describing the sensation aroused by 'il Duro' as 'a sadness that gleamed like phosphorescence'.

77:21–2 **Punch . . . Teddy Rainer's theatre** The traditional English puppet-show, Punch and Judy, was a common attraction at country fairs, especially in the nineteenth century. The show run by the Rainer family played at the beginning of the century in Eastwood. Cf. 149:26–7.

77:25 **'Maria Martin . . . Red Barn.'** Bloodthirsty and highly popular Victorian melodrama.

77:29 **tha h'arena** Thou (i.e., you) are not (dialect).

79:7 **camping in the desert . . . Egypt** Matthew ii. 13–14.

81:1 **The Reservists** In August 1914, on the outbreak of war, members of the peacetime reserve were immediately called up.

81:24 **quick-firing guns** Technologically sophisticated guns introduced into Germany and other European countries at the beginning of the century.

82:38–9 **captain . . . from Tripoli** The war of 1911–12 in which Italy seized Tripoli from Turkey; the war derived from the nationalistic idea of giving Italy 'a place in the sun'.

83:3 **Snyder fire** The breech mechanism invented by the American Jacob Snider in 1859 – adopted by the British army in 1866 – which allowed rifles to be loaded and fired much more rapidly. Although soon superseded, the system was very successful and one of the first examples of technologically sophisticated arms.

91:17 **The imperial processions** The Counter-Reformation's policies in the sixteenth and seventeenth centuries led to an increase in the Catholic presence, made more evident by the building of shrines and chapels.

93:22 **the mystery plays . . . feast of Frohenleichnam** [95:3] 'Mystery plays' are religious performances, often dramatizing a story from the Bible: see *Letters*, i. 411. Such performances are still common on the occasion of religious feasts; one of the most important in Bavaria is the 'Fronleichnam' feast on Corpus Christi Day, when the entire village winds in procession, in traditional costumes, through streets decorated with flowers. DHL misspelled

'Fronleichnam', thinking probably of the word 'froh' meaning 'happy' in German.

95:30 **"To be, or not to be,"** An allusion to *Hamlet* and an anticipation of the discussion of the line at 145:38–149:15.

97:39–40 **D'Annunzio's son . . . martyred saint** I.e., a Christ embodying morbid sensuality and spiritual rapture, posing in an aesthetically aristocratic manner.

98:15 **Hyacinth** In Greek mythology, Hyacinth was the handsome youth loved by Apollo and Zephyrus, and killed by the latter. From Hyacinth's love sprang the flower.

99:13 **eyes . . . have no seeing in them** A recurrent image in the book; cf. 'had no looking in them' (106:24) and 'eyes . . . terrifying sightlessness' (118:20–21).

99:28 **"Spring in the Austrian Tyrol"** *June in the Austrian Tyrol* by John A. MacWhirter (1849–1911) in the Tate Gallery, London. The same picture is mentioned (also with a wrong title) in *Mr Noon* (200:36).

103:1 **The Holy Spirit is a Dove, or an Eagle** In the New Testament the Holy Spirit is represented by the Dove (Matthew iii. 16); in the Old Testament the eagle's power and swiftness are often a symbol of God's qualities (e.g. Exodus xix. 4).

103:6 **Wren Churches in London** The English architect Sir Christopher Wren (1632–1723) designed St Paul's Cathedral (1675–1711), and over fifty other churches in London, using classical styles with great originality.

103:22 **the village** Villa di Gargnano extends on the lake shore just south of Gargnano and is part of its municipality. Nowadays the border between the two can hardly be defined, in spite of the two quays and piazzas. In Lawrence's time about 1,200 people lived in Gargnano, and rather fewer than 600 in Villa.

104:29–31 **tremendous sunshine . . . another world** The square in front of the church is a suspended balcony offering a breathtaking view over the lake and its surrounding villages. The flame-like cypresses around the sides of the square help to isolate the nest of San Tommaso from its surroundings, and increase the beauty of the view.

105:5–6 **Jacob's ladder** Genesis xxviii. 12.

105:21 **where heaven and earth are divided . . . the sky [105:26]** An image of creation; cf. Genesis i. 6–7.

107:28 **"The planet Mars is inhabited,"** In this acknowledgement of his inability to understand what 'to inhabit' might mean in connection with another planet, Lawrence anticipates some insights of contemporary criticism, in particular the deconstruction of a central point of view and a centralized system of values, and the assertion of multiple possibilities which are closely linked to the place where they develop.

108:5 **sometimes severed from her** An allusion to the creation of Eve from Adam's rib; also to the Platonic idea of male and female, originally one entity like the yolk and the white of an egg, and trying to reunite ever since their separation. Cf. 'Foreword', *Sons and Lovers*, ed. Baron and Baron (470:5–17) for the analogy of the apple.

109:18 **The school-mistress** Lawrence and Frieda were given Italian lessons by the local schoolteacher, Signora Feltrinelli, who belonged to a prominent Gargnano family.

113:17–18 **Eurydice ... Pluto** In Greek mythology, Orpheus descended into the underworld to bring back to the world of the living his wife Eurydice, who had been abducted by Hades (Pluto) to be queen of the underworld. She vanished as Orpheus did not respect the condition not to look back, but she was allowed to return to the world of the living for six months of the year, thus becoming a symbol of the arrival of spring and the change of seasons.

114:6 **The Signore ... the Signora** [122:15] Based on Pietro De Paoli (1845–1917) and his wife Silvia Comboni De Paoli (1868–1931), members of the minor, recent aristocracy (in contrast to Count Bettoni); they were landowning aristocrats in Gargnano, who prospered, like many aristocratic families, in the middle of last century (Casa De Paoli was built in 1851) and declined as a result of the setbacks of the citrus cultivation.

116:13–14 **Botticelli ... Michael Angelo** Sandro Botticelli (1445–1510), Florentine painter, illustrator and engraver; in the 'Birth of Venus' (*c.* 1485, Florence, Uffizi Gallery) Venus/Aphrodite emerges from a shell amid the foam of the sea. Michelangelo Buonarroti (1475–1564), Florentine painter, sculptor and architect; one of the main figures of the Renaissance. DHL's identification of Michelangelo as a turning point in the history of Western art emerges in his *Study of Thomas Hardy* and in the letters of the war period; see, for instance, his letter to Lady Ottoline Morrell of 7 April 1916 (*Letters*, ii. 592).

116:19 **old Mosaic position** A reference to the third book of Moses, Leviticus xxi. 16–23, which asserted that the physically blemished 'shall not ... come nigh unto the altar' to make offerings.

117:22–3 **Tiger ... night** William Blake's (1757–1827) 'The Tyger' in *Songs of Experience* (1794), opposed to 'The Lamb' in *Songs of Innocence* (1789).

118:2 **The will lies above the loins** Cf. *Letters*, ii. 471: 'we have a blood-being, a blood-consciousness, a blood-soul, complete and apart from the mental and nerve consciousness'.

118:37 **the Dionysic ecstasy** The climax reached in the rituals devoted to the Greek god of wine, Dionysus, characterized by wine-induced frenzy and by the uncontrolled explosion of instincts.

119:3 **Blessed ... heaven is perfect** [119:12] Respectively Matthew v. 3, 10, 39, 48 and Luke vi. 27–8.

119:33 **the Great Moloch** Canaanite fire god to whom children were sacrificed (Leviticus xviii. 21), consequently symbol of an image to which sacrifices are made. Cf. 138:5.

120:7 **love my neighbour as myself** Cf. Leviticus xix. 18 and Matthew v. 43.

120:14 **The Puritans ... Charles the First** [120:15] **... Cromwell** [147:21] Charles 1st, of the House of Stuart (120:34), was King of England 1625–49 when, as an extreme consequence of the conflicts aroused by the Civil War, he was executed by Oliver Cromwell's (1599–1658) New Model Army (DHL's 'Puritans'). His execution meant the beginning of the Commonwealth and the end of kings by divine right. See also 147:20–21.

120:21–2 **"Know . . . mankind is Man,"**   The opening lines of the Second Epistle in *An Essay on Man* (1733–4) by Alexander Pope (1688–1744).

120:36–7 **empirical and ideal systems of philosophy**   Empiricism and Idealism are two of the main trends in philosophy; according to the former, dominant in English philosophy in the seventeenth and eighteenth centuries, knowledge is confined to what can be perceived by the senses and verified. For the latter, dominant in the German tradition, knowledge is connected with representations and ideas more than with material objects, and all reality is centred in thought.

121:1 **Shelley, the perfectibility of man**   In *Shelley, Godwin and Their Circle* (1913), which DHL had read (*Letters*, ii. 315), Noel Brailsford discusses the influence of William Godwin's (1756–1836) doctrines of the perfectibility of man, universal benevolence and philosophical anarchism on the poet Shelley (1792–1822). See also 147:35–6.

121:4 **"Now I . . . am known."**   I Corinthians xiii. 12.

121:11–12 **skylark . . . filling heaven and earth with song**   Another echo of Shelley's poem 'To a Skylark' (1820) (see note on 58:3), in which the poet longs for unity with nature and with the energy that he feels as the very source of his poetry, so that his song can be as immediate as that of the skylark.

121:22–3 **Shakspearean advice . . . tiger**   Henry V exhorts his warriors to disguise their 'fair nature' in the 'terrible aspect' of the tiger (*Henry V*, III, i, 5–9).

125:16 **Fifty million children**   The figure is approximate; the official estimate in 1914 was 46 million.

127:23 **great floor of water**   Common in every lemon house for the irrigation of the plants, sometimes it took the form of little streams flowing down the layers of the construction.

133:14–16 **the cinematograph . . . grimace, agitation . . . chaos**   These words, with their flux of immediate change and innovation, echo the Italian Futurists' reaction against tradition and their exaltation of universal dynamism as a basic condition for a new perception of reality and life which had to be translated into a dynamic sensation in figurative language. The Futurist Movement had been founded by the poet Filippo Marinetti (1876–1944) in 1909, and had a great influence on European avant-garde artists; the cinema was one of its later focuses of interest. See also 226:36–9.

134:1 **portrait by a Flemish artist**   Franz Hals' (1580–1666) *Family Group in a Landscape* represents a patriarch in the centre with his family around him.

134:4 **republican**   I.e., with political ideas in favour of a republic. Italy became a republic by virtue of the national referendum of 2 June 1946, after which the king abdicated.

135:22 **dare not go alone** At the beginning of the century, public houses in Italy (like those in England) were a male domain.

136:9 **go away to America** From the second half of the nineteenth century, emigration to America or to northern European industrialized countries (see 'Italians in Exile') increased considerably. In 1913 some 872,000 Italians emigrated. Working in the factories allowed many labourers to free themselves from the landowner's dependence, earn some money to support their families at home and buy a piece of land or a house when they came back. See 'San Gaudenzio', 'Il Duro' and 'John'.

137:15 **a child crying in the night** Cf. *In Memoriam* by Alfred, Lord Tennyson: 'but what am I?/An infant crying in the night' (II. 17–18). See also 202:10.

138:1–2 **Strindberg** The Swedish writer and dramatist August Strindberg (1849–1912) inaugurated a new movement in European drama with his dramatic naturalism. In his most famous plays *The Father* (1887) and *Miss Julie* (1888) he overtly intertwined social conflicts with the corruption of human nature.

139:18 **Carnival ends on the 5th of February** The last day of Carnival (celebrated in all Catholic countries) is the Tuesday before the start of Lent.

139:35 **"the woman pays."** The title of Phase the Fifth of Thomas Hardy's novel *Tess of the D'Urbervilles* (1891).

141:22–3 **Galahad . . . Lancelot** Two knights of Arthurian legend: Galahad was celebrated for his perfect purity; Lancelot symbolized bravery in battle and was known for his love for Queen Guinevere.

143:20–21 **Queen Victoria of the Jubilee period** The Golden Jubilee of Queen Victoria's reign (1837–1901) was in 1887. From this year until 1892, coins were issued with the image of the 'Jubilee Head', representing Queen Victoria with a little toy-like crown on her head.

143:22–3 **new honours . . . new garments** Cf. *Macbeth* I. iii. 145–6.

143:40 **Forbes Robertson** The English actor-manager Johnston Forbes-Robertson (1853–1937), well known for his performance as Hamlet (filmed in 1913).

144:9 **Leonardo da Vinci** The universal genius of the Renaissance, Leonardo da Vinci (1452–1519), painter, sculptor, architect and engineer. In *The Crown*, DHL discusses Leonardo and Michelangelo's paintings of Leda and the Swan, presenting the subject as one of the symbols of divine flux of corruption. (*Reflections on the Death of a Porcupine and Other Essays*, ed. Michael Herbert, Cambridge University Press, 1988, 293: 15–18.)

144:26 **Orestes . . . Clytemnestra . . . Agamemnon** [145:4] In the *Oresteia* trilogy by Aeschylus (*c.* 525–*c.* 456 BC), Agamemnon sacrifices his daughter Iphigenia; on his return, he is murdered by his wife Clytemnestra, who in turn is killed by their son Orestes.

146:25–6 **the Davidian ecstasy** Cf. 2 Samuel vi. 14–16.

147:8 **Savonarola . . . Martin Luther . . . Henry VIII** [147:10] **. . . the State**

[147:11] All leading figures of the Reformation and the schism from the Catholic Church. The Italian religious reformer Girolamo Savonarola (1452–98), who attacked corruption in the Church and State and instituted a short-lived republic of terrifying severity in Florence, was hanged and burnt for heresy. The leader of the German Reformation Martin Luther (1483–1546) was excommunicated for his fierce attack on papal authority, wealth and abuse. Protected by the Prince Elector of Saxony, he translated the Bible and provided the basic creed of the Lutheran Church, thus initiating the Protestant Reformation in Germany. Henry VIII (1491–1547) declared himself 'Supreme Head of the Church of England' in 1535 when he was denied a divorce from his wife Catherine of Aragon by the Pope. His transference of papal powers to the Crown marked the beginning of the Anglican Reformation.

148:7–8 **Nietzsche ... old pagan Infinite ... the Pragmatist** [148:9] DHL is here considering two main contemporary trends in philosophy, both of which attack and reconsider traditional values. The German philosopher Friedrich Nietzsche (1844–1900) attacked the Christian virtues of pity and self-sacrifice and perceived the cultural flattening of the industrial era; William James (1842–1910), the founder of Pragmatism, saw the world as a plurality of continuous natural processes while truth is held to be relative and not attainable by means of metaphysical speculation.

148:11–12 *à la Sanine* The hero of the novel *Sanine* (1907) by the Russian novelist Mikhail Petrovich Artsybashev (1878–1927) declares his belief in a life of calculated pleasures, discrediting all conventional morality and political idealism.

149:35 **"O, that this too, too solid flesh would melt!"** *Hamlet* I. ii. 129.

150:21–2 **real Joseph, father of the child** Opposing Christian belief about the Virgin Mary.

151:19 **Agamemnon's soldiers ... seashore** I.e., waiting on the shores near Troy during the Trojan war.

152:3–4 **clerical party ... anti-clerical party** Up to a few decades ago, the distinction between the Communist Party, gravitating around the mayor (the Syndaco (152:7), traditionally identified with the colour red, and the Christian Democrats, identified with white, centred on the local priest, was a characteristic of many small Italian towns.

153:26 **Carina** The name in Italian means 'pretty' and is used also as a compliment to a lady.

154:3 **the Bacchae ... Phaedra and Helen** [154:4–5] The bacchanalia, feasts in honour of Bacchus or Dionysus, characterized by licentiousness and ecstatic rapture, were celebrated in ancient Athens. Phaedra was prey to an uncontrollable passion for her stepson, and killed him when rejected, while Helen, famous for her beauty, was abducted by Paris, thus causing the Trojan War.

154:21–2 **cypresses ... keep the darkness aflame** Cypresses look like an ever-burning, extremely compact flame. They are common in graveyards, but on Lake Garda they were often planted as windbreaks to protect the lemon plants, of which the wind is one of the most deadly enemies.

155:19 **hepatica** A genus of wild and cultivated flowers, often with blue or mauve petals.

155:22 **Bohemian glass** Bohemian glassmakers have been famous since the seventeenth century for their rich ruby-coloured glass with gilt decorations.

155:32 **many-breasted Diana** The Roman goddess of the woods, hunting, the moon and chastity (identified with the Greek Artemis); a special goddess of women and childbirth, a symbol of the female principle, represented sometimes (as at Ephesus) with many breasts.

156:5 **"Birra, Verona,"** A brand of beer.

156:17–18 **the Fiori . . . Felicina . . . partly inherited** [156:19] Based on Paolo (1853–1932) and Maria (1868–1939) Capelli and their children. The names Paolo and Maria are real-life names. DHL changed the names of the children, from Giacomo to Giovanni, from Riccardo to Marco and from Giuseppina to Felicina respectively. He turned the name of the family into Fiori (flowers), thus suggesting a connection with the blossoming flowers at the beginning of the essay. Paolo's family had worked there for generations without full ownership of the house (working the land of the landowner and occupying the house according to the share-cropping pact). His work in the gold mines in America allowed him to pay off the mortgage.

156:29–30 **hard clarity . . . Mantegna** The early Renaissance Italian painter and engraver Andrea Mantegna (1431–1506), a perfectionist in anatomy, draughtsmanship and perspective.

159:1 **polenta** A very common dish in the north of Italy, now fashionable (with meat or cheese), but at the beginning of the century the basic nourishment of poor families. It is made of ground maize flour, stirred continuously in boiling water till the whole mass thickens. It can then be cut into slices with a string (see 199:39).

159:32 **The earth was the . . . fulness thereof** Cf. Psalms xxiv. i.

160:17–18 **Signoria . . . God** For Paolo, the higher classes seem to be automatically characterized by a divine right; they are closer to God and have to be unquestioningly served and worshipped. DHL identifies the Signoria with the aristocracy, the elect of the old order. As a matter of fact the ruling families of the Renaissance Signorias ('Signoria' identifies a form of northern and central Italian government in the fourteenth and fifteenth centuries), such as the Medici family in Florence, were wealthy middle-class families, who had gained enormous power through commercial and banking activities and had then bought aristocratic titles. See too 165:4–5.

160:41 **first-fruit . . . on an altar** See Leviticus ii. 12.

161:34 **priest of Mugiano** Mugiano is a fictional name for the village of Muslone above San Gaudenzio. The priest Domenico Odorici (1859–1927) was a kind of eccentric spiritual leader in the community, who died when he fell down a cliff while leaning over the roadside fence. Although he was a habitual drunkard, local people still remember his ability to act as a midwife when a child was born, a boon for the community, whose members would otherwise have had to ride a long way to call for a midwife, who then would have had to be paid. He gained the reputation of having a mistress, as Tony Cyriax points out in *Among Italian Peasants*, Collins, 1919, p. 44; he may even have fathered a son. See too DHL's observations at 162:5–6; a red scarf would have been rather unusual for a Catholic priest (see note on 152:3–4).

162:30 **the old Furies** Like the Erinnyes in Greek mythology, these were Roman underworld goddesses personifying revenge.

163:34 **scandals about her** Her last child Felicina, born after Paolo had come back from America, was apparently not Paolo's child. See DHL's observations at 164:5–12.

163:38 **villages . . . ungoverned** In isolated places, especially in the mountains, local government (and even more so central government) was felt to be very distant.

165:21 **Pompeii** The ancient Roman port and resort buried by a sudden eruption of the vulcano Vesuvius (AD 79).

165:39 **the fighting . . . at the end of the lake** In the First World War, Italy fought against the Austrian troops occupying the region to the north of Lake Garda.

167:27 **the two English women** Frieda and Tony Cyriax, an Englishwoman staying with the Lawrences (see note on 161:34).

172:12 **the Adige** The river flowing through Verona.

173 **Il Duro** The character is based on Faustino Magri (1882–1974), whose nickname was 'Il Duro' (pronounced 'Düro' in dialect – in Italian the word means 'tough'). In the little towns on the shores of Lake Garda, it was a common habit – and still is – to use nicknames to distinguish families with the same surname who were linked by remote relations. Once the nickname was applied to one member of the family, all the descendants inherited that name, the men as well as the women. Il Duro's wife was thus called Giulietta 'la dura', and his daughter was Andreina 'la dura'. He was almost a legend in Gargnano, as a 'Don Giovanni', as an extraordinary personality taking obsessive care of his appearance, and as the best vine-grafter and wine producer of the area. In spite of his insistence on not marrying (176:5–29), he married Giulietta Tomasi on 14 January 1914. He was authoritarian with his wife and children, and constantly unfaithful to her. DHL presents him (177:30–34) as the personification of Pan, the Greek god of flocks and herds and the symbol of the energy governing nature.

174:33–6 **"Up, Jenkins." . . . guesses at the number of fingers** 'Up, Jenkins' consists of guessing who in the opposing team has concealed a coin passed between players and then brought up on the table at the cry 'Up, Jenkins' (Jenkins is actually the missing coin). The other game is the well-known, often dangerous Italian folk game called 'morra', where two players have to guess the combined number of fingers extended simultaneously from the fist. It is an exciting game which often arouses violent reactions.

179:4 **village . . . forgotten** Gardola di Tignale; see The Travel Routes.

180:1 **the Giovann'** Especially in North Italy, male Christian names are frequently used with the article. The title uses the nickname 'John', which sounds ambiguous in a collection of Italian essays. The presumed American is actually a poor Italian, based on Giacomo Triboldi (1894–1964), the son of a shopkeeper in Gardola.

185:25–6 **military service . . . forty** In Italy in 1912 military service was compulsory; it lasted for two years at the age of twenty-one. Up to the age of forty, men who had not served (because they had emigrated) were likely to be called up when they came back. Cf. the criticism of military service at 201:14–19.

186:3 **a funicular** A funicular was built in the early years of the century about one mile south of Gardola. It was (like many other funiculars in the area) the only connection between the isolated village on the mountains and the lake; it was shortly to fall into disuse with the completion of the road connecting Gargnano to Tignale.

189:17–18 **romantic past of High Germany . . . fairy tales and minstrels . . . the Meistersinger** [190:23] The medieval Germany of musicians singing, reciting and playing. The Meistersinger were poet-musicians of the fifteenth and sixteenth centuries, mostly citizens belonging to the middle class, grouped in local guilds, superseding the more aristocratic, court-oriented Minnesinger (love singers at court; cf. 45:39) of the three preceding centuries. The Meistersinger are mostly remembered through Wagner's music drama *Der Meistersinger von Nürnberg* (1862–7).

189:24 **a Niebelung** The folk heroes of the most famous of the medieval Germanic epics, *das Niebelungenlied*, which offers a portrayal of the Germanic ideal of faithfulness unto death, even beyond the grave. The saga forms the theme of Wagner's most famous musical drama, *The Ring of the Nibelungen* (1869–1874), in which the Rhine maidens guard the treasure of gold under the river.

189:28–31 **Schaffhausen the town . . . Falls . . . ugly** The city of Schaffhausen, situated on the north bank of the River Rhine, is an important rail and manufacturing centre. Near Schaffhausen is the famous Rheinfall, where the river, 370 feet wide, falls 80 feet in three stages; it constitutes an island of striking natural beauty and power in an industrialized area.

191:14–15 **the unbeautiful dialect** Swiss German.

192:38 **The Swiss . . . very free** [193:1] In Switzerland every male between the ages of twenty and forty was called up for military service one month a year. It was felt to be a duty to the country and not something imposed (cases of refusal were very rare). See Emil's words at 219:26–37 compared with Giuseppino's opposition to Italian military service at 202:14–19.

193:14 **shack-bags** Looking like tramps (dialect).

194:25 **Caruso** The plump Italian tenor of world-wide fame Enrico Caruso (1873–1921).

199:21 **odd Neapolitan cards** A pack of forty cards made up of four suits (sticks, cups, coins, spades) of different colours (green, red, yellow, blue, respectively).

201:33 **the Cirenaica** The eastern region of Libya: see note on 82:38–9.

202:25 *L'Anarchista* The title is probably misremembered as there is no evidence of such a paper in Geneva. Lawrence is probably remembering the anarchist beliefs of the people he met.

208:12 **crambling** Feeble, shaky (dialect).

208:17–18 **the meek, inherited the earth** Cf. Matthew v. 5.

209:1 **doctor from Graz** DHL is probably thinking of Otto Gross (1877– 1920), a psychoanalyst from Graz, who had had a relationship with Frieda in 1907–8.

209:19 **detestable Rigi** An isolated mountain rising precipitously, very high (5,905 feet) between Lakes Zug and Lucerne. The summit can be reached by rail or, with some difficulty, on foot.

209:36–7 **Lucerne . . . milk chocolate** 'It was beautiful, but Switzerland is too Milk Chocolaty and too tourist trodden' (Unpublished letter to John Middleton Murry, 30 September 1913).

211:23 **a fortnight he was let free** By the beginning of the century, employers in Britain had taken up the practice of paying holiday leave.

211:32 **Excelsior** The protagonist of the poem *Excelsior* (1841) by the American poet Henry Wadsworth Longfellow (1807–82) strives towards the highest (i.e., Excelsior), disregarding a woman's love and a series of warnings till, in his endless search, he dies in the snow.

212:26 **Streatham** A suburb of south-west London.

212:29–30 **Sadish . . . torture** 'Sadism', so named after the Marquis de Sade (1740–1814) and his satisfaction in violent sexual practices.

214:3 **the source of death overhead** Avalanches are fairly common in this area, especially in summer as a consequence of glaciers melting.

215:6–7 **tablet . . . many Russians killed** The Suvoroff Monument (1899) in memory of the Russian soldiers who died in 1799, fighting against the French.

215:20–1 **Skegness or Bognor** English seaside resorts.

216:29–30 **American oil-cloth** Waterproof material.

219:38 **soldiers in Bavaria hated the military service** The discipline imposed by the military code is demonstrated in 'The Prussian Officer' and 'The Thorn in the Flesh' in *The Prussian Officer and Other Stories*, ed. John Worthen and Brian Finney, Penguin Books, 1995, pp. 1–21 and 22–39.

221:24 **britching** I.e., stopping themselves being carried forward by the weight of their rucksacks, like horses against the breeching ('britching', dialect) strap while going downhill.

221:28 **"Kennst du . . . Citronen blühen?"** From Goethe (1749–1832), *Wilhelm Meister*, Bk III, chap. I, 'Do you know the land where the lemon trees blossom?' (German).

222:1 **Roman legions** The Romans conquered the area of modern-day Switzerland in campaigns in 58 BC and 15 BC.

232:7 **'Chocolate Soldiers,'** Cf. *Letters*, i. 452, an allusion to the popular musical *The Chocolate Soldier* (1910) by Oscar Strauss, based on the comedy *Arms and the Man* by George Bernard Shaw (1856–1950).

232:38–9 **our Christs . . . Tom Jones** In *Tom Jones* (1749) by Henry Fielding (1707–54), Tom is the victim of plots but forgives his enemies.

Glossary

The entries follow the sequence in which words appear in the text; page and line references are to first occurrences only. The words Mr, Mrs and Miss occur in the volume in German (Herr, Frau), French (Monsieur, Madame, Mademoiselle), and Italian (signore, signora, signorina), which Lawrence capitalizes when using as titles.

11:34 **Käfer** Beetle (German).

12:35–6 **Verboten . . . Strengstens verboten** Forbidden . . . strictly forbidden (German). The word 'verboten' is almost proverbial in relation to German obedience and rules.

13:12 **Aber** But (German).

13:20 **Graf zu** Count of (German).

13:28 **Kronprinz-Strasse** Crown Prince Street (German).

17:26 **"Kinder, Kuchen, Kirche,"** 'Children, cake, church' (German). DHL confuses 'Kuchen' with the German word 'Küche' (kitchen).

23:11 **Jawohl** Yes indeed (German).

24:6–7 **Bretzel . . . Kringel** Crisp salty bread with a particular twisted shape, a sort of winding 'B' and biscuits in the shape of rings (German). The Bretzel is often a symbol of bakeries in the south of Germany.

25:18 **Schnapps** Clear spirits (German).

30:23 **ex-voto** See Explanatory Notes.

31:31 **Maria hat geholfen** Maria helped (German, a conventional formula).

32:15 **Gott sey Danck gesagt** Thank the Lord (German, dialect forms).

32:40–33:2 **O Mutter Gottes . . . willen sey** O mother of the Lord of Röhrlmoos, let my son be freed from imprisonment, free him from fetters and bonds, if this be the Holy will (German; spelling sometimes wrong, sometimes corresponding to dialect forms).

35:14–15 **kreutzers . . . pfennigs** See Currencies.

36:1 **Kapelle** Chapel (usually small) (German).

37:2 **Quelle** Source, spring (German).

43:7 **Martertafeln** Wayside shrines, literally 'suffering boards', usually crucifixes (German).

43:8 **See** Lake (German).

44:22 **Klamm** Gorge (German).

45:14 **"Memento mori,"** 'Remember you must die' (Latin).

46:3 **"Couvre-toi de gloire, Tartarin—couvre-toi de flanelle,"** 'Cover

Glossary

yourself with glory, Tartarin – cover yourself with flannel' (French). A quotation from *Tartarin de Tarascon* (1872), a burlesque novel by the French novelist Alphonse Daudet (1840–97), where the main character Tartarin is modelled on the two popular figures of Don Quixote and Sancho Panza by Cervantes; hence the combination of glory and flannel.

51:1 *farouche* Untamed, unapproachable (French).

51:11 **piazza** The main square (Italian); in Italy the focal point of public life.

53:16 Si Yes (Italian). The correct form, here and elsewhere, has an accent: Sì.

53:18 **commune** Municipality (Italian); the spelling should be 'comune'. DHL was probably influenced by the French.

54:20 *kosen* Caress (German).

56:1 **Ecco signore** Here you are, sir (Italian). 'Ecco' as an exclamation, meaning 'here', 'look', occurs elsewhere: cf. 59:32 and 115:6.

56:10–11 *Strada Vecchia . . . Strada Nuova* See Explanatory Notes.

56:19 **Isola** Isle (Italian): here referring to the Isola del Garda in the middle of the lake. It is called 'the Island' at 110:39.

59:1 **padrone** Master/owner (Italian). The word is widely used in relation to any kind of owner, from the landowner ('padrone' of the land and the people working on it) to the owner of an industry. 'Padrona' at 69:26 is the feminine equivalent.

59:12 **Mais—mais monsieur—je crains que—que** But – but, sir – I am afraid that – that (French).

59:30 **La porte—la porte—elle ferme *pas*!—elle s'ouvre** The door – the door – it does *not* shut! – it opens (French). See also 115:3–4.

59:33 **l'Anglais** The Englishman (French).

60:5 **palazzo** Palace (Italian). Whereas 'villa' refers to a residential house, potentially belonging to anybody, 'palazzo' indicates a large house belonging to a powerful person. DHL underlines the fact that, judging by its exterior, Signor di P.'s house deserves the title.

60:32–4 **La Perseveranza . . . noi italiani . . . che allegri** A daily newspaper based in Milan (1860–1922); this article appeared on 20 January 1913 . . . 'we Italians, above all, are still too passionate: cheerful rather than happy, whereas English people are happy rather than cheerful' (Italian).

61:39 **merci monsieur—mille fois—mille fois merci** Thank you, sir – a thousand times – a thousand times, thank you (French).

62:2–3 **entre hommes** Between men (French).

63:24–5 **mais—voulez vous vous promener dans mes petites terres?** But – would you like to take a walk in my little estate? (French). Little is ironic.

63:34 **Perchè—parceque—il fait un temps—così—très bell'—très beau** Because – because – the weather is so – very beautiful – very beautiful (half Italian, half French: the accent should be acute instead of grave on the word 'perché').

64:35 **zoccoli** Clogs (Italian).

65:27–8 **Vouley vous . . . vouley vous entrer, monsieur** Would you like
. . . would you like to come in, sir (French). The mistake in 'vouley' (properly
'voulez') and the repetitions indicate the speaker's linguistic insecurity.

66:26 **maestra** Primary school mistress (Italian).

66:40 **Però** But (Italian).

67:12 **'Da Vendere.'** 'For sale' (Italian). Nowadays 'vendesi' would be more
common.

69:11 **chiesa** Church (Italian).

70:7 **'glotzend.'** 'Staring, agape' (German).

71:8 **'Grazia mamma!'** 'Thank you, mother/mum!' (Italian, the word 'grazie'
misspelled).

72:13 **contadini** Peasants (Italian).

72:30 **bellissimo, bellissimo** Most beautiful, most beautiful (Italian).

73:6 **Serata d'Onore** Evening of Honour, as translated by DHL at 73:10,
74:37, 139:24 and at 142:19, 22. A performance chosen in honour of the
starring actor, to exhibit his/her talent, it can sometimes correspond to the 'last
night'.

78:15 **"Questo cranio, signore—"** 'This skull, sir—' (Italian). Cf. the graveyard scene in *Hamlet* (v. i. 174–5). See also *Letters*, i. 505.

79:30 **Siciliano** Sicilian, here a nickname for a man originally from Sicily
(Italian).

91:9 **Grössenwahn** Megalomania (German).

94:39 **Gasthaus** Inn (German).

109:20 *perce-neige* Snowdrops (French).

110:20 **"Hued!"** Shouted 'Gee-up, go!' (Lake Garda dialect).

114:14–15 **Mais—mais, monsieur—je crains que—que—que je vous dérange** But – but, sir – I am afraid that – that – that I am disturbing you
(French).

114:29–30 **Voyez, monsieur—cet—cet—qu'est-ce que—qu'est-ce que
veut dire cet—cela?** Look, sir – this – this – what – what does this mean –
this? (French).

115:13 **non, monsieur, non, cela vous dérange** No, sir, no, that would
disturb you (French).

119:25 *raison d'être* The justifying reason for the existence of something
(French).

122:13 **nihil** Nothing (Latin).

127:1 **vous savez, monsieur** You know, sir (French).

127:4–5 **Perchè—parceque—il fait un tempo—così—très bell'—très
beau, ecco!** Because (Italian) – because (French) – the weather is – so – very
beautiful – very beautiful (French), you see! (Italian). For 'perché' see 63:34.

131:4–5 **così-così. . . poco, poco—peu** So-so . . . little, little (Italian) – little
(French).

131:24–5 **les richesses . . . vous savez** Riches . . . you know (French).

133:6 *un peu de divertiment* A little diversion (French). The Signore makes a French form out of the Italian 'divertimento' (fun) rather than using the French 'divertissement'.

139:30 **bella, bella!** Beautiful, beautiful! (with reference to a woman) (Italian).

142:6 *Amleto* ... **Non lo conosco** *Hamlet* ... I do not know it (Italian). DHL has problems in recognizing *Hamlet* in its Italian pronunciation with the accent on the second syllable. See also 75:8–11.

142:9 **Si** ... **una dramma inglese** Yes ... an English drama (Italian, the article should be 'un').

142:24 **"Sono un disgraziato, io."** 'What a miserable wretch I am' (Italian). *Hamlet* II.ii.538: 'O what a rogue and peasant slave am I'.

143:8 **la Regina** The Queen (Italian).

148:26 **"Essere, o non essere, è qui il punto."** 'To be or not to be – that is the question' (Italian, *Hamlet* III.i.57).

151:29 *gamin* Brat (French).

152:1 **ein frecher Kerl** A cheeky chap (German).

152:7 **Syndaco** See Explanatory Notes.

153:30 **Il Brillante** The brilliant one, i.e., an actor of light comic roles (Italian).

154:8 **cachi** Japanese persimmons (Italian).

157:25 **Il Paolo e me, venti giorni, tre settimani** Paolo and I, twenty days, three weeks (Italian; the correct spelling is 'settimane').

159:1 **polenta** See Explanatory Notes.

161:21 *Porca-Maria* Sow-Maria (Italian). One of the common Italian (religious) oaths linking the name of Christ's mother with a pig.

165:30 **Venga, venga mangiare** Come, come and eat (Italian; slightly incorrect, perhaps rendering a spoken form, or the way a native speaker talks to a foreigner).

169:18 **"bella bionda,"** 'Beautiful blonde' (Italian).

169:33 **E' bello—il ballo?** Is it nice – the dancing? (Italian).

170:28 **Venga—venga un po'** Come here – come here a moment (Italian).

171:17–20 **Si verrà ... far' l'amor** A very popular folk song in the area around Trento: 'Yes one will see the spring/ the almond buds will flower/ the women from Trento will come down to make love to Italian men.' Trento being part of Austria at the time, women from Trento were foreigners.

171:32 **Basta—basta** Stop – stop (Italian).

172:2 *proprio selvatico* Really wild (Italian).

175:28 **Peccato!—sa, per bellezza, i baffi neri—ah-h!** What a pity! – you know, for beauty, a black moustache – ah-h! (Italian).

175:34 **è triste** You are sad (Italian; DHL uses the polite form of address).

175:38 **Vuol' dire che hai l'aria dolorosa** He means you look sorrowful (Italian).

176:7 **Ho visto troppo** I've seen too much (Italian).

179:29 **Inglesi** Englishmen (Italian).

180:8 **Mio figlio ... bambino** [180:12] My son ... the child (male) (Italian).

181:9 **Evviva, Evviva!** . . . **Tripoli, sarà italiana,/ Sarà italiana al rombo del cannon'** [181:12–13) Hurrah, Hurrah! . . . Tripoli will be Italian,/ It will be Italian amid the roaring of the cannons' (Italian); see Explanatory Notes on 82:38–9.

181:28 **Bravos!** . . . **Caro—caro—Ettore, caro colonello** [181:30] . . . **Un brav'uomo. Bravissimo** [181:34–5] Good/Clever . . . Dear – dear – Ettore, dear colonel . . . He is a very good man. Extraordinarily good (Italian; the word 'bravo' properly means either clever or – in connection with man (brav'uomo) – someone honest and reliable; 'bravos' is misspelled).

189:24 **Niebelung** See Explanatory Notes.

190:26 **Abendessen** Evening meal (German).

190:29 **knoedel** Dumpling (German).

191:8 **Nacht, Frau Wirtin—G'Nacht, Wirtin—'te Nacht, Frau** Good night, landlady (German). The forms are colloquial and abbreviated.

191:24 **"schön"** 'Nice/good' (German). Rarely used as a compliment for the way one speaks a language; the landlady may be suggesting that – for a foreigner – he has a good accent.

192:1 **Bettler, Lumpen, und Taugenichtse!** Beggars, scoundrels, and good-for-nothings! (German).

194:12 **"Gasthaus zur Post."** 'The post inn' (German); every village or town in Germany had one, usually at the crossing of two main roads; it was the place where the carriages with the post stopped.

194:25 *trapu* Stocky (French).

199:31 **"Il sole, il sole!"** 'The sun, the sun!' (Italian). See 67:38 and 131:25.

199:40–200:1 **mezzo-giorno** . . . **campanile** Midday . . . the bell-tower (Italian).

200:28 **campanilismo** Extremely intense, almost fanatic attachment to one's native village (Italian, from 'campanile'/bell tower). See also 72:39.

201:10–12 **Sa Signore** . . . **l'uomo non ha patria** You know sir . . . a man has no country (Italian).

208:36 *angenehm* Agreeable (German).

218:41 **Sportverein** Sports club (German).

219:24–5 **Das ist schön** . . . **Hübsch** This is nice . . . pretty (German).

220:30 **Du lait chaud pour les chameaux** Some hot milk for the camels (French). The maid is punning on 'lait chaud' and 'les chameaux'.

220:36 **Encore du lait pour les chameaux** More milk for the camels (French).

221:28 **"Kennst du** . . . **Citronen blühen?"** See Explanatory Notes.

222:19–20 **Quanto costa l'uva?** . . . **Sessanta al chilo** How much are the grapes? . . . Sixty a kilo (Italian).

222:32 **Ja, dies ist reizend** Yes, this is very nice of you (German).

226:13–15 **Pardon, Mademoiselle** . . . **Vous avez laissé votre parasol** Excuse me, miss . . . you have forgotten your parasol (French).

Currencies

Before the decimalization of British currency in 1971, the pound sterling (£) was divided into 20 shillings (20s); each shilling was the equivalent of 12 pence or pennies (12d – the 'd' stood for *denarius*, an ancient Roman silver coin). The penny could be further divided into two half-pennies or four farthings. Therefore a price could consist of three elements: pounds, shillings and pence (£, s, d). The guinea was worth one pound one shilling and was used by professional men such as doctors or lawyers to charge fees. Since 1971 the pound has been divided into 100 new pence, the latter distinguished from old pence by the use of 'p' instead of 'd'.

In the German monetary system, a mark is divided into 100 pfennigs. Forty pfennigs, which DHL puts into the 'cash-box' (35:13), were in 1912 the equivalent of about 5d. The 'kreutzer' (35:14) was a small coin used in Austria, Germany and Hungary, with a cross on it (Kreuz = cross), which fell into disuse at the beginning of the century. The 'heller' was named from the German town Schwäbisch Hall where it was coined and was used in Austria till 1924.

On Lake Garda (near the border with Austria), Austrian, French, Swiss, German and Italian currencies (*Letters*, i. 464) were all accepted; DHL, like others, used 'franc' and 'lira' interchangeably. See Introduction, note 33. Twenty-five French francs were approximately equivalent to one English pound; a lira was divided into 100 'centesimi' and was the equivalent of about 9½d.

Further Reading

Very little criticism is available on the contents of this volume, published for the first time by CUP in 1994, and collecting Lawrence's early travel writing. The Introduction to the Cambridge edition is essential further reading, as it gives in full detail the history of the essays' composition and publication. Most published criticism has focused on *Twilight in Italy*, but the book's philosophical observations have been the subject of most of the discussion.

Anzi Cavallone, Anna, 'Lawrence a Gargnano', *Studi Inglesi*, II (2), 1975, pp. 401–24. (*In Italian; a vivid, detailed description of the people and the places mentioned in the essays set on Lake Garda, it offers interesting information about local people Lawrence was in touch with.*)

Black, Michael, *D. H. Lawrence: The Early Philosophical Works*, Macmillan, 1991. (*Chapter 7, pp. 228–329, presents a detailed analysis of* Twilight in Italy *in the context of Lawrence's philosophical thought.*)

Clark, L. D., *The Minoan Distance: The Symbolism of Travel in D. H. Lawrence*, University of Arizona Press, 1980, pp. 112–43. (*Extensive description of* Twilight in Italy *mainly focused on the North/South polarity; considers the earlier versions of the essays; argues for the superiority of* Twilight in Italy.)

Comellini, Carla, 'D. H. Lawrence and Italy', in *D. H. Lawrence: A Study on Mutual and Cross References and Interferences*, CLUEB, 1995, pp. 27–57. (*Through a detailed analysis of Lawrence's travel books set in Italy, it presents the influence of Mediterranean culture on Lawrence's work and vitalist philosophy.*)

Corsani, Mary, *D. H. Lawrence e l'Italia*, Mursia, 1965. (*In Italian; detailed study of D. H. Lawrence's relationship with Italy, of its importance in the development of his literary career.*)

Fasick, Laura, 'Female Power, Male Comradeship, and the Rejection of the Female in Lawrence's *Twilight in Italy*, *Sea and Sardinia*, and *Etruscan Places*', *D. H. Lawrence Review*, 1989, 21 (1), 25–36. (*Helpful discussion of the male/female relationship from a feminist point of view.*)

De Filippis, Simonetta, 'Lawrence of Etruria' in P. Preston and P. Hoare (eds.), *D. H. Lawrence in the Modern World*, Cambridge University Press, 1989, pp. 104–20. (*Although mostly with reference to* Sketches of Etruscan Places, *a profound analysis of Lawrence and Italy.*)

Eggert, Paul, 'D. H. Lawrence and the Crucifixes', *Bulletin of Research in the Humanities*, 1983, v. 86 (1), 67–85. (*Reconstruction of Lawrence's crossing of the Alps; photographs of the located Crucifixes.*)

Further Reading

Ellis, David and Howard Mills, *D. H. Lawrence's Non-Fiction*, Cambridge University Press, 1988. (*Chapters 2 and 4 offer a perceptive analysis of* Twilight in Italy, *as a problematic mixture of genres, and a discussion of the development of Lawrence's travel writing.*)

Gibbons, June, 'Twilight in Italy, D. H. Lawrence and Lake Garda', *Quaderni di Lingue e Letterature* (Verona), 1978–1979, 3–4, 165–171. (*Discusses Lawrence's response to Italy, comparing* Twilight in Italy *with his poems on his Italian experiences.*)

Kalnins, Mara, '"Terra incognita": Lawrence's Travel Writings', *Renaissance and Modern Studies*, 1985, 29, 66–77. (*An analysis of Lawrence's travel books as a metaphor for his inner development, paying particular attention to* Mornings in Mexico *and* Sketches of Etruscan Places.)

Lawrence, D. H., *Mr Noon*, ed. Lindeth Vasey and Peter Preston (Penguin Books, 1996). (*A semi-fictional, semi-autobiographical account of Lawrence's journey to Italy through the Alps.*)

Mehl, Dieter, 'D. H. Lawrence in Waldbröl', *Notes and Queries*, 1984, 229, 78–81.

Merlini, Madeline, 'A Priest of Love on the Shores of Lake Garda', in E. Kanceff, *Il Garda nella cultura europea*, Comunità del Garda, 1986, pp. 525–34. (*Proceedings of the international conference on Lake Garda in European cultures, September 1982; the article about Lawrence focuses on the central role of Italy in his works.*)

Meyers, Jeffrey, *D. H. Lawrence and the Experience of Italy*, University of Pennsylvania Press, 1982. (*Examines the importance of Italy in Lawrence's work.*)

Meyers, Jeffrey, 'Lawrence and Travel Writers', in J. Meyers (ed.), *The Legacy of D. H. Lawrence*, Macmillan, 1987, pp. 81–108. (*Lawrence's aesthetic of travel and his influence on later travel writers.*)

Nehls, Edward, 'D. H. Lawrence: The Spirit of Place', in F. J. Hoffman and H. T. Moore (eds.), *The Achievement of D. H. Lawrence*, University of Oklahoma Press, 1953, pp. 268–90. (*Discusses the travel books set in Italy as reflecting three main phases of Lawrence's literary career, among which* Twilight in Italy *is the most obscure and depressing.*)

Owen, Frederick, 'A Chapel Among the Mountains' and 'San Gaudenzio Today', *The Human World*, 1973, no. 11, 39–49 and 1974, no. 15–16, 75–83; 'D. H. Lawrence's Italy: Allurements and Changes', *Contemporary Review*, 1985, 247, 261–8. (*Vivid autobiographical sketches following Lawrence's tracks, with the first offering a description of the ex-voto paintings Lawrence saw in the chapel.*)

Tracy, Billy T., *D. H. Lawrence and the Literature of Travel*, UMI Research Press, 1983, pp. 91–128. (*Extensive study of Lawrence's travel writing; chapter 3 discusses* Twilight in Italy *focusing on Lawrence's dualistic doctrine.*)

Wagner, Jeanie, 'D. H. Lawrence's Neglected "Italian Studies"', *D. H. Lawrence Review*, 1980, 13 (3), 260–74. (*An interesting comparison between the two versions of 'The Spinner and the Monks', 'The Lemon Gardens' and 'The Theatre' with a preference for the essays published in the* English Review.)

Further Reading

Worthen, John, *D. H. Lawrence, The Early Years 1885–1912*, Cambridge University Press, 1991. (*The chapter 'Abroad', pp. 393–432, describes the real-life events of Lawrence and Frieda's journey to Italy.*)